Animal Clinic
for
Dogs

Animal Clinic
for
Dogs

Jim Humphries, D.V.M.

GRAMERCY BOOKS
New York

This 1998 edition is published by Gramercy Books, an imprint of Random House Value Publishing, Inc., by arrangement with Howell Book House, A Prentice Hall Macmillan Company, 15 Columbus Circle, New York, NY 10023

(Originally published as: *Dr. Jim's Animal Clinic for Dogs: What People Want to Know*)

Printed in the United States of America

Library of Congress Cataloging–in–Publication Data

Humphries, Jim.
    [Dr. Jim's animal clinic for dogs]
    Animal clinic for dogs / Jim Humphries.
       p. cm.
    Originally published : Dr. Jim's animal clinic for dogs. New York : Howell Book House, c1994.
    Includes index.
    ISBN 0–517–18906–2
    1. Dogs—Miscellanea. 2. Dogs—Health—Miscellanea. 3. Dogs—Diseases—Miscellanea. I. Title.
    SF427.H925 1998
    636.7'083—dc21   97–29101
                                        CIP

Random House Value Publishing, Inc.
New York • London • Toronto • Sydney • Auckland
http://www.randomhouse.com/

Animal Clinic for Dogs

9 8 7 6 5 4 3 2

Contents

Acknowledgments

My career in both veterinary medicine and in the electronic media has been affected by many people. They all deserve a gracious thank you for their teachings, support, encouragement and belief in what I do. My fondest memories are of those people who saw into the future and knew that my sacrifices and crazy ideas would eventually gain recognition. Blazing a trail can be a scary venture, but the fear was eased, and good advice and direction were given by these true friends.

First I would like to thank my wife, Pat. A true animal lover, Pat has always impressed me with her compassion and caring for any kind of creature. Even though what I do is way out of her comfort zone, she has constantly supported my ventures since our meeting five years ago. Her most valuable contribution is keeping my feet firmly planted on the ground and helping me keep an eye on the real goal. She persuaded me to stop trying to steer the ship so forcefully and let God's universal plan take its course. As soon as I did, things began to happen. Pat is also responsible for much of the writing, proofing and editing of my works in both print and the electronic media. She has a natural knack for taking a complex subject and making it easy to read, hear or see on video. She is the most natural animal trainer I have ever seen as is evidenced by our four great pets, and her National Top Ten Arabian mare. The relationship I have with Pat is an accomplishment in life of which I am most proud.

My mother clearly had the most early effect on my life and on becoming a veterinarian. Her early teachings about compassion and respect for life, along with her encouraging my medical curiosity, lit the fire that still burns for this passion I have. To this day she never stops encouraging me and gets more pure joy out of my accomplishments that anyone. I'll never be able to repay you for all you've done. You'll probably never get tired of hearing me say, *Thanks, Mom.*

Dr. James Merle Baker was like a father to me. He taught me fundamental principles of veterinary medicine, client relations, animal care and compassion. Truly my best memories as a young adult was riding with Doc on calls, looking up complicated diseases and making textbook information apply to the real world. Doc made learning fun and practical. His kindness and encouragement were instrumental in my making it through the rigors of veterinary school. He is a true hero and a savior to countless thousands of animals in south Texas.

Next, because this book is based on my years as a talk radio show host, I must thank the man who gave me that initial break—Dan Bennett. He taught me radio formatics, the importance of hitting commercial breaks and keeping the show moving and high energy. His criticism always made the show better and today my show is both informative and entertaining because Dan taught me how to mix the two.

Dale Brandon is my media and public relations consultant—but more than that he is a true friend. He has taken the foundation and framework I've built over the past eight years and turned it into a truly multi-media operation that reaches hundreds of thousands of pet owners. Dale gets real joy from my success. Dale's belief in me and his incredible enthusiasm was the exact prescription this doctor needed to continue on into uncharted territory.

Several other very important people believed in me when self-doubt loomed. Betty White is a major television star and animal lover. Heaven knows, she is approached by thousands of people and organizations every year for endorsements and to make demands on her time. Yet from the beginning, Betty has agreed to be a guest on my radio and television shows and has encouraged me every step of the way. That meant a great deal and kept me going when it was tough. Thanks Betty! . . . and thanks to Gail Clark, her personal secretary.

From a business standpoint, Roger Winter is my mentor. Roger is a highly successful businessman and keeps common sense and fairness his top priority. Roger has given me valuable advice for years and never expected anything in return. His creativity and savvy help guide me through some difficult business decisions. Roger takes great pride in seeing other people succeed and I am lucky to call him my friend.

Dr. Karen Fling and Dr. David Goodnight are two colleagues who have always supported my media career when others scoffed at my attempts to reach the public. They have never flinched in their support of my public education efforts and help me stay current in an ever-advancing field. This is noteworthy because many of my colleagues have tried to make this difficult path even more so, but these two doctors are not only excellent veterinarians, they also know what's best for the profession.

Finally, I thank everyone at Howell Book House. Sean Frawley and Madelyn Larsen are top professionals and their input on this work was invaluable. They have been there every step of the way on every project and I would not have been able to keep up the pace without their positive expectancy. They know the true value of pets in our lives and were eager to help me with my first two works! Thank you for making these dreams a reality.

And thank you, Father, for the dramatic display of power once I finally shed the yoke and let the universal auto pilot take back control.

Foreword

What ever happened to the concept of asking a simple question to get a simple answer? In light of the growing mounds of information being poured into our "mindfill" every day, it stands to reason that something has to go to make room, or we will be on overload. Just when we need it most, straightforwardness seems to have made the endangered list.

That is why I found this book and Dr. Jim's approach to his subject so refreshing. There are some very good dog books around, but one doesn't always have time to wade through extraneous material in search of help with a particular problem.

In *Dr. Jim's Animal Clinic for Dogs*, Dr. Jim Humphries has laid out the categories so they are easy to find, and the question-and-answer format manages to put you in direct personal contact with him. It also helps clarify what you need to tell your veterinarian, should it be deemed necessary.

This is an invaluable reference book. Keep it handy! After I read it from beginning to end, I was amazed at how many new things I learned—even after a lifetime with dogs—and all couched in common sense language that will help me retain the information.

We've come a long way in realizing just how important a role our companion animals play in our lives. We are at last beginning to appreciate the fact that our relationships with our pets are two-way streets—we benefit each other inordinately. Doing everything we can do to keep our animal friends healthy and lengthen their all-too-short lives is, in truth, doing something for ourselves.

BETTY WHITE

Introduction

I have always loved animals. I am always amazed when I hear people say they don't like animals, because for me it has always been such a natural thing. My best pal in junior high school was Toro, a little Beagle dog with the greatest personality I've ever seen. In fact, Toro was responsible for my first ever front-page picture and story in the local newspaper.

I had taught Toro to ride on the back of my motorcycle. He would brace both back legs on the rear edge of the seat and clamp both front legs around my neck and off we would head to do my paper route. I guess that scene was too much for the local reporters and soon everyone in town knew my dog rode with me on my route.

I worked with Dr. J. M. Baker, our hometown veterinarian, for many years. Doc was a kind man who worked harder than anyone I had ever seen. He went out of his way to accommodate my great interest in veterinary medicine. More than anyone, Dr. Baker is why I became a veterinarian.

I love both large and small animals. Each group has its own unique set of problems, cures and environmental setting in which to work. However, small animal medicine is special to me because I am able to spend more time with each case and it offers more opportunity for me to use my knowledge of internal medicine and diagnostics. It affords me the opportunity to practice advanced and detailed surgeries, as well as study interesting animal behavior.

I practiced for about six years in various settings: government work, medical center practice, emergency clinic specialty and private practice. After moving to Dallas, I became involved with the local humane society. Here I learned firsthand of some of the terrible situations many animals find themselves in. It seemed strange that I had never come across these issues. They certainly were not discussed in veterinary school. I became more sensitive to overpopulation, animal abuse and neglect.

In addition to humane issues, I became fascinated by the subject of human and animal interactions. I read books and articles and learned about the tremendous, almost miraculous, benefits of animals' interactions with cancer patients, recovering heart attack patients, the elderly, autistic and handicapped children, prisoners and head-injured people.

I began a mobile veterinary practice partly to serve these people and found those years to be very rewarding. I became very close to many of my clients—closer than one ever gets by seeing them in the sterile environment of an animal hospital. I was visiting their homes and they felt like I was a true friend.

Because of the unique nature of my practice I was asked to be a guest on a local radio program on KLIF, a newly formed all-talk station in Dallas–Ft. Worth. After two appearances, the program director, Dan Bennett, called me into his office and asked me if I'd like my own show! Of course I jumped at the opportunity. The thousands of times I had gone over the flea control message or told the heartworm disease story to one person at a time in the clinic raced through my mind. I thought of the hundreds of hours I had spent with people in their homes going over pet care items. Now, when I told these things, thousands of people would hear and benefit. I was ready.

A large pet-products manufacturer based in Dallas convinced me to try to take the radio talk show to a national network. Eventually I was able to line up just the minimum amount of sponsorships needed to pay for the very expensive satellite linkup time, and my show went on the air in 35 cities as "Dr. Jim's Animal Clinic."

Today my show is heard every Saturday afternoon in almost 100 cities and I have answered over 35,000 calls on talk radio. I have developed the talent for sizing up a question very quickly and delivering a highly focused and concise answer, *and that is the basis for this book*.

I feel I know better than anyone what people want to know about their pets. I have invested years of study and research into developing the proper answers for medical, surgical, behavioral and training topics.

In this book I answer many questions that are consistently asked week after week. In Part I, Common Questions, you will learn the right way to choose a puppy, *and* a veterinarian to care for it. Basic training and manners are different from obedience. Your dog may not be "officially" obedience trained, but still be well mannered. A dog who has no manners ends up in a shelter more often than not. I am a strong advocate of adopting dogs from a humane society or an animal shelter; therefore, I cover key points in proper adoptions. And, as you can imagine, I do not believe people should breed their pets, so I have spent an entire chapter on the questions people ask about birth control and reproduction. Having lost many beloved companions and having gone through the flood of deep emotions many times, I have included in Chapter 7 some of the ways to handle the loss of your pet friend.

In Part II, the home-care grooming tips are presented in enough detail so that you will be able keep your dog buddy smelling good, looking good and more fun to hug. Some of the products discussed have a direct bearing on your dog's health and, when used properly, will save you hundreds of dollars in grooming and veterinary bills.

Part III covers behavior and training. These topics generate the most calls on the show. From introducing dogs to new babies, to surefire ways to housebreak puppies, this section is packed with real world, common sense advice that will help you and your pets "get along." Even though this is not surgery or breakthrough medicine, it may be just as life-saving for a dog that barks, bites, forgets its housetraining or is just plain out of control.

Everyone is concerned with controlling fleas and ticks, worms and mites. Flea-bite dermatitis is the number one complaint in veterinary offices nationwide. New technology is released every day, and a great deal of bad information gets passed along as well. With Lyme disease all over the United States, you need solid advice on controlling parasites and you'll find it in Part IV.

The pet-food business has changed completely in the last ten years. With hundreds of new brands, some claiming they are not only the best, but also that all the others are bad for your dog, it is very confusing! Part V attempts to bring some sanity back to the issue of pet nutrition and explains how to choose a pet food that will be good for your dog and not break your budget.

As a veterinarian, I am most interested in true medicine and surgery for pet animals. Part VI covers the most common medical questions people have asked me. From vaccinations to cancer, from heart disease to heatstroke, you will get the same easy-to-understand advice that will steer you in the right direction with your own veterinarian. Also, itching and scratching dogs are so common that not a radio show goes by without someone asking my first, second or third opinion on how to help their dog. I have offered up the best information available today to deal with this maddening problem.

Finally, every time it is Saturday and the moon is full, I get the weirdest and funniest calls. I thought you would enjoy reading about some of these calls in Part VII, in the chapter called Full-Moon Saturdays.

Just a word about my philosophy. I hate wishy-washy advice. Far too many talk show hosts, especially in how-to fields, are under the impression they cannot be specific. They are afraid to step on someone's toes, or mention a brand name, or be too specific because someone will come along and point a finger saying they were wrong. Many times it is easier to be general and vague and not make waves. But in my opinion, *that is not helpful*.

When you are in a dark room, you want to know where the light switch is, not a lecture on light-emitting particles. You want to know what is the best switch, the name, the color, the shape, where to get it and how much it costs. You don't care that there are some forty switches at your hardware retailer and you don't want to hear, "Ask your friendly sales associate which one's best for you." That's why people call a talk show with an expert host!

Therefore I am proud of my concise, to-the-point, helpful, how-to answers. I am happy that my listeners get "golden nuggets" of advice on everything from dogs that mark the stereo speakers, to when it's time to say good-bye to a beloved family pet. I don't worry about what some company or manufacturer might say about my comments concerning their product. My only concern during a talk show is that I give the best advice I can muster at that moment.

No doubt there are doctors and animal behaviorists who know more about a specific subject than I do. But this book is not about details, or about the Nth degree, *it's about helpful golden nuggets of information*.

Dr. Jim's Animal Clinic for Dogs and the companion volume, *Dr. Jim's Animal Clinic for Cats* are compilations of the most frequently asked questions on talk radio and my very focused, easy-to-implement solutions. I've organized the information in such a way that you can access it without having to read the whole book. All of the quotations at the beginning of each chapter are actual talk-radio calls—*they're not made up*! All of the questions in each chapter are actual talk radio callers' questions.

Not every category could be covered in this book but eventually will be with subsequent editions. I hope my years of experience and proven techniques are helpful to you and your dogs. I know how much pets have meant to me personally, and I have seen firsthand how important they are to thousands of singles, young couples, parents, children and seniors. It is my greatest wish that you and your family will enjoy the relationship with your pets more because of this book. Enjoy.

Now let's go to the next caller. . . . Hi, you're on the air with Dr. Jim. . . .

PART I

Common Questions

CHAPTER 1

Choosing a Puppy the Right Way

Margie's call was about third in the first hour of my show. She and her husband had been out that Saturday buying a new puppy. She called my show asking my opinion of their choice! She had always had small dogs as a child, and he, like many men, felt like big dogs were best.

She was very proud that she had won the battle of small over large and announced they had brought home a Basset Hound puppy for her.

Bassets are, no doubt, one of the cutest puppies in the world. The only problem is they grow up into one of the more trouble-some breeds in terms of acquired and genetic medical prob-lems. They also grow to be quite large, sometimes tipping the scales at sixty pounds!

After hearing this, she thought briefly, then said, "Here is my husband, give him some tips on taking care of his dog!"

Dogs are very popular pets and have been companions to humans since the days of the caveman. The doggie census currently counts fifty-four million dogs in America. Over half of the country owns a dog, yet 70% of all dog owners are not happy with their pet's behavior. Much of this discontent can be traced to the owner making a bad decision about which dog to acquire in the beginning.

I am always happy when someone calls asking for a few pointers *before* they go out and buy a family dog. Far too often the calls I hear go like this: "Hi, Dr. Jim, we just bought a St. Bernard. What do you think?"

Other people call my show and ask how they can find a specific purebred, such as a Shar-Pei, because they are so cute. In fact, this is the number one mistake people make when choosing a new dog or puppy. They choose based on the way the puppy or dog looks.

What they don't consider is that each breed of purebred dog was originally developed with a specific purpose in mind (i.e., hunting, herding, etc.) and therefore, has been bred for certain personality characteristics. They also don't consider that many purebred dogs have more than their share of expensive medical problems.

If people took greater care in their initial choice of a puppy, there would be far fewer dogs given up to the shelters because they outgrew the families' expectations of size or time commitment. So, while it's important to know how to choose the puppy who will be right for you, it is most important to first be sure you have the time, desire and facilities to provide that puppy with a good home for many years to come.

Q: *My wife and I are recently married and would like to get a new puppy. We both work long hours and aren't home much. Any suggestions?*

A: Yes! Don't get a new puppy. You may not be good candidates for even an adult dog at this time and might consider another type of pet. Before you consider a new puppy you should ask yourself an important question. Is someone going to be home during the day?

A young puppy (three to four months) can be left alone for only a few hours at a time. You will need to make arrangements to come home every couple of hours or have a friend or neighbor come in to care for the puppy. Once the pup is four to five months old, he can be left alone for four to five hours only, so you will still need someone to come in once each day while you are away.

Young puppies are very much like babies. They need a great deal of care and attention. This is also an important time in the development of a pup's personality. He should have lots of interaction and not be isolated. If you are away a lot or don't have a lot of time to commit, an adult dog would be a better choice for you.

Q: *I have always wanted a Brittany Spaniel because they are so pretty. How do I know if this would be a good dog for me?*

A: Brittany Spaniels, like most all breeds, can be great pets given the proper training and environment. But will your life style and home fit a Brittany's disposition?

The single biggest mistake people make when choosing a puppy is picking a breed based on looks. You must realize that purebred breeds were originally developed for a specific purpose, and that purpose required the dog to have certain personality characteristics to be successful.

Take for instance, the Brittany. This dog was bred to hunt birds for hours at a time, over large areas. Brittany's have extremely high energy levels and need daily exercise, preferably the chance to run, and run, and run! If you're not a hunter and your idea of exercise doesn't include lots of time in the great outdoors on a near daily basis, then the Brittany may not be a good choice for you.

When you consider what breed of dog is right for your family, ask yourself these questions:

- What sort of energy level should my dog have? Are you a senior citizen who likes to read and maybe take short walks, or will your dog accompany you on hikes and jogs? Maybe he will need to keep up with three active kids.
- How much time can I devote to grooming? Some of the most beautiful and charming canines require almost daily grooming at home and others must be clipped on a regular basis, usually by a professional groomer.
- How much time do I have to spend with my dog? Some breeds are more "people oriented" than others and become bored and lonely if they are left alone for long periods. This can lead to anxiety and stress, which the dog may display by excessive barking, digging or other unwanted behaviors.
- What size of dog will fit into my life style? How much room you have in your home and yard is a consideration although not necessarily the most important. Some medium-sized dogs have extremely high energy levels and require lots of yard or a daily opportunity to run, while some large and even giant breeds tolerate smaller homes and yards very well.

You should consider that a large dog is more expensive to feed and typically costs more to board, medicate and groom. If you are a small or frail person, remember that even after obedience training, there may be times when you will have to physically restrain your dog. Can you control a ninety-pound German Shepherd? Do you have a vehicle which allows you to transport a large dog to the veterinarian, groomer, obedience class and on outings?

• How much time do I have to devote to obedience training my dog? While all dogs should be obedience trained, it is absolutely essential that large, aggressive breed dogs be well-trained so that they are always under control. Some breeds are more willful and stubborn by nature and take more time, patience and experience to train. These breeds may be a poor choice for first-time dog owners and those who have not successfully trained a dog before.

Once you have honestly answered these questions, you will have a good idea of what size and temperament of dog will fit into your life style. Next learn all you can about the breeds you are interested in. There are books available on every breed.

A good book to check out is *The Perfect Puppy: How to Choose Your Dog by Its Behavior* by Lynette and Benjamin Hart of The School of Veterinary Medicine of The University of California, Davis. In their book they rate each breed on a scale from one to ten on a long list of characteristics including: demand for affection, trainability, aggression, playfulness and tendency toward destructiveness.

Resist the temptation to buy any puppy, no matter how cute, that doesn't fit your situation. If it doesn't work out, it can be heartbreaking for you and the pup will have little chance of getting a good second home after he has outgrown the cute puppy stage and has perhaps developed some bad habits to boot!

Q: I want to make sure I pick the right puppy for me. After I decide on the breed, what's the first thing to look for?

A: First and foremost, pick a healthy puppy. Until you take the pup to your veterinarian, you won't know for sure, but avoid picking any obviously sick pups. The pup should be alert and active, but not crazy. He should have clear, shiny eyes with no discharge. His nose should not be runny or crusty, and he shouldn't be skinny (most young pups are a little potbellied). He should have a soft, full haircoat with no bald or crusty spots. Puppies should have bright white teeth with no stains.

Arrange ahead to take your new puppy immediately to your veterinarian for a complete check. If no major health problems are found, you are all set to take the little guy home. If any major problems are found, return the pup right away and look for a new pup. Resist the urge to be a hero and take on a major medical problem. It can be very expensive, financially and emotionally. Remember, there are thousands of pups who need homes. Pick one who can be a happy and joyful addition to your family for years to come.

Q: *Are there differences in personalities among litter mates? Is there a way to tell which puppy would make a good pet?*

A: There can be considerable difference in personality among puppies in the same litter and especially among different litters of pups within a breed. There are some things to look for when choosing a pup that can give you insight into the pup's personality and its potential to be a good pet.

Choose a puppy that was with its mother and litter mates for at least six weeks. It is during this time that the puppy learns how to socialize with other dogs, how to play without hurting and to respond to reprimands from mom when he gets too rambunctious. A puppy removed from his mom and litter mates too early may never learn to socialize well.

Once you have picked out two or three puppies that you like, you should take each one individually to a quiet room away from the distractions of the other pups and mom. Here you can do a few simple tests which will give you some idea of the pup's personality and potential as a pet.

First, just place the puppy on the floor and observe him for a few minutes. Does he start exploring? Does he come over to you for attention without being called? Does he seem afraid and try to hide or does he just sit where you placed him without moving?

The pup should be curious and active. He should begin to

explore his new surroundings after a few minutes. If he comes to you for attention without calling, that's a good sign as long as he's not out of control, jumping all over you and biting roughly. All young puppies mouth, but very hard biting could indicate he wasn't socialized well with his litter mates or he could be very aggressive and may be difficult to train. A very scared or timid puppy could be distrustful of people. A puppy who just sits where you put him without moving may be sick.

Next, call the puppy to you. Sit or kneel to get near his level. You can use a small ball or squeak toy to get his attention if necessary. He should be interested in you once he has checked out his new territory. Does he run to you with his tail up and a happy face, or is his tail tucked and his demeanor fearful? You should choose a confident, happy puppy.

Stand up next and walk around the room. Does the puppy follow you? Can you get him to follow you if you call him? A puppy that comes to you, but immediately leaves and ignores you may have little interest in people and would make a poor pet. The puppy you choose should be interested in you. This indicates he has good potential to bond to you.

Sit on the floor again and call the puppy to you. Does he let you pet him? Does he seem to want to stay near you without you holding him there? Your puppy should enjoy your affection and petting, but should not be out of control and jumping all over you.

Try restraining the puppy lightly. All puppies will struggle and wiggle a bit, but he shouldn't get angry or panicked. Next, turn the puppy on its back and gently hold it in that position. Again, all puppies will struggle at first. The puppy you choose should struggle for a while, but then relax and accept this position. This is a good indication that your pup will accept that he is in a submissive position to you, that you are the "alpha dog" or his leader. A puppy that will not tolerate this position at all may be very dominant and may grow to be a very dominant dog who will be difficult to train.

Individually test each puppy you are considering. Look for a happy, confident puppy that is alert and active without being wild. Pick a puppy that will come to you when you call it and that you can get to follow you. Your puppy should enjoy petting and affection and tolerate restraint. He should not be out of control, but neither should he be lethargic. He should be playful and active without nonstop jumping up and rough biting.

CHAPTER 2

Choosing a Veterinarian

Donna did exactly what I had asked her to do the week before when she called my show. However, she was almost in tears when she called today. She had just returned from a second veterinarian's office for the second opinion I had sent her for. Her dog, Muffie, had terminal kidney failure and wasn't expected to survive long without heroic, immediate and expensive treatments. The second doctor had done a complete physical exam, ran a few specific blood tests, and made an accurate diagnosis of an all too common form of fatal kidney disease.

The reason Donna was feeling especially guilty was the wasted time and money incurred at the first vet's office. This "doctor" had a reputation for using unconventional treatments and having pet owners come from many states for such treatments.

In Donna's case, he had his assistant hold various bottles of different colored liquids in one hand while he pressed on her outstretched arm to check the "resistance." With this and the curious results of another "test" where they all stood in a circle around the dog with joined hands, he pronounced the dog with a disharmony of the humors and prescribed Formula B as the cure.

It was after a week of Formula B's lack of results that Donna had first called me with the unbelievable story. I sent her immediately to a second veterinarian in the area that I knew to be of the highest quality.

Unfortunately, Muffie was too far gone and died over the weekend. It was not the last I would ever hear of "Dr. Disharmony."

The relationship between you and your veterinarian is extremely important. You will trust this person with the life of one of your best friends, one who often cannot tell you if he is hurt, or where.

Generally, veterinarians are very professional and dedicated people who make a big commitment in time, and sacrifice the possibility of greater income, just to work with animals.

Besides a professional-looking clinic that is clean, well lit and odor free, I feel the most important criterion is a veterinarian who stays up to date with the latest advances in animal medicine. Veterinary medical information doubles every six to seven years. This means a veterinarian must continue to study by attending continuing education seminars and by reading professional journals, or in a few years he will know only half of what he should.

It takes real commitment for a busy doctor to keep current. Ask your veterinarian if he regularly attends continuing-education courses, or look to see if the doctor displays continuing-education certificates on his walls. Check to see if the hospital is certified by the American Animal Hospital Association (AAHA), as they certify only the best.

Q: *We had an appointment with the vet this morning and were kept waiting thirty minutes. We are not happy about it. Don't you think he should have seen us right away?*

A: I understand your frustration at having to wait to see the veterinarian, but it could be that your doctor was unexpectedly delayed by an emergency or had to spend more time than expected with another client ahead of you. He may have a very busy practice, which could be a good sign that he is highly thought of. If this happens occasionally it's best to be understanding. If you consistently have to wait past your appointment time, talk to your doctor about it. Perhaps he can recommend a different time of day or day of the week when he is usually not as busy. Saturday mornings are typically very busy times at clinics nationwide!

Q: *We really like our vet, but he seems to be gone a lot. The last several times we've gone in we've seen someone new each time. We'd like your opinion.*

A: I recommend you talk to your doctor about your concerns. Try to tactfully find out why he is gone so often. If he's gone fishing all those times, then he may not be very committed to his practice, and the level of care is sure to reflect that. On the other hand, he may be gone to veterinary continuing-education seminars or could be working toward an advanced degree in surgery or another specialty. This would speak highly of his commitment to staying current on the latest advances in animal medicine.

Talk to your doctor and make it known to him that it is important for you to develop a consistent relationship with one veterinarian. Your doctor may be able to tell you certain days or times when he is always available. You will have to decide for yourself, after speaking with him, if it is a situation you can live with. If not, you may want to consider developing a relationship with the veterinarian who fills in for him, or changing clinics altogether.

Q: *Our doctor sees a lot of cows and horses. When we take our dog to see him, he seems to want to get through with us and move on to the next cow. What should we say to him?*

A: This is a common complaint among dog owners who go to a "mixed-practice" veterinarian, one who sees both large and small animals. Horses and cattle often comprise the bulk of these practices. Usually the veterinarian has to go to these patients rather than them coming to him, so he is often out of the clinic. Add to this the considerable monetary value of some of these equine and bovine patients and you can see why most mixed practice veterinarians concentrate more on their large patients, than on dogs and cats. It is also difficult enough for a doctor to stay current on medical advances in either large or small animal medicine, without trying to stay up to date on both.

All this is not to say that there are not some veterinarians who provide excellent care for both large and small animals, there are. If your veterinarian gives the impression that he much prefers cows to dogs, then that will probably reflect in his work as well. You, as the client, need to be happy with your veterinarian and feel that he is interested in your pet. You may want to consider changing to a small animal doctor. In some cases, there is only one veterinarian in a large area and so he must see all animals, small and large. In such a case, talk to your doctor and see if he sets aside special times to see only small animals, such as Saturday mornings.

Q: *We've moved to Los Angeles from Phoenix and need to find a new vet. Our vet in Phoenix didn't know of anyone here to refer us to. Can you help?*

A: Start by asking friends, neighbors and co-workers who own pets which veterinarian they go to. Find out what kind of pets they have, how well they like their doctor and why. Then develop a list of these doctors and others that are within your area.

Next call each clinic and ask if the doctor specializes in any particular type of pet or problem, what their office hours are and how they handle emergencies after hours. Notice how you are treated by the office staff on the phone. If they seem warm, friendly and helpful on the phone, that's a good sign they will treat you and your pet well in person. If you don't have a good feeling about the clinic from your phone call, eliminate it from your list.

Next, review your notes from your phone calls and note which clinics seem to best fit your particular needs. Pick a clinic whose office hours are convenient to you and which is close enough to your home in case of emergency.

Choose a clinic or two to visit. You might take your pet for a routine procedure such as yearly vaccinations for your first visit. On this visit, notice how you are treated by the office staff. They should be friendly and helpful. Notice if the clinic is clean, well lit and odor free. Ask about payment policies, if cash is required at the time of treatment or if credit cards are accepted.

Notice how the technicians and the veterinarian handle your pet and how they relate to you. Do pick a veterinarian you feel comfortable talking to, one who takes time to answer all your questions and one who seems caring and relates well to your pet. If the first clinic doesn't meet your needs, try again.

Q: *When we visit the animal hospital, the nurse or technicians seem to do most of the work. We like our doctor, but we'd like to see him once in a while. Is this normal?*

A: No, it's not normal. You need the opportunity for good two-way communication with your veterinarian. You will have some questions you want to ask him, and it's important that he have the opportunity to examine your pet in your presence so that you can both discuss any concerns. Some very busy doctors have to use technicians more than they would like, but it's important that you voice your concerns to the staff. Ask to speak to the doctor and make it known to him that you would like him to make an effort to spend more time with you when you bring your pet in. If the situation doesn't improve, you may want to consider finding another veterinarian.

Q: *My family has been going to the same vet for years. When we go in, he never talks to us much, just prescribes pills. Do you think we should look for a new vet?*

A: Yes. Loyalty is one thing, but to keep going to a veterinarian just because your family has always used him is not a good reason. Since your family has used this doctor for years, I imagine he is probably an older veterinarian and may be burned out on practice and not have an interest in communicating with his clients.

Good communication with your veterinarian is a must. He should explain thoroughly any illness or disease your pet has. He should discuss treatment options with you and explain why he recommends a certain course of treatment. You should be shown any X rays or test results and these should be explained to you. In short, you and your veterinarian should be a team, caring for your pets together. If it doesn't feel like that, you need to find a new doctor.

Q: *Our dog has cancer, and we've seen our vet many times for his treatment. Now she wants to send us to a specialist at a university. Do you think we should go?*

A: Yes. This is a good sign that your doctor stays up-to-date on the latest advances in animal medicine, that she communicates with experts and is not afraid to refer difficult cases to the appropriate specialist. Your veterinarian knows that veterinary teaching hospitals have access to the latest technology and equipment. Much of this type of equipment is extremely expensive, far beyond the scope of a private clinic. This is much the same as having your own family doctor refer you to a specialist or to a hospital for advanced treatment.

Q: *My vet doesn't seem to like my dog. It really bothers me, but I don't know how to say anything about it. What should I do?*

A: First of all, if you're not comfortable talking to your veterinarian, you need to find a different doctor. It is essential that you feel you can communicate with him at all times.

There are some veterinarians who like cats but don't care for dogs, or who like large animals but could do without small ones. If your doctor doesn't seem to like your dog, I would definitely find a new doctor. A veterinarian's entire job requires him to deal with animals, he should clearly like them. You wouldn't want to take your child to a pediatrician who didn't seem to like children. Your dog is, after all, your buddy, someone very important to you. You need to feel confident that his doctor likes him and cares about him.

Q: *Dr. Jim, we really like our vet, but we just went in for yearly shots and a checkup and got a bill for $150! We were shocked. Isn't that too high?*

A: That depends on what was done for $150. If your dog received only his yearly vaccinations, then that may be too high. If, however, he received an examination, heartworm testing, deworming, nutritional counseling and perhaps heartworm medication or a prescription diet, you may have gotten quite a bargain.

If you consider what you pay for health care for your pet compared to what you pay for yourself you will find you are getting a great value indeed. Most veterinarians work long hours and do not make a great deal of money. Their focus is on being able to provide good medical care to their patients. Medical costs have increased dramatically in the past years in all areas, veterinary medicine being no different. The difference is that human medicine has third party insurance payments to help recover part of the costs. The good news is there are now a few companies who are beginning to offer medical insurance for pets.

CHAPTER 3

Traveling with Dogs

Lucy called my show one day and showed great concern about a topical ointment her veterinarian gave her for a skin rash on her Poodle. She wanted to know how to use it correctly and seemed especially concerned because they were leaving for Florida in two days. I explained she should just apply it to the skin as directed, no big deal.

"But Doctor," she insisted, "we are going to Florida in just two days! Surely it won't get better by then." "Probably not," I replied, "just keep putting the medication on the rash until it gets better."

"But Doctor, you don't understand, it says right here on the label apply locally!"

Americans take almost five hundred million minivacations of four days or less every year. With sixty million cats and fifty-four million dogs out there, you can have trouble finding a pet-sitter or kennel space on short notice.

Many people simply don't like to leave their pets with strangers, in a kennel or at home, for days or even weeks at a time.

Traveling with your pets can be great fun. After all, they are part of the family, and many family vacations can be enhanced when your pets go along. On the other hand, taking your pets along on the family outing can be a real nightmare if you are not prepared. Therefore, planning ahead is important.

Q: I'd like to take my Miniature Schnauzer with me on short trips to see my family, but I don't know how she'd do. She isn't always friendly with other people.

A: Traveling with your dog can be a lot of fun or a huge headache, depending on the dog and the situation you'll be in. To travel with you, your dog should be well trained in all the basic obedience commands: sit, down, stay and especially, come. Make sure your dog has been well socialized. In other words, she should get along well with new people and other animals. She should be easy for you to control at all times. It's important that you can trust her around strangers, both adults and children.

It wouldn't be fair to your dog or your family to bring a nervous, unfriendly dog into a house full of strangers, especially if she doesn't mind well.

Try taking your Schnauzer on short trips to the park, flea markets or other places where there are lots of new people and new sights. Start with short outings and increase them gradually as she gains confidence. Try to let lots of new people talk to her and pet her if she seems relaxed and friendly. Don't push it, though, if she seems nervous and scared.

For everyone's sake, postpone traveling with her until you know she can handle it.

Q: *We have a six-month-old Lab puppy. When we take him in the car he drools the whole way—is that normal?*

A: Most puppies will drool excessively and may even vomit on their first car ride. This is absolutely normal. It's caused by a combination of the excitement of the new experience and the unfamiliar, unstable movement of the vehicle. Most puppies outgrow this reaction but with some dogs it persists into adulthood.

Motion sickness in dogs can usually be overcome using behavior modification techniques. If that doesn't work, your veterinarian can prescribe medications that will help. Tranquilizers are often prescribed to calm the dog and avoid the overexcitement that usually triggers the onset of nausea and vomiting. They also have some antivomiting effect. Don't try using human motion sickness drugs on your dog, as some of these are not safe.

Q: *Our Cocker Spaniel, Precious, gets very excited and nervous when we take her anywhere in the car. She usually ends up vomiting. Besides drugging her, what can we do to help her?*

A: You've already keyed in on a big part of the problem. Overexcitement is usually a triggering factor of motion sickness vomiting in adult dogs.

Here's a behavior-modification technique that works well with many dogs. Start by letting your Cocker sit with you in the car for five to ten minutes each day. Don't go anywhere, just sit in the car. Don't even start the car at first. Assume a very casual and laid-back attitude about the whole thing. Don't reassure her or pet her. Just talk to her in a calm and happy voice. (By coddling and reassuring her, you are actually confirming her fears that this is a scary situation.) Depending on how severe the problem is, you'll need to continue this daily for five to ten days.

Once your dog is calm sitting in the car with you, drive her to the end of the driveway, sit with her a few minutes and then pull back up. That's it. Get her out of the car, and she's done. Remember to stay very up-beat and happy. When this is no problem, start taking short drives around the block. Gradually lengthen the drive each day, and your dog should become accustomed to the movement and relaxed about being in the car.

Q: *My husband and I will be moving this summer and will be driving from Texas to California with our Dalmatian, Patches. What things should we pack for him?*

A: Good question! You'll want to be well prepared for this trip to make it as pleasant as possible for you and your dog.

Since some dogs may vomit when traveling and many drool excessively, it's a good idea to take some blankets to let Patches lie on in the car. Take along some paper towels and carpet cleaner, in case you need to clean up. I recommend an enzyme odor remover, such as Simple Solution or Nature's Miracle. They remove both the stains and odors and can be used without diluting or mixing.

His leash should be handy at all times. Make it a habit to snap his leash to his collar before you ever open a car door. Imagine how horrible it would be if he dashed out of the car and was lost in some totally strange location halfway between Texas and California. Make sure he has identification tags securely attached to his collar, with your name and phone numbers for your California destination. (If you don't know that yet, put the name and phone number of a friend or relative. Don't forget to tell them that you've done that.)

It's a good idea to have some sort of portable tie-out. You can let Patches relax in safety at a park or roadside stop while you and your husband enjoy some sandwiches. I like a tie-out called Ring Around a Tree, made by Four Paws Products and available at pet stores. It has a loop of vinyl-covered cable, which can be looped around a tree or car tire. The length of cable attached to the loop by a ring has a snap on the other end to attach to the dog's collar. There is also a large, heavy corkscrew-type tie-out which you secure in the ground and attach to a length of cable. It has limitations, though. If the ground is hard, it's tough to secure properly; some places where you'll stop there may be only pavement and if the ground is too soft, a strong dog can pull it out of the ground.

Pack plenty of his regular food. Don't rely on buying his food on the road. You may not be able to find his usual brand, and he doesn't need the stress of changing food added to the stress of the trip. You could end up needing *a lot* of paper towels.

Pack food and water dishes, and bring along a jug of water from home. A good idea is to freeze some ice in an old plastic butter tub with a lid on it. This allows the dog to lick and get some water, but not drink too much. On shorter trips it's also less messy. Don't forget a pooper scooper and some plastic bags for cleaning up after your dog. Bring along a couple of his favorite toys. Remember to pack any medications you may currently be using on Patches and bring a copy of his rabies vaccination certificate. Have a good trip!

Q: *We plan to take our dog traveling with us, but we will probably go only by car. Do we need one of those travel kennels? And which kind should we get—wire or plastic?*

A: Yes! A travel kennel is the safest way for your pet to travel. It not only keeps him out from under foot, making driving safer, it increases his safety and sense of security.

Depending on your type of vehicle and size of dog, it's not always possible to use a travel kennel for car trips. (You cannot fit a Rottweiler-size travel kennel in a Honda Civic.) But if possible, it's always the best way to go. Dogs tend to feel more secure and relaxed in their own kennel while traveling. You'll want to secure the kennel with seat belts or straps to eliminate movement. With your dog in a travel kennel he can't unexpectedly dash out of the car and get lost when you stop to fill up with gas! Your dog will also be much safer in the event of an accident. In case fire or ambulance personnel have to retrieve your dog from an accident scene, a kennel makes the job quicker and safer.

Many people like to use wire kennels for travel, especially those who have crate trained their dog in the wire kennel from puppyhood. I prefer the fiberglass type kennels for travel. They are lighter than wire kennels and won't scratch your car's interior. They make the dog feel more secure because they are more enclosed and help reduce motion sickness in pets that have that tendency.

Q: *Is it safe for dogs to travel on commercial airline flights? I've heard so many horror stories.*

A: Air travel for pets is certainly safer now than it was many years ago. There is now a federal law that makes airlines responsible for the health and safety of their animal passengers. All pets must be shipped in travel kennels which meet federal regulatory standards, and a veterinary health certificate is required before any pet is accepted for a flight.

Delta Airlines was nice enough to let me spend an afternoon with them to see their pet-handling process. You should check to make sure the airline you choose follows these procedures. Pets, in their travel kennels, should be hand carried to and from the planes. They should never be put on conveyor belts or baggage carousels. The pets should be placed by hand in a pressurized, temperature-controlled compartment, and the kennels should be secured to prevent movement during turbulence.

(By the way, there is no such thing as an unpressurized compartment in today's modern jets. All compartments are pressurized due to structural concerns.)

The pets should be checked to be sure there is adequate ventilation between kennels and that two adjacent animals aren't going to growl and snarl at each other during the trip.

Pets should not be left out in the hot sun or cold wind. They should be hand carried to secure, safe places until either loading or delivery to you is accomplished. All airlines must follow regulations about care of the animals during layovers and must take special precautions if the weather is bad or face fines.

Even with most of the major carriers trying to better train their employees who handle animals, accidents do happen. Most pet deaths result from suffocation or heatstroke. Animals have escaped from their kennels and have been lost or killed in traffic. Pets have been sent to the wrong location and have been left out in the heat or cold.

If you have a very small dog, you may be able to take it in the cabin with you in a special carrier designed to fit under the seat in front of you. This is certainly the safest way to go, as your dog never leaves your control. If you plan on traveling this way, make arrangements early. Most airlines limit the number of pets in a cabin to one or two. Some airlines do not allow pets to travel in the cabin at all.

If your dog must travel by air in the baggage compartment, use these safety tips to minimize the risk:

- Book a direct flight to minimize the chance of your dog ending up in the wrong location. If you must switch planes, allow plenty of time for your dog to switch planes as well.
- Book an early morning or late evening flight to avoid extreme heat. In very cold winter conditions, book a midday flight.
- Stay with your dog as long as you can before they load him. It wouldn't hurt to tip the baggage handler well.
- Freeze water in a margarine dish and attach it to the inside of the carrier so your dog will have access to some water. By freezing the water, it won't slosh during loading, but will begin to melt by the time your dog needs it. Line the carrier with something absorbent such as towels. This will allow spilled water or urine to be soaked up, and your dog will stay drier and more comfortable.
- For trips longer than twelve hours, attach a Baggie containing dry food to the top of the kennel with feeding instructions for airline baggage handlers.
- Put your name and phone number both on the outside of the kennel and on the inside, in case the outside tag gets torn off.

• Don't attach any tag by string or cord. It could fall into the kennel and your dog could get tangled in it and strangle. For the same reason, don't attach a leash to the kennel.

Q: *Our family would like to take our four-year-old Golden Retriever with us on our two week vacation. We'll be spending some time camping in national parks and some time staying in motels. Do you see any problem with taking her?*

A: If your Golden is well trained and well socialized, she should be a nice addition to your vacation as long as you prepare well.

Check well ahead of time to see if the national parks you want to visit allow dogs. Some don't. All national parks will require a rabies vaccination certificate and will insist that your dog be leashed at all times. (I'd also highly recommend you get this dog vaccinated for Lyme disease well before this trip.) You'll need a good tie-out chain, that won't get wrapped around a tree, to keep her close and safe while you're in your campsite.

Not all motels allow pets, so check ahead. You don't want to leave your dog in the car all night. It's a good idea to plan out where you'll stay each night well in advance and make sure each place will allow your dog to stay in the room with you. She'll need to be well behaved so that she doesn't bark or destroy the room while you're all gone to dinner. If you leave her in the room during the day for any reason, be sure to hang out the Do Not Disturb sign. This will prevent the maids from getting a surprise, and prevent your dog's possible escape.

To make your planning easier, The Annenberg Communications Institute publishes a hotel and motel directory called *Pets R Permitted*. This book lists over 3,000 hotels and motels that allow pets to stay with their owners, over 1,000 ABKA approved kennels for day-kenneling along the way or for extended kennel stays, theme parks that accommodate pets, special veterinarian and pet-sitter-location service information and travel safety and etiquette rules. (For information call (310) 217-0511.)

Q: *I will be taking a three-month trip overseas and would like to take my small dog with me. I know nothing about making these kind of arrangements. Can you help me?*

A: Traveling with your pet to a different country requires a great deal of preparation and homework. What is required will vary dramatically from country to country. You will be required to have a veterinary health certificate and a rabies vaccination certificate. The health certificate will need to be an official international health certificate and may need to be stamped and approved by the official state veterinarian. Some countries require their own special certificate and it may need to be stamped by the foreign consulate from that country. So, you'll need to check ahead with the foreign consulate for each country you wish to enter to see what will be required.

Be aware that there are some countries that require long periods of quarantine for any animal brought in. Even Hawaii, although part of the U.S., requires a *four-month* quarantine. This is because Hawaii is rabies free and extreme steps are taken to prevent the disease from being introduced. England is one such country with strict and long quarantine restrictions.

The cost of the transport varies greatly, depending on your destination and the size of your dog, but can be quite expensive. Your dog will be required to spend a great deal of time in a small kennel. You should consider if the stress to your dog and the expense incurred is worth having your dog with you on your trip. Remember, he will not be allowed in most restaurants and hotels.

You may find that it is impossible or just not practical to take your dog with you overseas. If you are determined though, the services of a professional pet transportation expert can make things much simpler. They will know or can find out the restrictions in the countries you will be visiting and will make arrangements for your pet's transport. You can find one by looking in the phone book in most large cities.

CHAPTER 4

Humane Societies, Abuse and Neglect

Pat called my show on Saturday quite upset over a stray Chow Chow that had been dumped at an equestrian center called Chadleigh Park. After about a week of the dog making friends with all the clients, the stable's owner had the dog picked up by the county animal shelter in hopes of finding it a home. When she asked the animal control officer about the adoptability of the dog, she was told that the shelter's insurance did not allow it to adopt out two potentially aggressive breeds of dogs, Akitas and Chow Chows. If the dog's owners did not claim it within three days, it would be destroyed.

Pat was quite upset. She knew the dog had been dumped and so would not be claimed by its owner. She had handled the dog extensively and knew it to be exceptionally sweet. It even got along well with the stable's dogs and cats.

I suggested to Pat that she first contact any private, no-kill, humane associations in her area and explain the dog's sweet personality and present predicament. If she could get one of these groups to agree to take the dog, then he had a chance. Once that was done, the stable owner would need to contact the director of the county shelter, explain that she was the person who had surrendered the dog and basically beg that it be released back to her custody for placement in the no-kill shelter. She would probably need to present proof that the other shelter had accepted the dog and would have it neutered prior to placement.

Pat called back the next Saturday and cheerfully reported that the county shelter had allowed her to pick up the dog and

she had taken it to a private, no-kill humane association.
Chadleigh, as they had named him, had been groomed,
neutered and featured on a local news' animal-adoption spot.
He was promptly adopted to a new home, and his new owners
were thrilled with him.

Local humane societies provide an essential service in the struggle to end animal suffering. They are the front-line soldiers in the fight to educate the public about humane and responsible pet care. They sponsor educational programs in schools and use community awareness campaigns of all sorts. They provide personnel to investigate cases of animal abuse and neglect. They rescue and rehabilitate abused animals and care for staggering numbers of homeless pets.

Happily, humane society volunteers are able to adopt some of these pets into new homes. A few have the heartbreaking job of humanely euthanizing most of them. If the caring, hardworking people of these organizations could send out one clear message to the country, it would be: SPAY AND NEUTER YOUR PETS. In this country, we must destroy fifteen and a half million dogs and cats year in and year out. There simply are not enough homes for them. Every person who allows their pet to breed is contributing to the problem.

Q: *Our neighbors have a Doberman in their back yard. It's tied to a tree with a chain and looks very thin. No one is ever out there with it and I've seen it standing and shivering many cold days and nights. Can't the humane society do something about this?*

A: Yes, your city or county will have laws which cover cases of animal abuse and neglect. Who enforces these laws will vary from area to area. It may be the animal control department, the police department or state humane officers. You can start by calling your local humane society. They will be able to assist you. The proper authorities will investigate and take action to see that conditions are improved, or remove the dog from its owners.

Neglect often causes more serious damage and suffering than does intentional abuse. Especially at risk are dogs that have been relegated to the back yard and may be just fed and watered once a day. Sometimes these types of careless owners forget even those essential needs for days at a time. Since little to no time is spent with these dogs, they may sustain injuries which go undetected and untreated until it is too late. They certainly suffer by lack of interaction, a harsh cruelty to such a social animal who craves companionship.

Your involvement is the first and most important step in getting this unfortunate animal some help. So much abuse and neglect is hidden from the view of all but a few people. If those people don't care enough to report it, the poor animals involved haven't got a chance.

Q: *We just got a puppy from the humane society. We love him and he seems very sociable, but our vet says he has mange. We're not happy with the humane society about this. What should we do?*

A: Your new puppy probably has demodectic mange. This is the kind that occurs most often in young puppies. Demodectic mange is transmitted to young puppies by their mothers as the puppies nurse. It usually first shows up at a few months of age as little hairless spots around the puppy's nose and forehead. It is not an animal care or sanitation problem. It occurs in even the best of puppies. In fact, the demodectic mange mite is found in normal skin, even normal human skin!

Your veterinarian can treat the pup for this mange using a dip called Mitoban. I wouldn't be upset with the humane society about it. I would let them know you are having the problem as they may want to look closely at the other pups in the litter.

Q: *We wanted to adopt a puppy from the local humane society, but they began asking so many questions, it surprised us. Many of the questions were personal. They also require a visit to inspect our house before we could be "approved" for a puppy. We became so offended, we left. Is this normal procedure?*

A: Don't be offended. Everything you just told me indicates that this is a highly responsible humane society with excellent rules for adoption. Good humane societies realize that the chances for a successful adoption are directly related to a successful match between adopted dog and new owner.

These humane societies typically have a long questionnaire to fill out, including questions about the age and number of family members, other pets in the home, size of house, size of yard and type of fence. They also ask about your previous experience with pets, what type of pets you have had and what has happened to them if they are not still with you. If they have the personnel resources, many good humane societies will require a "home inspection" visit to confirm that you have a safe, fenced yard.

You may think these extreme measures, but they're really not. Puppies that end up in humane societies have already been through a rough time. Although their basic needs are met while there, they don't have the security and comfort of a "home." They are deprived of the special attention that comes with being someone's special pet. There's a very good chance that these pups will recover quickly from their deprived beginnings if they get adopted to a good home, where they will fit well into the family life style.

The last thing these pups need is to be adopted to a home, then returned to the shelter six weeks later because "it didn't work out." Not only will it be very difficult for the pup to bond as well again, his sense of security is devastated. He never knows what to expect and could become quite neurotic. Not to mention, he will have passed his cute puppy stage and be much less likely to be adopted again.

The humane society staffers will know that certain types of dogs will fit best into certain family types. By learning all they can about you, they can point you toward a choice of puppy with the greatest chance of making a good pet for you. They are also able to eliminate people who would be unable to properly care for a pet, either because they lack the proper facilities or don't have the financial resources to assure proper food, shelter and veterinary care.

Q: *My wife and I went to the humane society today to adopt an adult dog. There were several wonderfully friendly dogs we just loved. There was one dog though that was so scared and timid. It just froze and trembled if you even tried to pet it. It got so scared it even looked as if it might bite. We're half considering adopting it because we feel so sorry for it. What do you think?*

A: I think what you're feeling is absolutely normal and understandable. I also think you'd be making a huge mistake. Think about it this way. A large percentage of those wonderfully friendly dogs won't get homes and will have to be put to sleep. If you adopt one of these more well-adjusted guys, you not only save a life, but you stand an excellent chance of having this new relationship work out great. One of these guys should be able to bond well to you and your wife and become a cherished family member.

I know its tempting to pick the saddest case in the shelter and adopt that dog. But you could be setting yourself up for tremendous emotional, physical and financial risk. It takes a long time and a great deal of expertise to successfully rehabilitate a severely abused dog. Many are so severely damaged that emotional and mental recovery is just not possible.

If, after investing huge amounts of time, patience and money, you are not successful, it would be a devastating experience. You might not even feel like trying again with a healthier dog. Then, not only would one of those wonderfully friendly dogs miss out on a second chance, you would miss out on the chance for a great relationship with a great dog.

Q: *We went into a humane society the other day looking for a dog. The smell almost knocked us out, and the people there acted as if we were bothering them. We left not wanting to adopt a dog from them but knowing there were homeless dogs in there in bad conditions. Should they be reported?*

A: Yes. While most humane societies are well run and staffed by caring, knowledgeable people, there are certainly some where the opposite is true.

Most humane societies, even well-run ones, are trying to care for more animals than their facilities can comfortably handle. This is because the pet overpopulation problem is so overwhelming. Most humane societies are also chronically short of funds because a good portion of their operating expenses must come from donations. Volunteers usually make up a part of the staff at any humane society, and this can result in unpredictable reception and responses to questions. For these reasons, I like to give each of these humane societies the benefit of the doubt.

There are, however, some which are just poorly run and clearly not doing a good job of caring for and adopting out pets.

I do think you should report what your experience was on your visit. You may need to do a little investigating in order to find the best authority to report to. First, try to contact the chairman of the humane society's board of directors. If the humane society is city owned, you can report them to the mayor's office or the city council.

Q: *A friend of mine is a member of a large national animal-rights group. She is trying to get me to join her at some of the group's protests. I believe in humane treatment of animals, but these people are frankly a little far out in left field. What do you think?*

A: Most animal-rights groups started out with the best intentions. However, with the tightening of the economy, contributions to all types of charities are down nationwide. As these groups compete for shrinking donations, many of them have resorted to sensationalistic, headline-grabbing tactics.

If you don't agree with all the stands taken by your friend's group, by all means don't support them, either by your presence or your donations. Only by supporting groups that represent your beliefs will animal humane groups get back on track.

If you'd like to do something to help animals, I strongly suggest volunteering and donating money at your community level. The pet overpopulation problem accounts for the needless destruction of over fifteen and a half million dogs and cats every year. Local humane societies tend to focus on this important problem. They work tirelessly, educating the public to spay and neuter and adopting-out homeless pets. A good number of the national groups ignore this problem altogether, focusing instead on sensationalism that will attract media attention. If you are not comfortable with your friend's organization, you may want to keep your donations of time and money closer to home.

CHAPTER 5

Reproduction, Spaying
and Neutering

Betty was one of my first callers this particular Saturday. She said they had a family dog named Bertha. Bertha was such a great dog that they wanted to have a litter so they could have a Little Bertha!

"How do we go about breeding her?"

Deep sigh. . . . "Well Betty, have you ever gone through the process of having a litter of puppies before?"

"No."

"Then let me take a moment here and explain what you are about to get into. You know, Bertha is going to have more than one puppy. What are you going to do with the other ten?"

"We thought we'd sell 'em and make some money!" she said proudly.

"Betty, the best advice I can give you, after fifteen years of practice, is not to breed Bertha!"

"Why?"

"OK, I'll just go down the list.

1. We put to sleep as many as fifteen million dogs and cats in this country every year because of overpopulation. Many of these animals come from litters just as you are about to generate."

She interrupted . . . "Oh, we'll find homes for them all!"

2. "If Bertha does have ten or eleven puppies, you're looking at having all of them dewormed, first shots, dewclaws removed and tails docked, perhaps second and third shots if you don't find homes for them all right away . . . plus food for them all, Bertha's medical expenses during pregnancy and after the litter comes . . .

the possibility of a Cesarean section and so forth. In other words Betty, I guarantee you will lose money on this venture!"

Now even more perturbed because I wasn't helping her with her question, "Well I want my children to have the experience of seeing a birth!"

3. *"And that is the worst reason to have a litter! Because you are not experienced in this process, not only are you going to be under the stress of puppies around the house and possible extraordinary medical expenses, but what kind of message will this send to your children? That animals are here just for our use or amusement, just so we can see a litter being born?"*

We heard the loud click of the phone as Betty hung up on me.

4. *"Not to mention that Bertha will never be the same, her breasts will enlarge, sag and forever hang down and her appearance will change. Her vulva will be forever more swollen. Statistically, spayed females live three years longer and they are less likely to get breast cancer."*

Most people have no business breeding the family dog! The only people that do are the ones that *have a business breeding dogs*, i.e., professional breeders. Pets are not breeding machines. There is no obligation attached to pet ownership that requires you to make more!

In my opinion, pets should be enjoyed for what they offer *as individuals*, not for what their offspring potential is. Additionally, I can say with some authority that inexperienced people who try to have a litter are in for much more than they imagine. In almost every case these people lose money and far underestimate the time commitment required for the venture.

What typically occurs after people lose money on a litter or two, is they will begin to cut back on sanitation, nutrition, vaccinations, de-worming and other essentials just so they can make a profit with the next litter. Puppy mills are a large-scale example of this. The result is thousands of puppies in pet stores with medical problems *you* get to pay for. Some of these problems last a lifetime, if the pup gets to live to adulthood.

Q: *I heard what you said to Betty, but our Agnes is such a special dog and so beautiful that we really want one of her offspring.*

A: I can understand this feeling. I have had many great dogs over the years and I've felt the same way about all of them. But if I had an offspring from all of them, I would be not only overrun with dogs, but I would have been responsible for hundreds, even thousands, of dogs that I could not keep.

We forget that dogs have many offspring in one litter, and these offspring go on to have offspring and so on. In fact, one litter can turn into 4,372 dogs in just seven years. When you look at it that way, it really opens your eyes.

I suggest this: love Agnes for herself but don't try to replicate her. Each new pet is a new and unique individual. I guarantee your next dog will be just as special in a different way.

Q: *Our dog just came into heat and is acting very strange. When will she be out of heat?*

A: Dogs have an estrus or heat cycle of eighteen days. She will have a bloody discharge for about the first nine days. The discharge then turns to a straw-colored, clear liquid for the last nine days. It is during this last nine days when she is most likely to stand for a male dog and become pregnant. But remember, she will attract male dogs during the entire eighteen days because she is emitting pheromones. Every male dog within a ten-mile radius will know the news! Keep a careful watch over her when she is outside.

Q: *Our vet has told us there is a birth-control pill for dogs. Can you tell us about that?*

A: Yes, it is called Ovaban. It is given to many show dogs to keep them from being in heat during a dog show (which could cause quite a ruckus). It is used when breeders are planning to breed a dog but are waiting for some reason. The "doggie pill" is safe and effective but is only to be given under prescription of your pet's doctor.

Q: *I caught my male Rottweiler "doing it" with a neighborhood Labrador this morning. When I tried to pull them apart, I got bit fairly badly. What's the best way to pull dogs apart?*

A: The best way not to be injured by two dogs caught up in the heat of the moment, is never let your dog get into that position. If you must break up dogs in "the act" use water, either from a bucket or a hose, and soak them good. That'll take the wind out of their sails.

Never use your hands to pull dogs apart. The male dog has an enlarged area midway up his penis called the glans penis. It is a large knot that swells during the erection and even more so during copulation. It actually ties up the male with the female. This is nature's way to assure semen stays in the vagina, and it provides the female with sufficient stimulus to cause pulsation in the vagina to get the semen into the uterus.

It must be very painful for both animals to have this romantic link pulled apart by you. In fact, when you think about it, you can understand why he bit you.

Q: *(After some discussion with this male caller about the importance of neutering his dog he finally admitted his major objection.)*
I can see spaying the female, but I just can't bring myself to castrate ole Joe Bob!

A: Many men in our society have a real anxiety about castration. I can't say I blame them. In fact, that is why, long ago we veterinarians began calling the procedure neutering! But even so, many men will not allow their male dogs to be neutered for no other reason than their own fear of castration. They actually feel the anxiety, fear and regret that would go along with such a thing in humans, when they think about it happening to their male dog.

I'm no human psychologist, but I've certainly spoken with many of these men on my talk show. I can only make the case for all the good that neutering male dogs does.

If you know one of these men, have them read this:
- Neutering a male dog does not change his personality.
- Neutering a male dog does not make him gain weight.
- Neutering a male dog does not decrease his natural protectiveness.
- Neutering a male dog does not hurt him.
- Neutering a male dog does not deprive him of the "joy of sex."

- Neutered males recover very quickly, with a minimal amount of discomfort.

Here's what neutering dogs does:
- Neutering a male dog does decrease their roaming and therefore prevent unwanted litters, accidents, injuries, poisonings and annoyed neighbors.
- Neutering a male dog does decrease fights and motor-vehicle injury.
- Neutering a male dog does decrease urine marking of every vertical object within the dog's environment.
- Neutering a male dog does stop dogs mounting your guests' legs.
- Neutering a male dog does decrease the strong smell of your dog's urine.
- Neutering a male dog does decrease that offensive discharge from the dog's penis.
- Neutered male dogs do pay more attention to their owners, are more affectionate and make much better pets for the rest of their lives.

Q: *We have a four-year-old Chow who just had seven puppies. She lost three. Now she is not eating. She's under the house and won't come out. What can we do?*

A: First, do whatever you have to do to get her out from under the house and to a veterinary hospital. She probably has some sort of uterine infection or metabolic imbalance because she should be healthy and feeding those puppies.

From what you've told me, my guess is that this dog doesn't have the best of clean environments in which to have a litter and raise healthy little ones. If you are going to take on the responsibility of bringing seven new lives into the world, you need to be serious about it. Be sure the mother is on the best possible nutrition during her pregnancy, be sure she is up-to-date on all her vaccinations before she gets pregnant. Make a clean, sanitary environment for her whelping and subsequent nursing of the litter. Make sure all puppies can stay warm and out of harm's way during the first four weeks of their life, and be sure you have a relationship with a veterinary hospital, because you're going to need it.

Finally, after you're through all this, *please* spay that dog. Neither you nor she have any business having any more puppies.

Q: *How long after our dog is in heat can we spay her?*

A: Good question. The uterus is inflamed and more vascular for several weeks after an estrus or heat cycle. I would recommend waiting two to three weeks after you know she is out of heat before spaying her.

Q: *Our Schnauzer–Poodle cross is about to have puppies. What are the signs that she's ready? Any tips on taking care of the litter would help, too!*

A: A female about to have puppies will begin to act differently twenty-four hours before whelping. She may whine, pace and act anxious or afraid up to a few hours before whelping. You should have already made a safe, quiet place for her to have her litter. A professional whelping box is a simple box where one side is cut down low for her easy passage. You can either buy one of these, or make one out of a cardboard box. There should be plenty of clean rags or towels, and you should place the box in an area where you can look in on her but not bother her with the traffic of family, neighbors and kids.

Right before she has her puppies, she will nest. She'll circle and lay down in it many times when choosing her spot. She may very well choose a spot other than her whelping box to have the litter, but it will have to suit her. Don't let an expectant mother outside without keeping an eye on her constantly. She could get under a shed or house or otherwise become trapped, secluded or lost during a very critical time.

Finally, when puppies begin to come, do your best to leave her alone unless she has a problem. She can push on a puppy for ten to thirty minutes and be quite normal. Once a puppy is actually in the birth canal, she should have no more that ten minutes of strong, active pushing. If a puppy is in the birth canal and she pushes for longer than about ten minutes, you may want to get her to the vet hospital. I would suggest you notify your pet's doctor that she is expecting so he can be prepared. Dogs have puppies one at a time. In fact, she may have a puppy, get up, drink a little and look like she is finished, then go back into her whelping box and have some more. So don't be surprised at that, it's normal.

It is also normal for her to want to eat the placental sacs. Don't let her. Even though wild dogs do this to protect the litter from attracting predators, domesticated dogs usually get pretty sick from them.

Most dogs don't need much help, but if she doesn't get the sac off the puppy fairly quickly, you may help her do that. You can take a clean towel and rub the puppies vigorously to get them breathing and crying a little.

I highly recommend a visit to the veterinarian the next day for physical exams on all the puppies and for mom.

Q: *Our five-year-old Scottie, Ashley, is pregnant. She's on a standard grocery-store-brand food. Is there any diet change we need to make to help her?*

A: Pregnant dogs should have the best nutrition possible. I recommend a high-quality, premium pet-store food such as Hill's Science Diet, Iams or Nature's Recipe. They have the highest quality ingredients and are easily absorbable. I do not recommend supplementing her with vitamins or calcium unless your veterinarian specifically prescribes it. There may be other supplementation he suggests for Ashley's case.

Q: *Our dog has just been bred by a neighbor's dog. Can we get her a shot or something to abort this pregnancy?*

A: Yes, as a matter of fact that is recommended in cases where the stray male is much bigger than your female because that will cause your dog serious, if not fatal, complications in about sixty days.

Although giving dogs the so-called "mismating" shot is not without risk, it can be used safely in cases like this. It is a large dose of female hormone which makes the uterus not receptive to implantation by the fertilized ova. It should not be given repeatedly, for example, every time the dog comes into heat and gets bred. Anytime you use large doses of hormones you run the potential risk of secondary problems.

I'd suggest getting your dog spayed and then keeping her in her own safe back yard! I would have animal control patrol the neighborhood and pick up the offending male, he may be causing other unwanted litters nearby.

Q: *We were going to spay our dog, but in the meantime she got pregnant. We cannot afford to have a litter. Can we go ahead and spay her now?*

A: If your dog is in her first trimester of pregnancy, you can spay her while she is pregnant. Remember, anytime you do this, the surgery is more complicated and carries with it a higher risk. The uterus is active, vascular and more likely to bleed. There is more fluid loss and a larger change to the dog's hormone cycles. But it is a safe procedure and is especially recommended in a case like yours.

CHAPTER 6

Senior Pets

"We have a wonderful Poodle that's been in our family twenty years! She eats just fine, is fairly perky and every now and then she actually wants to play."

"That sounds great, Judith, how can I help you?"

Her voice begins to quiver, "Well, Dr. Jim, I hope you can help me, everyone tells me to put her to sleep, she's just too old."

"Judith, is there anything wrong with her?"

"No! Nothing, she's just old! But several friends say because she's old I should have her put to sleep."

"Then you tell all those other people to go jump in the lake! That's your pal and your lifelong friend. She may live several more years. I've known small breeds of dogs like that to live to twenty-five! Absolutely NOT. You enjoy her, take her to the doctor's every six months for checkups, put her on the best senior diet you can buy, enjoy the time you have left together and don't let anyone talk you into doing anything for their own reasons!"

"Oh, Dr. Jim, God Bless you, I was hoping you'd tell me she was OK."

As veterinary medicine advances, just as with human medicine, our pet dogs live longer. The average dog now lives to be thirteen years old, with many dogs living into their mid to upper teens. It's not uncommon for small breeds of dogs to live eighteen to twenty years.

Many owners are upset at the thought of their precious pet aging, the time seems to go so fast. A dog's life span progresses so much more rapidly than a human's. But his senior years can be some of the best for you and your dog. It takes a degree of devotion on your part. Older dogs need some special attention and care to keep them healthy, happy, comfortable and active in their senior years.

Q: *Our twelve-year-old Beagle snapped at our eight-year-old son the other day while the dog was resting. What do you think caused that?*

A: Most dogs will have some degree of hearing loss by about twelve or thirteen years of age. Old dogs also sleep more soundly than they did when they were young. They're less aware of what's going on around them and are, therefore, easy to startle if awakened suddenly. Everyone in the family should know this and be careful to wake the dog gently, perhaps by calling his name at a moderate volume while standing about four feet away.

If you have a large family and many children, then you should call a family meeting and let everyone know that your Beagle is a senior citizen and deserves a certain amount of respect and special care. This will be easier on the dog and prevent such potentially dangerous situations.

Q: *Our twelve-year-old Irish Setter is having more and more trouble getting up from sleeping. Do you think she has arthritis? Is there anything we can do to help her?*

A: She most likely does have some arthritis. Depending on the breed, many dogs begin developing arthritis in their joints as early as six or seven years old. Most dogs have some arthritis by the time they're ten.

Moderate exercise twice a day for fifteen to thirty minutes will help her keep her muscles in good condition and her joints lubricated by movement. Pick activities such as walks at a moderate pace and low-key games of fetch. Avoid any activity that would make her jump up in the air, like Frisbee-catching. Swimming is great exercise for older dogs when the weather is very warm. Keep the swimming sessions short. Her endurance will be decreased, and sometimes dogs "keep going" to please their owners past the point of being tired.

Make sure she has a warm place to sleep indoors at night and on all but the mildest days. Cold and damp weather aggravate arthritic conditions. You might get her a nice "egg-crate" foam bed covered with artificial sheepskin. This type of bedding helps alleviate pressure on joints.

Finally, keep her weight at a good level. Excess weight compounds the problem of arthritis by putting extra stress on her joints. Don't forget to visit your veterinarian more often now that you have a senior dog!

Q: *Our thirteen-year-old Boxer named Big-Guy has been developing bumps all over his body. Can you tell us what those are?*

A: Many older dogs develop lumps and bumps that are visible. Thankfully, many times these are benign growths, usually of fatty tissue origin, and won't cause the dog any serious medical complications. Lipomas, as they are called, are common in older dogs and usually do not require surgical intervention unless they involve, or are near, an important anatomical structure.

If these lumps become numerous and appear to grow over several months, then I believe they should be removed. If the lumps do turn out to be benign, then good surgical technique should be the last of them. However, new ones might form and may require further removal.

Some bumps and lumps are not benign. Malignant tumors may show up as a lump in the skin and many times grow faster and more irregular than the benign types. Boxers are a breed of dog known for its susceptibility to various forms of cancer. I would highly recommend you have Big-Guy taken in immediately and let the doctor do a biopsy of one of the spots. Only by this test can you tell if the bumps are benign or malignant.

Q: *Our thirteen-year-old Pug has a whitish opaque look to his eyes and doesn't seem to see as well as he used to. Does he have cataracts? Can we have them removed?*

A: Cataracts are quite common in older dogs. It simply means that the normally clear lens of the eye has clouded up due to dehydration or protein accumulations on the inside of the structure. Dogs with cataracts generally do very well until the last stages of opaqueness. Even though they can't distinguish sharp edges and small shapes, they can follow general movements and actually compensate very well.

It is when the cataract becomes severe that you'll notice the dog losing all sight. Cataracts can be removed by various surgical procedures. I would suggest you get a specialist to do the surgery. Most large metropolitan areas have veterinary ophthalmologists who can expertly remove cataracts. However, some general practitioners who have a special interest in ocular diseases may have developed sufficient interest and experience to do a good job of cataract removal.

The doctor will either remove the lens by extraction, or by a process called phacoemulsification, where he will use ultrasound to liquefy the lens material and pull it out, replacing it with sterile fluid to give the lens its shape again. The postoperative result is excellent and reduces many serious secondary complications that can occur in dogs with mature cataracts. Also, most veterinary medical teaching hospitals at universities will do these procedures if you happen to live near by. You may ask your veterinarian for a referral to one.

Q: *It seems that since our Poodle has been getting older, he doesn't seem to hear as well. Could he be going deaf?*

A: All older dogs experience hearing loss to some degree. It's often the first sign of aging that owners notice, especially in the small breeds. Some sounds are more difficult to hear than others, leading many owners to call it "selective hearing loss." It seems dogs can always hear food going in their bowls but not always their owners calling them.

Most dogs have some hearing loss by age twelve or thirteen. Although most dogs have gradual loss of hearing, rarely do they go totally deaf. Hearing loss can also be caused by ear infections, wax buildup in the ears and overgrowth of hair in the ear canal. Have your veterinarian check your dog to rule out a possible medical problem.

If all is OK at the doctor's office and your dog does have old-age hearing loss, remember, you will have to begin communicating with him differently. Move more slowly around him, and don't forget to touch him more to get his attention. Use soft toys or bean bags thrown near him to get his attention and to correct misbehavior. Deaf animals usually compensate by learning to use sight and their sense of vibrations more. Take advantage of this.

Q: *What should we do about our eight-year-old Basset Hound's body odor? It seems to be getting worse as she gets older."*

A: It's an unfortunate side effect of aging that many dogs have more odor problems. The odors originate from several sources, the most common being the mouth.

Older dogs need their teeth cleaned more often to remove tartar buildup. Between cleanings by your veterinarian, you need to clean the teeth at least twice a week, using a special dog toothbrush and a special toothpaste designed for dogs. Your veterinarian can show you how.

Older dogs often have more skin odor because the secretions of the sebaceous glands in the skin contain more wax and oils as the dog gets older. A good brushing with a soft bristle brush every other day and a weekly bath using a gentle medicated shampoo will help a lot.

Ears are another "odor culprit." If you notice a foul smell coming from your Basset's ears, have her checked by your veterinarian to rule out an ear infection. Then, you can clean her ears gently with a cotton ball and a little baby oil every couple of days.

Finally, make sure there are no open sores that have become infected, check her feet and between her toes very well and "end up" with her anal glands and perianal area. This can be a source of very bad odor. You may want your vet to do this job, but you'll have to follow up with proper hygiene at home if there's a problem. She's worth it!

Q: *Dr. Jim. Why do small breeds live so much longer than the big breeds such as Great Danes?*

A: The average size of the typical mixed breed is thirty to sixty pounds. When dogs are bred indiscriminately for many generations, that's the size range that typically results. Selective breeding, such as is done in the pure breeds, is targeted at increasing certain characteristics in the breed. In the giant breeds, such as Great Danes, St. Bernards, Irish Wolfhounds and Great Pyrenees, breeders have bred so much for size that these dogs are way above the norm. Their abnormally large size puts great stress on their musculoskeletal and cardiovascular systems, and this dramatically shortens their expected life span. These dogs are old by five or six and rarely live past eight or nine.

Interestingly, small dogs reach physical maturity early in life, say about six months, but live the longest. Giant breeds reach physical maturity late in life, at about eighteen months, and don't live much past eight years of age.

Q: *We have a thirteen-year-old mixed breed, mostly Beagle I think, and he seems to waddle more than actually walk. Do you think he is too heavy?*

A: By your description, I think he certainly is. If you can't feel your dog's ribs with gentle pressure on its rib cage, then your dog is overweight, or obese actually, and he needs to reduce. Elderly dogs are less active and have a slower rate of metabolism, so they require fewer calories than they did when they were younger. If you continue to feed your dog the same amount and type of food as he ages, he'll begin to put on excess weight.

Obesity is a serious problem in dogs, especially as they get older. The extra weight puts added stress on the muscular system and on arthritic joints. It greatly compounds heart problems such as congestive heart failure. In the "long and low" breeds such as Dachshunds and Basset Hounds, excess weight can increase spinal-disc degeneration, leading to pain and possible crippling. Obesity greatly increases the risk of surgery should your pet require it. Other increased risks include diabetes, skin-fold dermatitis, impaired liver and kidney function and digestive problems.

There are some medical conditions that can make a dog look fat when he isn't. An abdominal tumor or fluid retention secondary to congestive heart failure may mimic obesity, so have your veterinarian give your dog a thorough checkup before you put him on a diet. Your veterinarian will also recommend the best diet to help your pet reduce. You'll need to increase his activity level as well to help him lose weight. Slow or moderately paced walks for ten to fifteen minutes several times a day will work best.

Q: *Our Sheltie, Cricket, is eight years old and is starting to become noticeably less active. Do you think it would be a good idea to get her a new dog friend?*

A: Yes, one of the best ways to keep an older dog active, happy and, therefore, healthier is to get her a young dog as a companion and playmate. You'll notice a big difference in her activity level as she teaches this "youngster" the ropes. A similar breed of dog and one of the opposite sex is usually accepted the best by an older dog. Head to the humane society today and find her a buddy. (Review Chapter 1 before you go.)

Q: *Since our Boxer, Mike, has gotten older, he's really having a lot of gas, if you know what I mean! Is there something we can do about this?*

A: Trust me, I know what you mean! As our dogs get older, their digestive systems change. Sometimes they can't handle the food ingredients they once did. Many pet foods contain soy or whole grains. These ingredients contain complex sugars that Mike may not be able to digest anymore. After a meal, these sugars ferment in Mike's intestine and produce the unpleasant gas. And you know what happens then!

You can change brands of pet food and be sure the new brand contains less soy or wheat ingredients. I would also recommend buying the highest-quality food you can find, not only to assure that the nutrients will be more absorbable, but because senior dogs need higher-quality nutrition than what is provided by many standard grocery-store brands. It will be quite hard to find a dog food that does not contain these complex sugars because 95% of all commercial dog food diets have the gas producing ingredients. But you may very well find a brand with a formula that is more easily digested by your dog.

The best help comes through enzyme chemistry. AkPharma Inc. makes a product called CurTail, which is a natural-source food enzyme that aids in the digestion of these complex sugars found in pet foods. The enzyme acts on the sugars before they become a problem. You simply put a few drops of the product on your dog's food immediately before each meal. It can be used on any type of dog food.

Interestingly, your dog, a Boxer, is in the top ten of the gassiest dogs! The top ten breeds are: German Shepherd, Mutts, Labrador Retriever, Boxer, Doberman Pinscher, Poodle, Cocker Spaniel, Rottweiler, Beagle and Dalmatian. Sorry Mikie!

Q: *I've noticed that lately my Collie seems to dribble urine on the rug when she sleeps. She never used to do that. Is it because of her age? She's ten now.*

A: This is a common problem in older dogs and especially in females. It is called urinary incontinence and may be caused by many things. First you should probably have your veterinarian rule out a urinary tract infection. If she can somewhat control the flow of urine it may be an infection. If she continuously dribbles, then it could be a physical or hormonal problem.

If it is an infection your veterinarian can put her on very effective antibiotics that should clear up the infection within two weeks. Some bladder infections are very persistent and may require repeated treatments with various antibiotics. So be prepared to be patient with the doctor's treatment regime.

If it is not an infection, then the next thing on the list is to determine if the dribbling can be controlled by the use of supplemental estrogen hormone. This determines if it is estrogen sensitive. If so, then you simply supplement her with an estrogen hormone (DES) for the rest of her life. This usually works very well once you and your veterinarian have found the exact dosage that will control the symptoms.

If the dribbling does not respond to estrogen, then it may be neurological. This could mean either a brain lesion or a spinal cord or sacrum area problem. These are harder to diagnose. Many people with older dogs with such a problem aren't willing to spend the time and money required to determine if it is a neurological tumor or dysfunction. And if it is, treatment is limited.

If the dribbling occurs only when she is sleeping, you may want to spread a sheet or some towels out where she sleeps and wash these on a regular basis. Don't punish her for this dribbling. She has no control over it.

Happily, most of these cases are estrogen sensitive and plac-ing her on DES will usually solve the problem.

Q: *I've heard you talk about the importance of diet in senior dogs. My Pomeranian, Lady, is in good health, but she's fifteen now. What would be the best diet for her?*

A: First, eliminate table scraps and human food "treats" from Lady's diet, no matter how much she loves them. Even small amounts of table scraps can become a significant percentage of a dog's diet, especially a small dog. This can upset the balance of fats, proteins, carbohydrates, vitamins and minerals she needs to be healthy.

Because her appetite is probably still very good, but she's not as active as she used to be, she needs a food with fewer calories but the proper balance of nutrients of the highest quality.

For a healthy older dog, I recommend a premium-brand senior dog food such as Hill's Science Diet Canine Senior, Iams or Nature's Recipe Senior. These have lower protein amounts but much higher-quality protein content than do puppy or high performance foods. Because your dog is healthy, she does not need a diet that severely limits protein. These diets are intended for dogs with kidney dysfunction and may have too little protein for a healthy dog. Look for a premium senior dog food with 14% to 21% protein and 10% fat. Stay away from low-cost or bargain brands!

Q: *Our old dog, Charley, is getting on in years. What special preventive measures should we take to keep him healthy, and how often should he see the vet?*

A: Charley should now be checked by your veterinarian *every six months*. Due to the fact that dogs age at a more rapid rate than humans, significant changes to your dog's vital systems can occur in as little as three to six months as he gets older. In addition to his veterinary checkups, here are some important points about caring for Charley in his senior years.

- Keep Charlie's weight at a good level and feed him a good quality senior dog diet recommended by your veterinarian. Remember that older dogs don't need as many calories because they're less active. But they need the highest quality food you can buy.

- Give him daily exercise of a moderate type, such as walking or fetching, for fifteen to thirty minutes. This will keep his muscles, joints and cardiovascular systems in good shape.

- Charley will need more frequent grooming to keep body odors down and to prevent health problems. Pay special attention to his teeth. Tooth loss is common in older dogs, especially small breeds, because their teeth are more crowded and the bone anchoring their teeth is thinner than in large breeds. Your veterinarian will need to clean his teeth more often, and you will need to brush them several times a week.

- Keep his nails well trimmed. Some older dog's nails become very long and may curl under, making walking difficult or painful. His nails should be trimmed every other week, either by you, your groomer or your veterinarian.

- Check for lumps and bumps on his body when grooming. These may be tumors which may be benign or malignant. Your veterinarian will need to check Charley if you discover any lumps.

- Remember that older dogs are less tolerant of heat or cold. In the summer, leave Charley inside with the air conditioner on during the day or leave a fan blowing outside where he can get in front of it. He'll need good shelter and a warm blanket in cold weather and needs to be out of drafts, preferably in the house. Cold, damp weather also increases arthritic pain.

- Give him lots of love and affection. Try to keep his routine fairly consistent. As he gets older, he will rely more on you and will feel more secure with a stable routine. Let everyone in the family know you need to interact with Charley a little differently now that he may not move as fast or hear as well.

CHAPTER 7

Euthanasia and Pet Loss

Don't be dismayed at good-byes. A farewell is necessary before
you can ever meet again. And meeting again, after moments or
lifetimes, is certain for those who are friends.
                              —Richard Bach, from *Illusions*

It is never easy to lose a friend. Even though it is not the loss of a
human life, the loss of a pet can sometimes have a greater impact
on our daily lives because some pets are with us every day and pets
offer unconditional love. The loss can leave a huge hole in our lives.
The feelings of grief, emptiness and loneliness are the same when
we lose a pet as when we lose a human friend.

One of the most difficult decisions a pet owner can face is
whether it is time to end a pet's suffering through humane euthanasia. As a veterinarian and talk show host, I have helped hundreds
of clients and callers face this decision. It is never easy.

Q: *Our thirteen-year-old Boxer, Sarge, has cancer and is weaker every*
day. Now, just this week, he has begun not being able to hold his
bladder at night and he occasionally moans. When do we know it's
time to . . . we can't make that decision.
A: First of all, thirteen years old is very old for a Boxer. Boxers are
one of the breeds of dogs that simply don't live long enough. It is
rare to meet a thirteen-year-old Boxer. That is testimony to the
fact that you have taken excellent care of Sarge.

This is one of the most difficult decisions you will ever make
as a pet owner—and it's painful. My rule of thumb on deciding
when it's time to put a beloved pet to sleep is to ask yourself this
question: is life fun for Sarge anymore? If he can get up and

down without too much pain, eat and eliminate without too much trouble, respond to your petting and be interactive, then he probably still enjoys being with you.

However, if he cannot exist within these necessary and dignified boundaries, life probably isn't fun for him anymore and the most humane thing you can do is let him go to sleep and be rid of the pain and discomfort.

By itself, not being able to hold his bladder, is not reason enough, in my opinion, to put Sarge down. There are some good nursing things you can do to help this problem. You can let him sleep on disposable sheets or cover his bed with plastic. You can even buy or make doggie "Depends" for him. Many dogs live for years with urinary incontinence.

However, if in addition to the urinary problem, Sarge seems to be in pain, has difficulty walking and appears to be in misery, then it is time.

Animals have a way of communicating this to us. Allow yourself to be open to his communications, and you may be surprised at the feelings and insight you receive. If you decide it is time, remember this: Sarge has given to you, unconditionally for thirteen years. Now you have a chance, one last time, to give to him some final peace and rest.

Q: *My eleven-year-old German Shepherd has heart failure and has been very sick for the last month. It's the hardest decision I've ever made, but I've decided it's time to put her to sleep. I want to be sure that it isn't going to be painful for her. Can you tell me how it's done?*

A: Bless your heart, I've been through this many times with my own pets as well as hundreds of times with client's pets. It is always hard. You can rest assured that euthanasia is not painful when done by a professional with the proper equipment and medications.

Most veterinarians use a simple overdose of a general anesthetic. It is injected slowly in the vein so that she simply goes to sleep, as if she were going into surgery. The overdose ensures she will drift into deep sleep, then slowly her heart and respiratory functions will stop. It is a very peaceful way to go.

I've seen hundreds of animals give a deep relaxing sigh during the procedure, as if to say, "Thank goodness, I don't have to struggle anymore, I'm free to move on."

Q: *My thirteen-year-old dog is very ill and is in pain. I know I need to let him go now. I don't want him to feel like I've abandoned him. Do you think the veterinarian will let me stay with him while he puts him to sleep?*

A: I know this is a difficult and painful decision. I completely understand your wanting to be there for your pet to the end. I think it's a good idea. Your dog will know you are there and that you love him. It will make him more calm. The thoughts of the years of love and memories you two have shared will drift with him as he goes.

Discuss your wishes with your veterinarian. Some veterinarians either don't like for you to be in the room for this procedure, or simply won't allow it. I think this is because they feel it may be harder on you to witness the death, or because they are uncomfortable with the outpouring of emotions that naturally follow. If your veterinarian won't allow it, I would suggest finding one who will. You should not be robbed of this important time by someone else's inability to handle it. I suggest you call first and see if your doctor will let you be there.

The doctor should counsel with you, answer all of your questions and give you plenty of time in a quiet room with him before it is done. Once injected, the doctor should leave the room and let you have some quiet time with him. My thoughts are with you and I sympathize with your loss.

Q: *We have to take our Poodle, Sam, in to be put to sleep on Monday. We want to know what will be done with his body and what options we have.*

A: Most veterinary hospitals have made arrangements for either disposal by cremation at the hospital, or they may have an area pet cemetery pick up animals that die or are euthanized for proper burial. It is unfortunate that most city regulations won't allow burial of animals in household back yards, because that's where I'd like to have my pets. But it is an important law in place to protect human health. If you live in the country you can have your own pet cemetery area under a favorite tree—I like that idea.

If the hospital does not have such arrangements made, then I suggest you call ahead, today, and find a pet cemetery or crematorium. If you wait until Monday, your emotions will keep you from thinking clearly. Ask if the facility is a member of The Pet Loss Foundation or The International Association of Pet Cemeteries. IAPC is based in South Bend, Indiana, and can refer you to a reputable cemetery.

Q: *I lost my twelve-year-old Sheltie, Charley, last month. I still can't get over it. My friends are now trying to get me to buy another dog—I'm not ready. What can I tell them? I need more time.*

A: If you're not ready, you're not ready. Politely tell your friends: you know that one day you'll be ready for a new puppy, but that you are not prepared for that commitment right now. I think you are very smart in taking your time to grieve over your Sheltie. Far too many people give in when well-meaning friends try to "cheer them up" by pushing a new pet on them too fast. I've found that people have difficulty bonding to a new pet if they haven't had adequate time to grieve over their loss.

There is no textbook time for recovery from a loss—human friend or pet companion. There will come a day when you'll decide you'd like to have another wagging tail and happy dog face around the house. Just remember, the new dog will not replace Charley, no dog could do that. You will, however, develop a brand new relationship with the new guy that will, over the years, be just as special and meaningful as was the one you had with Charley.

Q: *When we lost our twenty-year-old Poodle, Bentley, it hurt so bad we've decided never to get another dog. We don't ever want to go through that kind of pain again!*

A: I can really relate with that feeling! It does hurt bad, but that's good! It means you care, and will allow yourself to truly enjoy animal companionship. Many people never allow themselves to experience the joy of human–pet bonding and the priceless enrichment of their lives pet animals can bring.

But you should know, after twenty years with Bentley, how valuable having a doggie face around the house is! Don't deny yourself that joy based on fresh pain. Give yourself a proper amount of time to heal. Be happy you and your family had Bentley, and take pride in the fact that he had you!

Soon, you'll begin to miss the life a dog brings to the house, the constant, unconditional companionship a new pet pal will offer. Then and only then, why not head down to the humane society and save a life. That new dog will generate his own special place in your heart and his own special memories for all of you.

A few years ago, my wife Pat and I lost our German Shepherd, Zeus. He was the most special dog either of us had ever known. We were devastated by his sudden death due to an acute illness at age six. My wife tells me that she has never felt such intense pain as from this loss.

No dog can ever replace Zeus in our hearts, but today we have two dogs who are wonderful in their own ways, a German Shepherd, named Bravo, and a Welsh Corgie, named Penny. Whether it is true or not, no one knows, but Pat and I find comfort in the thought that when our time comes to go, Zeus will be there waiting for us, tail wagging.

Part II

General Care and Grooming

CHAPTER 8

Bathing, Shedding and Scooting

"Dr. Jim, our dog has a real odor to him, what can we do?"

"Well, Bob, what kind of odor is it? Is it coming from his ears, or tail, or is it intestinal gas? What?"

"I don't know. I can't smell much anymore, let me get Mabel on the line." (Mabel gets on the extension.)

"It's real bad dog smell, it's all over his body, it's all the time. Bob can't smell it, but it drives me crazy!"

"Well, Mabel, how often do you bathe him?"

"Oh, every now and then."

"How often is that . . . once a month?"

"Oh no. Maybe once every six months."

"You folks need to bathe your dog more often! Get a good medicated shampoo from your veterinarian or pet store and bathe him every week!"

"Every week!"

"Yes, it sounds like he needs that at first, then you may be able to cut back to every two to three weeks."

"Well, Mabel, you'll have to bathe him, you know. I can't smell it!"

"He's your dog too, you know. I can't bathe him all by myself 'cause of my rheumatism."

"Bye, Bob; Bye, Mabel. I think I just started a domestic dispute. Let's go to our next caller."

With as much skin disease as there is in dogs, bathing them is essential, both for general cleanliness and as part of their medical therapy. Not to mention that a clean, good-smelling dog is more fun to hug! Bathing also helps remove dead hair and so decreases shedding.

Dogs shed. It is as regular and as certain as the sunrise every morning. *Seasonal shedding* occurs in the spring and fall. This is the normal cycle of haircoat turnover. *Nonseasonal shedding* occurs at all other times and is lighter, but constant. Shedding can be increased by allergies, disease and low levels of skin inflammation from various causes. What we dog owners must learn is how to keep the shedding to reasonable levels.

There are some breeds of dogs that are heavy shedders and some that are low shedders. The known heavy shedders are: Belgian Sheepdog, Belgian Malinois, Curly-Coated Retriever, Collie, Sheltie, Alaskan Malamute, Samoyed, German Shepherd and Keeshound. The light shedders are: Irish Water Spaniel, Basenji, Schnauzer, Poodle, Maltese, Greyhound and terriers.

Scooting is an annoying habit of dogs that aren't properly groomed on a regular basis. Many people think it is funny, but a dog's bottom must itch pretty bad for them to contort themselves into the scooting position and drag their rear on carpet, concrete or anything else that will relieve the pain. It is usually a malady we can easily correct, and I'm sure your pet friend would appreciate your quick attention.

Q: *How often should I bathe my Rottweiler? She goes to the stable with me several times a week, and she can get smelling pretty bad sometimes.*

A: Some dogs will need a bath every week, while others can go months with just an occasional good brushing. It depends your dog. Some dogs are fairly fastidious, they like to stay clean and seldom get dirty. Other dogs love to romp in the mud and roll in foul-smelling things. Short-haired dogs such as Rottweilers typically require less bathing and overall grooming than long-haired dogs.

Just use your common sense. If your dog smells bad, you'll want to bathe her so she's nice to be around. If she has fleas, she'll need to be bathed, probably weekly throughout flea season. If her coat begins to look oily or dull and lackluster, she could use a good bath and conditioning rinse.

If she is scratching a lot and her skin has a bad smell to it, she needs a bath and would probably benefit from a medicated shampoo. In the spring and fall, when she goes through her major shedding, a good bath can help accelerate the process by helping get rid of loose hair.

If your dog doesn't seem to need a bath, then don't bathe her on a regular basis just to be doing it. Regular brushing is more important to the health of your dog's skin and haircoat. Too much bathing can rob the coat of natural oils and moisture.

Q: *Our Basset Hound has a real bad, oily smell to her skin. What would cause that, and is there any way to get rid of it?*

A: Your Basset may have a seborrheic skin condition. Chronic low-level inflammation of the skin causes increased production of fatty acids. Bacteria grow more easily in this bed of extra fatty acids, and they create the "doggie" smell. You can treat mild cases using a medicated antiseborrheic shampoo once a week. Moderate to severe cases will probably need to be seen by your veterinarian, who can prescribe steroids and other medications that will help to decrease the inflammation in the skin.

When using medicated shampoos, remember to let them sit in contact with the skin for ten minutes. I know it is no fun sitting with an upset, wet, lathered dog for what seems like ten hours, but it is necessary for the medications to have their desired action.

There are many types of medicated shampoos on the market. I prefer you buy one from your veterinary hospital. However, if your doctor prescribes one from the pet store, that is also OK. Just be sure you get the directions for its use from the doctor. Don't rely on the pet store clerk to give advice on this condition.

Q: *Our neighbors are using Selsun Blue "people" shampoo on their dog. They said their vet told them that was the best. What do you think?*

A: Selsun Blue certainly is a good product to treat many forms of low level dermatitis where there is a high turnover rate of the external skin layers. It helps slow this exfoliation and decrease the itching. Many board-certified veterinary dermatologists recommend its use.

There are also many other high quality medicated shampoos

that have been specifically formulated for dog's skin. I recommend Bio Groom's BioMed Tar–Sulfur Shampoo, BioGlan's Dermaplex, and Tomlyn's Nova Pearls Coal-Tar Shampoo for seborrheic dermatitis in dogs. Most of these can only be found at pet stores or grooming shops.

Most medicated shampoos are variations of coal tar extract, which smells pretty bad, but works well. Others have salicylic acid, aloe vera, ti-tree oils and the like. Most are nonprescription and are a good adjunct to other therapy from your pet's doctor.

Q: *How do I know what kind of shampoo to use to bathe my dog? There must be a hundred different brands.*

A: Of course any special shampoo prescribed by your pet's doctor is the one you will need to use. These medicated shampoos really help as an aid to fighting dermatitis and allergy-related skin disease. Most of them don't smell very good, but use them anyway.

For dogs that don't need a medicated shampoo, the decision is whether or not to use a *flea* shampoo. I suggest a good flea shampoo *if* you are having to fight fleas. It will help kill the fleas on the pet and have some small residual effect.

However, if you are *not* having a problem with fleas, there is no reason to use a flea shampoo as they can be harsh and drying. I'd suggest a nice conditioning shampoo instead.

A conditioning rinse is also good for dogs, especially those with long or thick haircoats. These dogs need some hair conditioning in order to comb them out.

Do not use household products such as dishwashing detergents to wash your dog. These products contain harsh detergents that can irritate the skin and strip the coat of natural oils. They may also leave an irritating residue which can result in scratching and encourage infections.

I also don't care for the inexpensive pet shampoos you'll find in grocery stores. They are very drying and may even be irritating to your pet's skin. Stick with shampoos that you can find in pet stores or from your veterinarian.

Q: *I've heard you say to be careful about a dog's eyes and ears when you bathe them. What precautions should I take?*

A: Use a little eye ointment or mineral oil in each eye before you begin. This helps prevent any chemical irritation some dogs show to various shampoos. Also, use a wad of cotton in each ear to prevent water accumulation in the deep canine ear canal which may spark irritation or an infection.

When you lather the dog, begin behind his head and work backward. Do the same when you rinse the dog. On the face, I like to lather very sparingly, using a washcloth, and then use the washcloth to rinse the face as well. You are a lot less likely to get either shampoo or water in your dog's eyes or ears doing it this way. Don't forget to remove the cotton from his ears when you're done!

Q: *Please don't laugh, because I'm sure this is going to sound like a really dumb question. How exactly do you bathe a dog? I've never done it before. I just adopted an adorable Sheltie from the humane society and she really needs a bath!*

A: Don't worry, that is not a dumb question. As a matter of fact, if you've never done it before it can be an overwhelming task. Begin by getting all the things you will need and put them within easy reach before you ever start.

You'll need a brush, shampoo, rinse (if you like), eye ointment or mineral oil, cotton balls, a hose with a spray attachment, a washcloth and three or four towels.

First brush your dog thoroughly to untangle the hair and to remove loose hair and debris. Carefully work out any mats with your fingers, because they will tighten more once they get wet.

After putting a little eye ointment in the eyes and cotton balls in the dog's ears, thoroughly wet the dog using lukewarm tap water, starting at her feet and working up to her back and along her neck. Next, use ample amounts of your shampoo. Dog hair seems to take more shampoo than human hair, so be liberal. Scrub it in and make a good lather. Medicated shampoos will need to sit in contact with the skin for about ten minutes.

Start shampooing at the neck and work backward. Work the lather through the coat down to the skin. Then work on the head using a washcloth. Wash the ear flaps, but don't get soap into the ear canals. Go slowly around the eyes. Avoid getting shampoo in the mouth. Don't forget to get between the toes, behind the ears and under the chin, favorite hiding places for fleas and ticks. If you need more lather, try using a little more water first before you use more shampoo.

Rinse the head first, using your washcloth, then the rest of the body, using the sprayer. Rinse very well getting all the soap out from every crack and crevice. If your dog was very dirty or smelly, I'd repeat the whole process. Now is the time to use a conditioning rinse if you'd like. Do a final safety rinse to make sure all soap lather is gone. If left in contact with skin, soap can cause a localized area of irritation.

If it's a nice summer day and you're outside, let your dog run and air dry after a rubdown with a large towel. However if not, use several large towels and dry the dog well. It will take a few hours to finish the job. In cool weather, keep your dog indoors until he's completely dry.

Some dogs will let you use a blow dryer to dry the haircoat. This is very scary to other dogs, however, so be careful and introduce your dog to this new procedure slowly. Be careful to use a low setting. High settings may burn sensitive skin.

Q: *Is it OK to use flea shampoo on my new Malamute puppy? She's six weeks old.*
A: You'll need to read the label on the shampoo and see if it's approved for use on young puppies. Most flea shampoos are not, although there are some that are, as well as some mild flea soaps that can be used on puppies.

Unless your new puppy has a severe flea infestation, I'd prefer you simply use a regular shampoo which is approved for puppies. I like to keep chemicals away from young animals as much as possible. The bath itself will probably drown most of the fleas.

Q: *Our dog got squirted by a skunk. Can we use tomato juice to get the smell out?*
A: It does work. In fact, I've had the occasion several times to send the technician out to buy several quarts of tomato juice so we could soak a client's dog to get the smell out.

Not to be outdone by such homespun practicality, commercial companies have produced chemicals that claim to immediately neutralize the skunk odor. Skunk Out is one such product, and again, it seems to work fine. Good luck!

Q: *My dog sheds constantly. We have him on a standard grocery-store dog food. What else can we do?*

A: The first thing I suggest is switching your dog to a higher-quality dog food. One of the premium brands available from a pet store or your veterinary clinic will provide your dog with the best quality nutrition. The healthier your dog's skin and coat are, the less he'll shed.

You may add a teaspoon of vegetable oil to your dog's food two or three times a week to add a fresh source of fatty acids to her diet. These fatty acids are responsible for skin and haircoat health. They are also the molecule that may go bad in dog food that sits too long on the store shelf, and what is deficient in many of the low end brands.

The rest of the prescription is *regular* grooming. Bathe her once a week with a good medicated shampoo and brush her daily. This will stimulate the circulation to the hair follicles and remove old hair and skin flakes.

Q: *Our vet says our dog needs an infusion of the "an-all" sacks. Can you tell me what that is?*

A: Your doctor is talking about *anal glands*. These are two small sacs on either side of the dog's anus. They were intended to squirt a little very pungent smelling material onto the stool when the dog defecates. This helps mark territory.

However, with our domestication of the dog, and his diet, these glands have become a problem. The material can become thick and pasty, or the gland may become impacted or infected. This can cause the dog itching, pain and eventually even an abscess near the anus.

When these problems occur, medical attention is required. The main symptom seen is scooting, but sometimes you may just notice the dog doing a lot of licking the rear and even straining to defecate. The doctor will express the glands and, depending on what's seen, may decide to infuse them with an antibiotic and steroid medication.

I usually show my stouthearted clients how to do this at home so they can do the job without coming into the clinic. Many people don't want to do it—and I don't blame them. It's no fun!

Q: *I have a four-year-old Lhasa Apso. She has been scratching a lot lately, and I notice she has some pretty bad mats behind her ears and underneath her belly. Why does she get these mats? Is that why she's scratching?*

A: There are a number of reasons why your dog may be scratching. She could have fleas, dry skin, insect bites, or she could just have irritated skin from being dirty. The mats indicate you need to do a better job of regular grooming.

If, as your dog sheds her coat, the dead hair is not removed, it will form mats. She will scratch in an attempt to remove the dead hair. This scratching not only irritates the skin, but makes the mats worse. Irritated skin becomes inflamed, and this causes it to ooze more oils. These excess oils on the skin are the perfect place for bacteria to grow. This bacterial growth causes a secondary bacterial skin infection and the spot gets worse. As you can see, this can become a vicious cycle very quickly.

Your dog depends on you to keep her healthy and comfortable by grooming her regularly. It's one of the responsibilities you take on when you get a dog. Obviously, long-haired dogs and those with thick haircoats require more grooming than short-haired breeds. You should thoroughly brush your dog each week, making sure all mats are carefully worked out. A quicker, daily brushing in between makes this job easier and keeps more hair off your furniture and floor.

I like to simply stick a slicker brush in my back pocket when we go to the park. We play a little fetch, then I let her rest and brush her. This makes the job more fun for both of us!

Q: *Our dog, Goldie, scoots. We know her anal glands are done every time she is groomed. Why do you think she still scoots?*

A: There are several possible reasons. It could be your groomer isn't doing a proper job of taking care of the glands. It may be that your grooming interval is fine for her haircoat, but the anal glands are becoming swollen during the interval. It may also be that her bottom itches for another reason besides anal gland impactions.

Another cause of such itching could be an allergy. Many dog allergies inflame the very sensitive skin areas like ear canals, between toes, eyes and lips and even the perianal area. It can also be a simple local dermatitis caused by an initial bit of scratching that has now become a chronic irritated spot that she is keeping inflamed with her scratching.

In any case, I'd suggest your veterinarian look at her. The doctor can quickly decide what it is and probably get her some quick relief.

Q: *How often is it necessary to groom short-haired dogs? We have a Doberman who stays in the house with us when we're at home.*

A: Short-haired breeds such as your Doberman obviously don't require the amount of grooming that long-haired, thick-coated breeds such as a Collie would. However, short-haired dogs also need to be brushed. Their coats shed out as well, and a good brushing removes dead hair and stimulates the skin's natural oils.

Regular grooming also gives you a chance to check your dog over on a regular basis and look for health problems. While grooming, you should feel for any lumps or bumps. Early detection of cysts or tumors gives your dog a better chance to recover from these. Minor injuries such as cuts, insect bites and abrasions can be hidden under a dog's coat, but you'll be sure to find them with a thorough grooming.

Q: *We have an Old English Sheepdog. It gets really hot and humid here in Texas in the summer. We'd like to have him shaved for the summer. Is that OK?*

A: In your case, yes, I think that would be OK. I'm not in favor of shaving every long-haired or thick-coated dog as soon as summer arrives.

Nature will signal your dog's body to start shedding its heavy winter coat when the time is right. You'll need to help this process by daily brushing during this shedding season. A couple of good baths will also speed the removal of dead and loose hair. As long as the dead, loose hair is removed by brushing, most dogs' coats actually provide good insulation from the heat. A well-brushed haircoat enables air to circulate between the hairs and down to the skin, increasing the dog's natural cooling mechanisms and making him more comfortable in hot weather.

There are some breeds, however, with very heavy, thick coats that do seem to be more comfortable in a short summer cut, *if they live in very hot, humid climates*, such as Florida or south Texas. Besides Old English Sheepdogs, Chow Chows, Malamutes and Huskies sometimes do better when clipped for hot weather.

A word of caution though, the haircoat needs to be long enough to protect the sensitive skin from sunburn. Don't let anyone clip it too short.

Most importantly, use your common sense in keeping your dog cool and safe in hot weather. Make sure he has lots of fresh water, good shade that won't disappear as the sun moves and an area with good air circulation. You can get him a child's wading pool and fill it with about a foot of water, so he can get in and cool himself off or put a fan in a safe, covered area where he can get in front of it. If he can be inside the house with the air conditioner on during the hottest part of the day, that would be best of all!

Nails, Teeth, Eyes and Ears

"Doc," the caller said, "I need a second opinion on treating ear mites in my dog Rascal! I've used the old family cure on him for a few weeks. Now he seems to really shake his head and appears to be getting worse. What can I do?"

"Well, Bob, I'd first recommend letting a veterinarian take a look just to be sure you really are dealing with ear mites, it could be something else, like an ear infection. If it is ear mites, your doctor will give you some Mitox. Just treat both ears by the label directions."

"OK, do I first need to get all the mashed potatoes out?"

"What?"

"Well, ya see, that's the old family fix. Ya just keep mashed potatoes stuffed in there for about a week and them critters are supposed to be gone!"

Animals' ears are very sensitive. In dogs, the ear canal is long and takes an almost ninety-degree turn. The slightest bit of inflammation or irritation makes the ear canal produce excessive amounts of ear wax, called cerumen, which is the perfect place for bacteria to set up housekeeping and grow large colonies. Before long this can lead to a moderate to severe external ear infection that can cause a dog constant pain and stress.

Well-meaning owners will sometimes put things in the ear canals thinking it will help with mites, ticks or infections. However, the tissues inside the ear are very sensitive. Harsh chemicals, rough treatment or even mashed potatoes can do more harm than good.

In dogs, the ear is a vital organ. It is very sensitive and when inflamed can cause the dog a great deal of discomfort, stress and even hearing loss. Be careful when treating ears. Let your veterinarian do the poking around. Then have the doctor advise you on how you can treat the condition at home with proper medications and methods.

I think the most overlooked parts of a dog's body are the teeth and gums. Lifting up a dog's lip and looking at the teeth is just not something most people think about doing regularly. Yet teeth need regular attention and if ignored, will cause problems.

Nails are another overlooked part of normal grooming. They grow relatively fast and if the dog does not normally walk or run on rough surfaces, will need trimming every two to three weeks. I've seen nails so neglected that they have grown out, around and back into the dog's foot pad, creating a badly infected foot.

The eyes are the most delicate tissue in the body. Happily, we look into our dog's eyes almost daily, so when they become red or cloudy we usually notice it and can take some immediate action.

Q: *Our Poodle seems to tear a lot and the stains on the hair at the corner of his eyes are becoming permanent. Anything we can do about that?*

A: These tear stains are common in white breeds of dogs. They result from the pH level of the tears, which evaporate. There are several brands of tear stain removers available through pet shops and groomers, which will lighten these stains. In addition, if the tearing is excessive, your veterinarian can prescribe antibiotic eye drops, which can decrease the amount of tearing. Some tearing will always occur, however.

Q: *I've noticed that our puppy has a loose baby tooth next to one of her new permanent teeth. Will that come out OK?*

A: It probably will. As the new permanent tooth grows into place, this baby tooth, or deciduous tooth, will be loosened and eventually come out with chewing and wear. However, some of these do not ever come out and are retained. This can cause a problem.

When the retained tooth is adjacent to the permanent tooth, it is the perfect place for food particles to become trapped and for tartar to form. This area often remains mildly inflamed and therefore is more susceptible to infection.

I've seen retained baby teeth in dogs eight years old. This simply means a veterinarian has never seen it before, because if the tooth has not fallen out within a few months, it should be removed. How firmly attached the baby tooth is will determine how much work is involved. Very loose baby teeth are easy to remove and require little aftercare. However, some are firmly implanted in the gum and bone and may require a general anesthetic and surgery.

I'd suggest watching it for no more than a month. If it hasn't come out on its own by then, have your doctor look at it on the next puppy-shot visit.

Q: *My Springer Spaniel broke a nail today. It's bleeding badly. Is there something I can do here at home, or do I need to get her to the vet?*

A: For now you can put a little hydrogen peroxide on the broken nail area and wrap the foot in some bandages. However, I'd suggest getting her to the vet today. The nails are very highly vascular and when broken off near the cuticle can bleed quite a bit. Plus, with a piece of the broken nail still in place, the trauma that occurs with every step will keep the injury open and bleeding. This can cause susceptibility to secondary infection and a great deal of pain, not to mention little blood spots all over the house.

The veterinarian can remove the nail, check the bone that is inside the nail's shell and decide the proper action to take. Many times a new, although possibly deformed, nail will grown in its place.

Q: *I was checking the teeth on my four-year-old Doberman, Kelly, and I noticed one of her lower "fangs" is kind of purple colored. What do you think caused that?*

A: She has probably had some type of trauma to the tooth, possibly a fracture. A fracture causes a break in the protective enamel of the tooth and allows bacteria to enter. An abscess can form at the tip of the root which often allows bacteria to spill into the dog's bloodstream where it can cause problems to the organs, such as the kidneys or heart. Bacteria can also destroy the bone which anchors the root of the tooth.

When breaks are caught early, the tooth can usually be saved by treating the tooth with a sealer and covering it with a bonding material. An older fracture may require a root canal to avoid infection and preserve a tooth that would be lost if left untreated. The first thing your veterinarian will do is X-ray the tooth. The doctor will then know the extent of damage and whether an abscess exists.

A dog's teeth are his means of eating and of "handling" objects. Healthy teeth are essential for his health and well-being, so its important to check your dog's teeth regularly and correct any problems immediately.

While most veterinarians are able to perform routine cleaning and extractions, I'd recommend finding a board-certified veterinary dental specialist to deal with the more complicated procedures like filling cavities, or performing root canals, or tooth restorations, if one is available in your area. Check the yellow pages.

Q: *Our ten-year-old Beagle, Buffie, has begun getting a cloudy appearance to his eyes. Is that a cataract or something?*

A: It is either a cataract or a fairly common old-dog change to the eye called nuclear sclerosis.

A cataract is a cloudiness or crystalline appearance in the lens. The lens is the actual focusing structure of the eye and sits behind the iris. If you see a cloudy or crystalline appearance and it seems to be behind the iris or pupil of the eye, that is probably a cataract. Cataracts usually cause some degree of vision loss. Dogs learn to compensate very well when vision is only blurred or cloudy, but a mature crystalline cataract will cause blindness.

Some people call any cloudiness of the lens in old dogs a *senile cataract*, when in reality it is a condition called *nuclear sclerosis*. Nuclear sclerosis occurs when, over time, the fibers of the lens become more dense and light is reflected off the back of the lens capsule. This gives the lens a cloudy appearance, which looks very much like a cataract—but it is not. Nuclear sclerosis will probably not cause complete blindness. It does affect the dog's vision, however. These dogs learn to watch for blurred, unfocused movement and rely more on smell, sounds and vibrations for their sensory input.

Injuries or ulcers on the cornea will also cause a cloudiness. These can be serious and should be seen to immediately. The eye is a very delicate organ, and injuries can cause a rapid infection or deterioration of some of the most fragile structures. Never wait long before having an eye problem evaluated by a professional. I'd suggest a trip to the vet for a proper diagnosis and some good medical treatment.

Q: *I want to start trimming my dog's nails myself at home, but I'm afraid I'll make her bleed. How do I know where to cut?*

A: If your dog has white nails, you'll be able to see the line of demarcation where the blood vessels are. This is sometimes called the "quick." Cut well below the vessels using a good pair of nail clippers, either scissors or guillotine type.

If your dog has black nails, you won't have the advantage of being able to see the blood vessel and you'll have to estimate its length. A good way to estimate where to cut is to draw an imaginary line directly out from the bottom of the foot pad. Where this line intersects with the nail is where you cut. This is where the nail will just begin to contact the floor when the dog stands.

If your dog's nails are very long, just start by cutting a very small amount every three to four days. When you get the nails to a good length, then you can start trimming every one to two weeks, depending on how fast they grow.

Keep some styptic powder nearby, in case the nail bleeds. Simply push the nail into the powder, or touch some on the nail with a Q-tip, to stop the bleeding.

Q: *We've been told our dog, Dee-O-Gee, needs a dental prophy. Is that just like what we go in for?*

A: Absolutely! A dental prophy for your pet is just as important as it is for you. Because dogs' teeth are not seen as regularly, and therefore, aren't treated as regularly, they can become inflamed and infected due to the constant buildup of tartar. Although tartar buildup is considered normal, it creates some abnormal consequences: inflamed, swollen gums and secondary infection that can sometimes become so severe as to cause a blood-borne infection that can settle in the kidneys!

Your vet should tranquilize Dee-O-Gee and scale or scrape the surfaces of the teeth to remove the tartar. The doctor will then flush the gums, treat them if necessary and you'll have a pet with a clean set of teeth. However, they will only stay that way if you take on the responsibility of brushing them yourself.

Get a special toothbrush and toothpaste from the doctor or your pet store. Ask for a Petrodex dental kit. This kit, produced by St. Jon Laboratories, is excellent. The brush has a long handle and the bristles are four times softer than the softest human brush. This is important because inflamed gums are very sensitive and bleed easily. A human toothbrush would damage them and make the problem worse!

The toothpaste acts by enzyme activity. This means there's no need to scrub it around to make it work and no need to rinse it out. It is harmless for the dog to swallow and will not irritate his stomach.

Q: *We took our dog in for a tartar scraping. The vet sent us home with a doggie toothbrush and toothpaste kit. Exactly how do we brush our dog's teeth, and how often?*

A: A young dog, one to three years, needs its teeth brushed once every week. Dogs older than three should be done about three times a week. Senior dogs probably need it five times a week.

Start slowly. Don't expect your dog to accept this weird thing right away. I would not brush his teeth for a week or so after a dental cleaning. The gums will still be sore.

Pick a good spot where you can have access to water and good control of your dog. Train your dog to accept this brushing in stages. Begin by taking a little bit of the toothpaste on your finger and rub your finger along the outside of his teeth for a few seconds. That's it! Release him, praise him and give him a dog biscuit.

Next time take a little longer. Slowly you can introduce the toothbrush and brush gently for a few seconds. Increase the length of time you brush each time until you eventually work up to a few minutes.

Remember, with pet toothpaste the enzyme action does the work, not detergent or scrubbing action, as with human toothpaste. Therefore it's more important to get the toothpaste in every crack and crevice than to scrub it around.

Luckily, there is no gargling and spitting. I'm not sure I could tell you how to teach your dog to do that!

Q: *I think our three-month-old Labrador puppy, Sadie, broke a tooth. She doesn't seem to feel good and isn't eating. She still has her baby teeth. What do we need to do?*

A: You'll need to get Sadie to her veterinarian for immediate treatment. Broken teeth are a common occurrence in dogs. Puppies, with thin enamel on their baby teeth, frequently break a canine tooth by chewing on rocks or other hard objects. Just as with people, a dog's broken tooth with its exposed nerve can be very painful. It often causes enough pain to make the dog unable to eat and overall very depressed.

A broken deciduous, or baby, tooth usually requires extraction by a veterinarian. If not removed, the tooth may form an abscess which could affect the adult tooth and even spread infection, via the bloodstream, through the body. Broken teeth always need veterinary care.

Q: *Our West Highland Terrier, Max, began having difficulty walking on his front legs. When we took him to our veterinarian, we were told his nails were so long they changed his foot position. What did he mean by that?*

A: If a dog's nails are not trimmed regularly, they can grow very long and cause major problems, either by curling under the foot and putting pressure on the foot pads or by growing straight forward and forcing the joints in the dog's paw to bend backwards at an awkward angle. Either way, the result is pain and stress on the dog's feet and joints.

Dog's nails grow fairly rapidly. If a dog walks regularly on rough surfaces, he'll keep his nails worn down, but the typical pet dog spends most of his time indoors, on dirt, or grass. He'll need regular nail trimming to keep his feet healthy. Have your veterinarian show you how to trim Max's nails, and then do them at home every week.

Q: *I know that some puppies have their dewclaws removed. We adopted a mixed-breed dog from the shelter, and she has them. Should dewclaws be removed in adult dogs?*

A: No. As a puppy this little claw is very loosely attached by cartilage only and easily removed with a minor surgical procedure.
However, as the dog grows into maturity, this connection
becomes firmly attached by bone. The surgery to remove dewclaws in adult dogs is a major one. It involves disarticulating an
entire set of "finger" bones and is unnecessary and painful.

Unless this was a hunting dog that was constantly getting
them torn in rough terrain, I would recommend against it.

Q: *Our dog has a very bad smell coming from his ears. What is that?*
A: Probably an infection of the external ear canal, technically
known as otitis externa. This problem is seen in all breeds of
dogs but is quite common in Poodles, Cockers and their crosses.
It usually begins as a very minor infection and grows to a larger,
more out-of-control infection, with time and lack of treatment.
Once the bacteria have set up housekeeping in the moist, dark,
protected environment of the ear canal, they can become quite
stubborn and treatment may become long-term.

If it is a chronic infection, it would be best to have a veterinarian culture the ear canal to see exactly what bacteria is causing the infection. Then the doctor can prescribe the exact
antibiotic that will kill the infection. Many people just keep
putting the same old medication from infections past on such a
problem, and it does no good. A bacterial culture and sensitivity
test is essential in these cases.

Once the doctor has treated the ears, the follow-up care will
most likely fall on your shoulders. Be sure the doctor shows you
how to properly treat the ears, because it will have to be done
daily for months.

Q: *Doc, my old hound has a big fluid-filled sac on one of his ear flaps.
It's been there for several months. What is that?*
A: This is probably an aural hematoma, or blood sac, that has
formed inside the ear flap due to constant and repetitive trauma
or injury to the ear flap itself. We usually see these hematomas
in floppy-eared breeds of dogs with chronic ear infections.
Because they constantly flap their head due to the pain in their
ears, they will break blood vessels inside the ear flap and the

hemorrhaging will occur between the layers of tissue in the ear flap. This will cause the bubble or sac of blood to accumulate.

This is a condition that requires surgery to correct. The surgeon will carefully open an elliptical piece of skin on the inside of the ear flap and drain out all of the fluid. He will then suture the ear in such a way as to close up all of the cavities that may fill up with fluid later. Some of these require several surgeries to correct and some scarring to the ear flap may occur.

This problem is a sign of a deep-seated pain or infection in the ear, which must be corrected or more trauma will be done to the ear-flap tissue again.

Q: *Tito has developed a sore spot on the tip of his ear flap. It heals, then reopens; heals, then reopens. Now there is a V-shaped wound there. How can we get this thing to heal?*

A: This is a somewhat common, very frustrating condition called a fissure. Because the tips of the ear flap are very thin, they heal slowly after an injury. If the injury was a cut, as often occurs in dogs with long, floppy ears, it may not heal fast or completely at first. If chronic infection sets in, this will slow the process even further. The most common delay to healing in this type of injury is more trauma. Such a wound never gets a chance to really heal and the tissue begins to recede creating the V-shaped fissure.

This wound may eventually heal but the V-shaped deficit in the flap is there to stay. The only way to get rid of that is to surgically take the ear flap back and create a new contour to the edge. You can ask your veterinarian about that surgery.

Q: *Our vet has treated our Cocker Spaniel's ear infections for years. They always come back. Now the dog's ear canal is swollen shut! How are we going to get this treated once and for all?*

A: When you treat any chronic infection it is frustrating. You must first know that you are treating with the proper antibiotic that will kill the specific bacteria or other organism that is causing the infection. A bacterial culture and sensitivity test is essential. If a veterinarian is treating a chronic ear infection and has not done one of these tests, he is treating in the blind.

If you have done this, and you are using the most effective, most up-to-date antibiotics, then you have a totally refractory case that will not respond to medicine and will most likely require more drastic measures. A surgical procedure that opens up the ear canal to the outside can be done. That will allow the inner ear canal an opening to the outside, and allow medication and fresh air to reach the chronically inflamed and thickened tissues. Many of these dogs do very well after surgery, although there is a noticeable uncosmetic effect.

Q: *We bought a Doberman last week. Our vet says we should have his ears cropped. My wife and I don't really see a need for this because we're not going to show him. What's your opinion.*

A: My friend, if you do not see a need for it, then do not allow yourself to be talked into the surgery. In fact, the surgery is now so out-of-date, a lot of progressive veterinarians refuse to do it. It does nothing for the dog, it is only for the owners.

Cropping ears is a throwback from the breed standards set forth by AKC and other breed clubs. If you are going to show the dog, according to their rules, you have to have the ears cropped. But that is the only reason a dog should have half of its natural ear flap cut off! If AKC were more modern and progressive, they would delete the requirement and we'd see ear cropping fall out of favor with everyone. In fact, in a few states and many foreign countries, it is illegal!

Frankly I think the surgery is risky, cruel and a waste of money. After all this is done at a time when a young puppy is growing bones, cutting teeth, building muscle and developing an immune system. At that critical time in your pup's development, you put the dog under a needless general anesthetic, expose him to the risk of infection and other complications, then whack off half of his normal ear flap—just for cosmetics? In fifteen years of veterinary practice I've never done an ear cropping, but I've spent countless hours talking clients out of the procedure.

Q: *Our Lab has a tick down in its ear. He is shaking his head constantly and pawing at his ear. We can see the tick, how can we get it out?*

A: If you can see it, hold the dog still and carefully reach the tick with a pair of forceps or tweezers, and try to get it out. Pull steadily and slowly and the tick will release its mouth parts. If you jerk it out quickly, you'll break off the tick's mouth parts in the ear canal and this could cause an infection later on.

If you suspect there are other ticks in the ear, you should probably have your veterinarian examine the ear with an otoscope. This way he can look all the way down to the eardrum and remove any of the parasites that may be down that far. Putting some mineral oil in the ear may help, as this will cut off the tick's oxygen supply and may make him back out. Be careful, the ear is a sensitive organ.

PART III

Behavior and Training

CHAPTER 10

Introducing a New Pet or Baby

"Doctor Jim, we brought a new puppy into our home two weeks ago and our cat is freaked out! I don't believe his little kitty paws have set foot on solid ground since we brought the pup home. He's like Tarzan, going from bookshelf to chair to countertop all through the house. My wife wants to build him a few bridges so he can just stay up high. Now I know where the term 'catwalk' came from. Isn't there something we can do?"

How to introduce: a new baby to the dog; a new kitten to the dog; a new puppy to a cat; a new puppy to an existing dog. These are frequent questions I get on talk radio. First meetings are very important for future relationships, so think about a plan beforehand and take your time with the introductions.

The single biggest problem with introducing a new baby or a new pet to an existing pet dog is jealousy. This doesn't have to be a huge problem. Owners, unintentionally, cause a large part of the problem themselves by being too protective of the new arrival, or not giving enough attention to the existing pet. Stop and think about it a minute. Your dog lives for your attention. Anything that comes into his world and causes you to either not give him as much attention, or worse yet, reprimand and reject him, is going to cause him to feel very jealous.

Before introducing a new arrival, the whole family should sit down for a family meeting and be instructed in THE PLAN. Then, *everybody* sticks with it. By including your dog in the excitement of the new arrival you can make it a happy occasion for everybody.

Q: *My husband and I have just gotten a seven-week-old Welsh Corgi puppy, a female. We haven't brought her home yet. We already have a three-year-old, neutered German Shepherd, a male. He's been an "only dog" his whole life, is very bonded to us and gets along very well with other people. How do we introduce this new puppy?*

A: It is good that your German Shepherd is well socialized. In other words, he gets along well with strangers and other animals. You shouldn't have any problem introducing your new puppy as long as you follow a few rules.

Because your Shepherd is a large dog and your new Welsh Corgi pup is so small, you may feel the need to protect her, a common mistake people make in introducing their dog to a new puppy. If you get nervous and overly protective, grabbing up the pup and reprimanding your Shepherd every time he gets near your pup, the Shepherd is going to assume the pup is doing something wrong and needs to be punished, or that something wrong is definitely going on.

You need to assume a *very casual, up-beat attitude* about the introduction. The first meeting should be outside your Shepherd's territory, if possible, so he will feel less protective (perhaps at a park, or at least the front yard, rather than in the house or back yard). This neutral ground means they are meeting on more equal status.

Put your pup in a travel kennel, or better yet, a small wire crate. Put the crate on the ground and let your Shepherd investigate the pup through the wire. VERY IMPORTANT—praise your Shepherd and be very happy whenever he is around the pup. He will take his cues about this new arrival from you. If you're happy and relaxed, he will be too. If you're nervous and jumpy, he will assume there is good reason for him to be nervous and jumpy too.

The next meeting can be in your back yard or house, because you need a safe, enclosed area. Put your Shepherd's leash on his collar, but don't hold him tightly. First let him come up to the pup and sniff it, while one of you holds the pup on your lap. Praise your Shepherd and stay very relaxed and happy. Don't hold the pup over the Shepherd's head while standing. This could make the pup look like a toy you're about to throw for him or even be threatening. Next, put the puppy on the ground and let your

Shepherd nose him. Don't worry if he rolls the pup over or puts a paw on him, as long as your Shepherd continues to look happy and relaxed. If he looks aggressive or nervous, take a break and reevaluate your attitude. Were you happy and relaxed? Did you act excited and pet and praise the Shepherd?

Supervise all interactions between the two until the puppy gets older and your Shepherd has firmly "adopted" her. Feed the two separately and in different places. The puppy should have her own puppy crate (see Chapter 11 on housebreaking a puppy) and shouldn't invade your Shepherd's bed. Get her her own puppy toys as well. Don't interfere if your Shepherd takes a toy away from her or won't let her on his bed. Adult dogs will reprimand puppies when they get too rowdy and will teach them how to act around other dogs. Let him be a teacher, don't interfere.

Finally, make the same rules apply to the new puppy as to your Shepherd. If he is not allowed on your bed, don't let her sleep on your bed. She should have her own bed in her crate, next to your bed at night.

Q: *My wife and I are soon to have our first baby. We have a four-year-old, mixed-breed hound. Boomer has been like our child. How do we introduce the new baby?*

A: A new baby in the house is going to mean big changes for everybody, Boomer included. When a baby comes, there is often much less time for the family pet. You can make the transition easier for Boomer if you start preparing for it a little ahead of time. Think about how much time and attention Boomer gets now. If he is used to a lot of time with you and you know that will decrease when the baby comes, start decreasing the time you spend with him a couple of weeks before the baby comes, so that he doesn't equate the arrival of the baby with the change.

VERY IMPORTANT—I'm not suggesting you stick Boomer in the back yard and ignore him. However, if he's used to sitting beside you for hours in the evening while you watch TV and pet his head, you can start now to pet him and talk to him for several minutes, then get up and go do something. Give him lots of quality attention, but in shorter spurts.

Try *very* hard not to change the rules on him because you have a new baby. If Boomer is used to being in the house with you, don't stick him in the back yard. He'll be miserable and may associate the isolation with the baby and become jealous. If he's always been allowed on the couch, don't change the rules when baby comes. Just keep him well bathed and groomed.

After the baby is born, bring an article of the baby's clothing home from the hospital and let Boomer investigate the new little one's smell ahead of time. When the baby comes home, have a friend or relative carry the baby into the house the first time so that Boomer does not associate the baby's arrival with you. Let Boomer come up and sniff the baby while one of you holds her. Praise Boomer whenever the baby is around. You want him to associate praise and good things with the baby. Stay very relaxed, have an upbeat, happy attitude. Boomer will take his cues from you about how he should feel about the new arrival.

Make an effort to spend some quality time playing or going for a walk with Boomer every day. Never leave Boomer unsupervised with the baby. Expect him to be surprised the first time he hears the baby cry. He will want to investigate the source of this sound. Don't reprimand him or act nervous, but do watch him closely. Don't reassure him. Just talk to him in a calm, happy voice. (Reassuring a dog confirms in his mind that there is something to worry about.)

Once your dog understands that this is a new member of his "pack," he will probably get very watchful and protective of her.

One note of caution: When babies start to crawl and when they start to toddle are times for close supervision with your dog. A crawling or toddling baby does not look like a human to a dog, and may look like another animal. Once mobile, babies may also corner a dog, making him feel trapped. They also have a tendency to poke fingers into a dog's eyes and mouth. So, use good common sense and always supervise your pet's interactions with your baby.

Q: *How do you introduce a kitten to a dog? We have a four-year-old Cocker Spaniel, Laddie, and just took in a stray kitty.*

A: Introducing a kitten to a dog usually works pretty well. It's much more difficult to get a grown cat to accept a puppy. It does help if your dog is well obedience trained, so that you can control her well, and if she has been well socialized. In other words, she was exposed to lots of people and different animals when she was a puppy and so is calm about it.

Kittens are great, because they are very persistent in approaching an older animal, but they're not big enough to be threatening to most dogs. Once properly introduced, kittens and dogs often become great friends.

When you first bring your new kitten home, let her get accustomed to her new home one room at a time. Put her in a room with her litter box, bed, food, water and toys. Let her have a day or two to settle in and get to know you before you introduce Laddie. In the meantime, let Laddie get used to her smell under the door.

When you first introduce Laddie to the kitten, expect some hissing and running away on the kitten's part. Put Laddie's leash on him and have him on a down–stay if you can. Let the kitten into the room, but don't let Laddie approach her. Let the kitten approach Laddie. Laddie will probably whine, bark and try to rush up to the kitten. Keep him calm and make him stay with you, but don't overreprimand him. You want his association with the kitten to be positive. Maintain a happy, positive attitude and tone of voice. Try to keep him from barking, but distract him by talking to him in an excited voice rather than reprimand him.

The kitten will probably have hidden under a bed by now. Just stay in the room with Laddie on a leash with you. Stay happy and upbeat and give the kitten time to become curious about the dog. Don't ever force the issue by holding the kitten and bringing her up to the dog or the dog up to her. This is a very threatening situation for the kitten, and you're liable to be badly scratched.

You may need to do five or six of these little sessions before the two make nose-to-nose contact. Let the kitten do it in her own time, and supervise Laddie carefully. Always praise and pet Laddie when the kitten is around. This will let him know that you are happy the kitten is there and he should be too. He also associates the praise and attention he is receiving with the cat.

Once the two have met, let the kitten have extended periods of access to the entire house while Laddie stays near you on a long leash. That way, you can grab the leash and reprimand him lightly if he starts to chase the kitten. As long as he looks relaxed and happy, your kitten is probably not in danger. If Laddie appears aggressive or nervous, then you'll need to do more sessions. Remember to praise Laddie when the kitten is around and keep a happy, relaxed attitude. He takes his cues from you on how to feel about the new arrival.

Once used to a new arrival, most dogs are good around kittens. The two often play together and may even sleep together. The kitten should be good company for Laddie.

Q: *We have a four-year-old mixed-breed cat who is great, but we're bringing home a new Scottie pup in three days. How do we do that?*

A: This combination has a few inherent problems. Adult cats are not fond of change in their environments, and puppies are terribly rowdy. Let your cat first investigate the puppy on its own while the puppy is in its puppy crate (see Chapter 11). Most likely, the cat will want as little as possible to do with the puppy. The puppy, on the other hand, will probably be endlessly fascinated with terrorizing the cat. Let the cat avoid the puppy when it wants to. Puppies can be very rough and rowdy, and cats don't appreciate being pounced on.

You might even relax the rules a little and let the cat up on the counter in the kitchen so he can be in the kitchen with you, but be up out of puppy reach. You'll want to supervise your puppy when he is out of his crate until he is five to six months old (see Chapters 11 and 14). Try to distract him with another activity when he takes off after the cat, but don't reprimand him. If the cat fights back and scratches him, don't interfere. The cat needs to be able to set some limits on the pup's behavior. Do check your pup carefully and see that he wasn't injured. Any actual cat-scratch wounds would need immediate treatment with an antibiotic ointment.

Q: *My wife and I would like to adopt an adult dog as a companion to our Bichon Frise, Pepper, because he is alone a lot while we're at work. How do we introduce them to each other?*

A: I think a companion dog for your Bichon Frise is a great idea.

Dogs who must spend a lot of time alone get very lonely and can develop behavior problems out of boredom and loneliness. If you want to adopt an adult dog, the best combination is usually a breed of similar size and type and of the opposite sex. However, almost any combination can be successful when both dogs have been neutered or spayed. I wouldn't recommend putting two unneutered male dogs together. You'd be asking for problems.

When you pick out your new dog, make the first introduction to Pepper off your property so Pepper won't feel too territorial. Take both dogs to a park, in separate cars, or use a friend's yard. Keep both dogs on a leash and let them greet each other and go through their ritual of sniffing. It's very important that you communicate to Pepper that this is an exciting and happy event, so be happy and upbeat. Don't be overprotective of either dog, and praise Pepper whenever he is around your new dog, so he will associate her with positive things.

If the dogs seem to be calm around each other, and if you're in a enclosed yard, let both dogs off leash and let them play. The dogs will have to decide who will be top dog. There may be some dominant behavior on the part of one or the other. Don't interfere with this as long as nobody is getting hurt.

Once at home, feed the dogs in separate bowls in different areas to prevent fights over food. Be careful not to overdo the attention to the new dog so that Pepper doesn't get jealous. Sometimes the excitement of a new pet causes owners to ignore or reprimand the demands for attention from the established pet. Try to think of your new dog as "Pepper's dog" and give Pepper attention first, then the new dog. It's not mean to the new dog. It just establishes Pepper's seniority and will prevent possible jealousy and fights.

CHAPTER 11

Housebreaking a Puppy and Correcting Adult House Soiling

"Doctor Jim, my wife and I have wanted to get a new puppy for over a year, but because we both work, we have felt like we couldn't be around enough to teach the pup properly. Well, we finally broke down the other day and bought the cutest little Bichon Frise puppy in the world.

We listen to your show and know how important it is to let her have the chance to 'go' and that little puppies do have to 'go' quite often. However, our work schedules have not changed. So . . . I got the bright idea . . . if she can't go outside, we'll bring the outside in to her!

I've built a four-foot by four-foot by four-inch box. I filled it with potting soil, went to the nursery and bought some land-scape sod. She now has her own little 'yard' in the house. I'm so proud of my little invention. The reason I'm calling is to ask you: how do I get her to use it?"

This is definitely an area where many dog owners have problems. A large percentage of my talk radio calls have to do with puppies that are not housetrained. The problem does *not* lie with the puppy, but the method of housebreaking. *Housebreaking a puppy is not hard*. It takes effort and a good deal of time commitment in the puppy's early months. However, this time commitment is really an investment. You are investing in your puppy's next twelve to fifteen years, in its happiness, your sanity and pride in your new friend.

Housetraining puppies also requires you to be realistic in your expectations of your new puppy.

There is probably no other area of dog behavior so misunderstood or full of myths as the area of housebreaking. I receive calls every week from people who tell me that their adult dogs have accidents on a weekly, or even daily, basis. There is really no reason for this. Dogs are actually quite easy to housebreak. This is because all dogs, both wild and domestic, have a natural desire to keep their "den" clean. Dogs are also naturally anxious to please and, so, if taught correctly, should have no problems with house soiling.

Just remember the word *schedule*. Most adult dogs who house soil do so because of a messed-up schedule. Usually, if you can get their schedule back on target, they will be housebroken once again.

Q: *I've heard you talk about "great training or crate training" a puppy to housebreak it. What do you mean by that, and why does it work?*

A: It is *great* training, no doubt, but it is called *crate* training and is absolutely, without exception, the best way to housebreak a puppy. The "crate" is actually a wire or Fiberglas kennel, which becomes the pup's own little home.

Using this little "puppy home," we can actually simulate the dog's den. All dogs have a normal and natural desire to curl up in small places, get their backs up against something and feel safe and secure. This is why, in the wild, they seek out a den.

Crate training works wonderfully when you follow a few simple rules. The reason it works so well is this: Dogs in the wild live in dens. Dens offer protection from the cold, the heat and predators. It gives the wild dog a sense of security and well-being. All dogs, domestic dogs included, have a strong natural tendency to seek out a "den." It's a place to call their own. Just think of it like your room when your were a child.

In most homes, it is difficult for a dog to find a place of his own where he can retreat to be by himself, out of the traffic and activity of the home. A dog will attempt to find a spot by curling up under coffee tables, chairs and in corners. By giving a dog his own "den" in your home, you can take advantage of mother nature to quickly housebreak a puppy, control destructive puppy problems and raise a more well-adjusted, self-confident dog.

In nature, a dog does not defecate or urinate in its den. Therefore, a puppy will try to keep his "den" (his crate) clean. He will naturally hold his bowels and bladder while he is in his crate. It's like having a little valve on your pup's bladder. Of course, a new puppy cannot hold his bladder very long and, if left in his crate too long, will have to urinate and defecate. If he did this in the kennel, that would be *your* fault, not the dog's. Remember, very young puppies have to eliminate every thirty minutes to every hour. Don't worry, as they get older just by a few weeks, they can begin to hold it longer and longer and eventually will be able to go four to six hours in the kennel and not be in discomfort.

Q: I just bought a seven-week-old Miniature Schnauzer puppy. I want to start out right. I've heard you talk about crate training a puppy to housebreak it. How exactly do I do this?

A: Buy a crate that is large enough so that your puppy will be able to stand up and turn around when she is adult-sized. Don't buy too big a crate or your puppy may fail to see it as a "den." I recommend a wire crate rather than a Fiberglas travel-type kennel, because a puppy can see out of a wire crate easily and feels a part of everything around him. He can see you and won't feel isolated. It's just like putting a human baby in a playpen.

Start from the beginning having your puppy sleep and rest in his crate. Without any training from you, he will naturally begin to seek the security and safety of his little "dog room" when he is sleepy or wants to be off by himself.

When you first introduce your puppy to the crate, toss a little treat in to get the little guy to go inside. Don't force him in. You don't want him to be scared of his new home. Coax him with food and reward him with praise. At first, he may back quickly out. Don't worry, that's normal. Take it slow and encourage him to go in on his own. Again, an open, wire-type kennel is easier for this because it does not appear to be so closed in and dark inside.

I like to take the top off of the kennel and simply place the puppy in from above, again just like putting a baby in a playpen. Then when it's time for him to come out to play, you simply open the door and out he bounds. By putting the pup in from above, he learns to use the door on his own, and will have no anxiety about going in and out! It won't be long before your new pup thinks of the crate as his and begins to seek it out.

Let your puppy get used to his new home slowly. Don't just put him in there and leave him. A new puppy is going through a traumatic time. He's just been taken away from his brothers and sisters, and he doesn't know you yet. He's just a baby, and he's scared. Wait to bring your puppy home until you can spend a good deal of time with him for several days.

I recommend that your puppy be in his crate during all unsupervised times. Try to place the crate where he can see you, though. I like to carry the kennel into the kitchen while we are making meals, into the living room if we are watching TV and into the bedroom for the night. I put the kennel, with the top off, right next to the bed. This way, when he needs to go out, I can hear the whimper and take him out. Also, if he whimpers due to loneliness, I can simply hang my arm down into the kennel and make him feel more secure. During times when you can watch him carefully, let him out to play and explore, but keep your eye on him.

Your goal is to prevent any accidents. Be realistic though and realize that accidents will happen. They will be few, however, if you are careful to watch the pup anytime he is out of his crate.

While your pup is in his little "den," he will not urinate or defecate. This is mother nature's way of keeping the den clean. If he can see you, he won't feel isolated. Little puppies six to seven weeks old have to empty their bladders *at least* every two hours. Puppies eight to ten weeks old still need to "go" about every three to four hours.

This is where the time commitment comes in. You need to be on a strict schedule. Every two hours, at first, take the little guy to the door, praise him, and then take him outside to where you want him to eliminate. Put him down and wait. He will go, trust me. When he does, get all excited and really praise him. Give him time to defecate as well as urinate. He will probably walk around a little and pick another spot.

You can gradually increase the time intervals as he gets a little older and is able to "hold it" longer. I've always thought it would be great if puppies had a little red light on their forehead that lit when they needed to "go." Even without a warning light, you can count on certain times. Your puppy will need to "go" just a few minutes after eating and drinking, after vigorous playing and chewing, and after waking up. Basically, new puppies *always* need to "go."

By following a strict schedule, you are teaching your puppy that he is to hold his bowels and bladder until he is taken outside. This schedule will stay with him his whole life.

Q: How old will my puppy be before he can stay in his crate for eight hours while I am at work?

A: To answer your question, your puppy will probably be able to hold his bowels and bladder for eight hours when he is about six to eight months old. That is a long time, however, for a puppy to be in a crate. If he does stay in his crate all day, then all night as well, that's too long.

I'd recommend trying to come home at lunch and let the little guy out and give him some attention as well as letting him eliminate. If you can't do that, try to get a neighbor or friend to go over once during the day while you're gone, to let him out.

If you have a safe, enclosed yard, why not let the pup be in the yard during the day while you're gone. That way he can eliminate as he needs to and can be inside with you in the evening and can sleep in his crate at night. Just be sure to provide a good doghouse or shelter out of the weather.

Q: I've always heard you should put newspapers down for a puppy to "go" on in the house. I've never heard you mention this, don't you think that works?

A: No, I don't recommend that at all. Letting a puppy eliminate on papers in the house just teaches him it is OK to "go" in the house. It is very confusing for the puppy when later you decide it's time to teach him to go outside. For the same reasons, I don't recommend the housebreaking pads that you can buy at pet stores. Your puppy needs to learn it is simply against the rules to "go" in the house.

If my simple advice doesn't convince you, then statistics should. In the northern U.S. where climates are very cold in the winter, there is a much higher incidence of house soiling in puppies and adult dogs. Why? Because people paper train their dogs due to the bitter cold outside. It is simply no fun to stand outside while your new puppy is figuring out that she is supposed to "go" outside. So people take the easy way out and paper train. Because of this, more dogs up north think it's OK to eliminate inside, and therefore there is more house-soiling behavior problems in the north as compared to more moderate climate areas.

Q: *What if my puppy has an accident in his crate?*

A: Your puppy may have an accident or two in his crate until he figures out it is his "den." He may also have an accident if you do not take him out often enough. If he does have an accident, DON'T PUNISH HIM. Take him out to his elimination spot and praise him for urinating there. Take the bedding out of the puppy's crate and replace it with clean bedding. Then get back on your schedule. If your puppy has accidents it should be a signal to you that something is wrong with your scheduling.

Q: *What do I do if I catch my puppy "going" in the house?*

A: Accept the fact that you are going to have a few accidents. A new puppy has absolutely no way of knowing that it's not OK to just eliminate in the house. You have to *teach* him. The important word being "teach" *not punish*. New puppy owners tend to really overpunish in housebreaking.

At some point, your puppy is going to squat and start to urinate or defecate in the house. If you are supervising him carefully while he is out of his crate, you are going to see this happening. Clap your hands together and say a loud *"no."* DO NOT HIT THE PUPPY! Not with your hands, not with a newspaper, not with anything! Don't rub his nose in it either! Puppies will not learn a thing from these old methods. The goal is to startle him into stopping the urination. A clap of the hands and a loud sharp *"no"* will definitely startle him. That stops the flow. Then pick him up, take him outside to his elimination spot, put him down and praise him. Praise and pet him, even if he doesn't eliminate anymore right then. Give him plenty of time to finish the job if he needs to. It may take him a minute or two to get over the startle of the *"no."* Then take him back inside and put him in his crate while you clean up the accident well.

Don't forget to use an enzyme odor eliminator to completely get rid of the smell. Enzyme odor removers actually break up the urine molecules into harmless carbon dioxide and water. This way there is no residual smell that might attract him back to that spot. Be sure to follow label directions.

I recommend Nature's Miracle or Simple Solution, which will remove the odor and the stain as well. Most of the places where there is a puppy odor, there is a stain. Try not to let the puppy see you cleaning up the spot. Place his crate out of view while you clean up. Dogs have a way of wanting to investigate any spot you are fussing over, and you don't want to attract him back to that spot.

Q: *When I find a "puppy accident" in the house, I grab the pup, spank him with a newspaper and rub his nose in the mess. Then I throw him outside. My wife gets all upset at me, but I figure he'll learn!*

A: I figure you're wrong, *very* wrong. You're breaking almost every rule of housebreaking puppies, all in one fell swoop. Not only is your response ineffective, it's mean and the dog is simply learning to be afraid of you, and I don't blame him. He's being punished and has no way of connecting it to an action. This is similar to a policeman coming up to you and punching you in the nose for running a stop sign three weeks ago!

If you don't catch your pup actually in the act of having an accident, IT DOES NO GOOD TO PUNISH HIM LATER. He simply does not make the connection of his actions earlier and why you are punishing him now! If you would put the pup in a wire kennel when you can't supervise him, then accidents wouldn't happen without your knowing.

Spanking the dog for accidents increases his anxiety over elimination and he learns it's simply not wise to eliminate where you can find it. He will soon begin to look for a more out-of-the-way spot, like behind the couch. Spanking the dog does not make him understand that: a. it's not OK to "go" in the house and b. he makes you happy when he goes outside at his approved elimination spot.

Rubbing a dog's nose in the mess is just plain stupid. I have no idea who started this, but I'd like to "rub their nose in it." It serves no purpose whatsoever except to teach your puppy that you are unpredictable and irrational in your behavior. He is learning to be afraid of you and to stay away from you. In more dominate personality types and more aggressive breeds, you may be setting yourself up for a real showdown later. I've known people who have been severely bitten once the dog learns he's old enough to challenge you on this insult.

Throwing the dog outside does not teach him a single solitary thing either! In order to teach the puppy where you want him to go, you have to take him to the spot, wait for him to "go" and then praise him for "going" there. How else is your dog going to learn? Do you think he sits up at night and reads a book about fitting into your family? No. His input comes from you, the teacher.

You must communicate the rules by consistent positive reinforcement and humane, understandable, negative reinforcement only when appropriate. That would be when the accident takes place right in front of you, and then negative reinforcement should only be a loud sharp *no!*

Guide the pup to the door and out to the elimination spot. Accidents should also tell *you* something—that you have missed an important time in his bladder or bowel rhythm. You simply did not give him the opportunity to eliminate when mother nature told him he needed to go.

Remember this, puppies have a strong and natural desire to please you. Believe me, they do not have accidents just to make you mad. So, give the little guy a break. You are not doing anything to let him know what you want him to do. Raising a puppy takes a commitment in time and effort. It takes the desire to know how to communicate with him effectively. If you're not willing to make that commitment, then do yourself and this puppy a favor. Buy a stuffed animal instead.

Q: *Since puppyhood, our two-year-old Lhasa Apso occasionally has an "accident" in a back bedroom that we seldom use. Why would she do that?*

A: Since this has been going on from the time you got the dog as a puppy, it is clear she was never properly housetrained, probably because she was never really made to stick to a schedule.

The reason we can housebreak dogs is because it is in their nature to keep their "den" clean. It is difficult for a puppy to perceive that your whole big house is one "den." That is why you start housebreaking by confining the pup to a very small area at first, except when you can watch it closely. Then you gradually allow it access to a larger and larger area as it becomes older and more reliable with its elimination schedule.

It is common for dogs who were never properly housetrained to pick a seldom-used room for their toilet area. To them, this is perfectly logical. In nature, dogs never eliminate near where they sleep or eat, but always pick an out of the way area.

Remember that urination behavior is habitual, as well as smell and site oriented. You have to change the urination habit (by schedule), remove the smell and prevent access to the site in order to change this behavior.

Here's how:

SCHEDULE TRAINING

You need to go back to basic housetraining, just like she was a puppy. The most important factor in housebreaking is *schedule*. You need to take her outside and give her the opportunity to eliminate at the times she's most likely to need to. This is: 1. first thing in the morning; 2. fifteen minutes after each meal; 3. after vigorous play or chewing; 4. just before you go to bed at night.

It doesn't matter if that means four times a day or eight times a day. What matters is that you allow her the opportunity to eliminate at these times. You need to go outside with her. Guide her to the spot where you would like her to eliminate. Stay with your dog until she does her business. I find it helpful to teach your dog a command for it, like "Hurry up." Be patient, if you've never done this with her, she won't know at first why you're standing outside with her and will probably try to get you to play with her. If so, put her leash on her and let her wander in a six-foot circle around you. When she either urinates or defecates, I want you to really praise her. Tell her what a good dog she is. *This is how she knows that you want her to eliminate outside, because you praise her when she does.* Again, this takes patience, but remember you are creating behavior that will follow her for life and save your nerves and carpets.

At all other times that your dog is in the house, she needs to be confined to a small area, preferably a wire kennel, except when you can keep your eye on her. Housetraining should focus on preventing accidents and praising proper elimination.

Don't allow your dog free access to the entire house until you are sure her schedule is set and she understands where you want her to "go" (at least four weeks). Then allow her access to the house gradually, by letting her have a larger and larger area to be free in.

Removing the Smell

Before you let your dog have greater access to your house, you'll need to clean the spots in your back bedroom very well so that your dog is not attracted back to the spot. Use an enzyme odor remover.

Only by using an enzyme odor remover will you completely get rid of the odor causing molecules. These enzyme odor removers work by breaking down the urine molecule into odorless carbon dioxide and water. This way there is no residual smell to either you or the dog. Do not use vinegar and water or household cleaners such as Lysol. These leave enough of the smell behind for the dog to detect. If the dog can smell any urine on the spot, she will be attracted to urinate there again. Be sure the label says enzyme odor remover, and then follow the label directions carefully. Some of these enzyme odor removers require you to activate the enzyme action with warm water. Others are ready to use right out of the bottle.

Preventing Access to the Site

It also helps to block your dog's access to the spot by putting a chair or potted plant over the area once it is dry. By physically restricting the dog's access to the "scene of the crime," it will help remove the site-oriented motivation for urinating or defecating on that spot.

Q: *I have a six-year-old Springer Spaniel, Callie, who has always been well housebroken until three months ago, when she had a bladder infection. I took her to my veterinarian, and now her bladder infection is all gone, but she's still urinating in the house.*

A: This is not an unusual problem. Sometimes a well-housebroken dog will have a medical condition, such as your Springer's bladder infection, which causes it to be unable to control its bladder, and so it eliminates in the house. This type of elimination is usually small amounts of urine emitted frequently during the day and night. The bladder infection makes the dog feel like she has to urinate all the time, and she tries, even though her bladder may be almost empty.

Once she has started eliminating in the house, the dog sometimes loses the concept of the entire house being her "den." She will simply need to be *retrained*. You'll need to start again, on schedule, taking Callie out to her elimination spot and praising her for urinating outside. When you can't watch her every movement, she needs to be confined to her crate so she doesn't have an opportunity to have an accident. Clean up any spots where she urinated very well, using an enzyme odor remover. You may even have to get down on all fours and sniff the carpet to find areas where she has gone. It is important to treat all soiled areas so she cannot smell a previous spot. I'd also recommend you block her access to the spots using a chair or potted plant once the treated area is dry.

Take Callie out to eliminate first thing in the morning, fifteen minutes after each meal, after vigorous playing or chewing and just before you go to bed. Take her food and water up about two hours before you go to bed, and be sure she is in her crate, next to your bed, for the night.

You should follow this schedule and not leave Callie unattended inside for at least four weeks. When you start giving her access to the house again, do so gradually, a room at a time.

Q: *My dog is not housebroken! I know he can hold it because he holds it all day long while I am at work. When I come home I let him outside. When I let him back in, he'll defecate in the house.*

How long are you leaving him outside?

Oh, about five or ten minutes.

A: You are simply not leaving this dog outside long enough. A dog will often take some time to find "the right spot" to urinate and then will sniff around even more to pick another spot to defecate. The dog is probably happy and anxious to see you and wants to come back inside quickly, but he just hasn't had enough time to eliminate "a day's worth" of waste.

I suggest you put on your coat, grab your flashlight if it's dark, and go out with your dog. Watch him and make sure he urinates *and* defecates before you bring him back in! Don't forget to praise him when he defecates outside. This is how he will know that you want him to defecate outside. Right now, he probably thinks it's normal to hold his bladder and bowels all day, urinate outside after you come home, then defecate in your house— because that's what you've trained him to do.

If, after twenty minutes outside, he doesn't defecate, go ahead and bring him in, *but watch him closely*. He is now conditioned to defecating inside and may be holding it until he gets back in. Watch for warning signs such as sniffing the floor, circling, and starting to squat. If he does this, don't punish him, but shout a sharp *no!* so he will stop the action. Then quickly whisk him right back outside and wait with him until he defecates. Really praise him when he "goes" outside.

You'll need to do this every day until you're sure he has been reconditioned. After that, remember to give him more time to finish his business before you bring him in. Be sure you have cleaned all areas where he has defecated with enzyme odor removers.

Q: *My husband and I have a mixed-breed female named Sadie. When we come home, she seems real excited to see us and she urinates right there in front of us. My husband spanks her, but she just turns over on her back and urinates more. What can we do to stop this?*

A: Sadie is exhibiting what is called "submissive urination." *This is not a housebreaking problem* and so can't be cured using house-training methods. It is actually a submissive/fear reaction and spanking her is only making it worse.

In nature, if a dog gets nervous or anxious, especially around a more dominant dog, it will urinate as a signal of submission.

Many times the dog will actually flip upside down and expose its belly. This is the most vulnerable part of the body and by overtly exposing it to the perceived attacker, the dog is signaling that she is submissive and "gives up!"

This is particularly liable to happen if the dog thinks it may be attacked by the more dominant dog or human. It means, "I'm not challenging you, I acknowledge you are dominant over me, so please don't attack me."

You can see why the problem is worse when you spank Sadie. She is already excited and nervous and when she realizes an "attack" from your husband is eminent, she becomes even more nervous and tries to signal her submission even more by turning over and urinating more. Punishing her only sends the behavior into a vicious spiral, and the poor dog never understands what's wrong.

This problem should be handled by trying to decrease the excitement and nervousness associated with your coming home. Be very low-key and calm about coming home, and don't greet Sadie until you've been in her presence for ten or fifteen minutes. Then, greet her in a very mild, low-key manner. You may also give her a little food treat as you greet her. Food rewards help her feel calmer and she will concentrate less on the anxiety of the situation.

If she urinates or turns over, don't punish her, either physically or verbally. The best thing to do is simply turn your back to the dog and walk away. Don't ever pet her when she rolls over on her back. This is just rewarding her submission. Stand up and step back. If she gets up, pet her, but stay low-key. If she turns over again, stand up and walk away. Eventually she will learn that she doesn't get attention by being submissive.

In all your interactions with Sadie, try to avoid overexcitement as this will trigger her submissive urination. Certainly, she should *never* be physically punished. This is a very sensitive dog. I'm sure a harsh word is all she needs to know she has displeased you.

Also, I'd suggest *you* begin this work with her and have your husband keep his distance until you have made some progress. Then he can begin to go through the same process of decreasing her fears toward him.

Q: *I have a four-year-old Jack Russell Terrier, Riley. Lately, Riley has been marking my bed and my couch. He doesn't really urinate a lot, he just marks them. How can I stop him?*

Has Riley been neutered?

No.

A: Riley is urine marking your house to mark his "territory." He's saying "That's Mine!" Male dogs want to mark every vertical object in sight when they're outside or in a new, unfamiliar place. Most of the time they don't mark in their own house if they've been properly housetrained. However, there are some triggers that may cause a male dog to mark in his own home. A new dog in the house, or even a new dog in the neighborhood, may make him feel the need to label his territory as his. A new piece of furniture, a new cat or even a new child or visitor in the house may cause some male dogs to feel the need to mark.

This problem occurs primarily in intact males. Neutering stops the problem in about 60% of the cases, without any further behavior modification. When you combine neutering with some good housetraining procedures, you get 98% of it stopped.

I suggest you get Riley neutered right away. Neutering has many other positive side effects as well (see Chapter 5).

You will also need to clean any marked areas well using an enzyme odor remover to remove all traces of smell so that Riley is not attracted back to the spots. I also suggest using a pet repellent spray on the areas daily for several weeks. I like Repel, made by the Farnam Company. You'll find other products with names like Stay Away and Dog Off. Do not use ammonia. Many people believe that because ammonia is pungent smelling it will repel dogs. Remember what's in urine—ammonia. So it will actually act as an attractant instead of a repellent.

CHAPTER 12

Manners and Obedience Training

"Our dog doesn't know anything! She's always run off when we take her out and it can take hours to catch her. She's very friendly, but it's frustrating when she won't come when we call her."

"Well what kind of obedience training have you done with her?"

"Well . . . none."

"How do you expect this dog to know what you want her to do? It's not like she spends her evening hours reading a book and learning your family rules. You are her teacher, you are 'top dog' and she looks to you for leadership. Without any leadership she'll just do whatever she wants."

"Oh . . . I thought they learned that stuff from their mother. . . ."

It is in the area of basic manners that I receive a large number of calls to my radio shows. It is obvious that a huge percentage of pet owners have problems with their dogs' manners ranging from the annoying to the dangerous. While I understand the frustration these owners feel with their pets, I also realize that most of the time the owner has unintentionally contributed to the problem.

Everyone suffers in these cases. A dog that is out of control, jumping up on visitors, barking constantly, running off and not coming when called is not going to give much pleasure to his owner. This owner may even decide that dogs are not for him, and he will lose the opportunity to enjoy the very special relationship only a well-behaved dog can offer.

The dog certainly suffers. Many poorly behaved canines are relegated to the back yard and receive little attention. This is a sad and lonely life for a dog who is, after all, a pack animal, needing companionship and love. In fact, a dog so needs companionship that the lack of it can actually be the cause of many behavior problems. In the wild the dog's very existence depends on keeping the pack together. When he is separated from his pack, anxiety and fear become strong to motivate him to get back to his protective pack. When you take such a strong pack instinct from such a social animal you are dooming it to a miserable and sad life. It may become withdrawn, aggressive, fearful or simply starved for attention.

Saddest of all, many of these potentially wonderful pets are euthanized because of behavior problems. Behavior problems are the number one reason why people give their pets up to shelters and humane societies. Homes cannot be found for most of these pets, and they must be euthanized.

The good news is that these problems can be fixed or prevented altogether with some education of, and effort from, the owner.

There is no way I can emphasize enough the importance of obedience training for *every* dog. Both by personal experience and by the thousands of calls I get on talk radio, I know that dogs who are obedience trained are better companions, live longer and are more of a joy to own.

Obedience training your dog does more than simply make your pet easier to live with. It forms an important bond between you and your dog, establishing his trust in you and placing you in the position of leader and teacher. Dogs instinctively follow and respect the "leader." The fact that your dog will consistently see you as this respected leader is one of the most important benefits of this training.

Q: *I recently adopted a mixed-breed female puppy from the humane society. This is my first dog and I want to start out right. I've been told it's important to show your dog you're the boss but I'm not sure exactly what that means or how to do it.*

A: I'm glad you called. The process of teaching your puppy how to live by your rules will be much easier if you understand a little about the nature of dogs and how they communicate and learn.

First understand that dogs are pack animals, even domesticated dogs like your new puppy. This means she is naturally sociable and needs the type of companionship and structure that a pack would provide. In the wild, a pack is lead by the "alpha dog." This is the dominant dog, usually a male, but sometimes a female. This dog makes the decisions about where the pack travels and when they hunt. He keeps the peace among the lesser pack members. The other pack members are confident and secure in his leadership.

You, and your family members, are now your dog's pack. In order to feel confident and secure, she needs to see you as pack leader, or "alpha" to her. She will then take your direction, respect your reprimands and seek your approval. There are several ways that you communicate to your dog that you are the leader. Harsh punishment—yelling or physically striking the dog—is not one of them. *Never hit your dog or punish out of anger.* This will only teach your dog to fear and avoid you. Alpha dogs in the wild are consistent, fair and forgiving.

Here are some of the ways you communicate to your puppy that you are the leader.

- Teach her things, such as basic obedience training and tricks. (Leaders are teachers.)
- Reprimand her for bad behavior. Do it immediately. Do it fairly and forgive quickly.
- *Praise, praise, praise* her when she does what you want.
- *Be consistent.*

Q: *Our dog, Shelly, is in the house with us whenever we are home. I don't want to have to put her outside when we eat, but she won't stop nudging our arm and begging while we're trying to have dinner. How can we stop that?*

A: I think it's great that your dog is in the house with you enjoying your companionship whenever you're home. Dogs are very social animals and crave the company of their human "pack members." This is actually an excellent opportunity to teach your dog some manners and self-control.

If your dog has not received any obedience training, then this is the first thing she needs. In order for us to exert control over our dogs' behaviors, we need a language of communication that both dog and owner understand. That's what obedience training does. It teaches the dog what you mean and what you expect when you give it basic commands such as sit, down, stand, stay and come. Once your dog has learned to consistently respond to these basic commands, controlling unwanted behaviors such as begging is easy.

Start by practicing putting your dog on a down–stay. Gradually increase the time you expect her to stay until she is reliable for thirty minutes. Then at dinner time, when your dog starts to nudge your arm or beg in any way, say *"no,"* in a firm, low voice. Guide her to a corner of the room, or other out-of-the-way place where she can still see you. Command her to down and stay. Return to your dinner. If she gets up, tell her *"no."* Guide her back to her spot and make her lie down. (Don't repeat the command stay; she was already told what to do.) Be consistent! If you let her get up every once in a while and either don't notice or don't take the time to correct her, she'll learn that she doesn't always have to mind. Then, she'll test you. When you're finished eating, don't forget to release her from the stay with the command *OK*. There must be a start and an end to each stay command.

Q: *Our little six-year-old Poodle, Sweetie Pie, whines all the time. Is she in pain or is she just trying to get our attention?*

A: You should first eliminate the possibility that your Poodle is hurting. Look her over carefully and feel her gently from head to tail and down each leg. If you're not convinced that she's OK, have your veterinarian check her.

Whining is commonly an attention-getting behavior, especially if this has worked in the past. If she whines because she spends a lot of her time outside alone while you're inside, she is probably lonely and wants to join you in the house. I think you should let her. If she is whining while inside with you, she is probably a bit spoiled and feels like she should have your full attention at all times.

Tell her, *"No, enough,"* and give her a little tug on her collar. Then distract her by giving her something else to think about.

Tell her to sit or down. When she does, praise, praise, praise her. She will probably be quiet for a second or two and then start back up. Repeat the process, praising her when she is quiet, even for a few seconds. She will start to figure out that she gets your approval and praise when she is quiet. Don't forget to praise her at times when she is sitting quietly beside you or other quiet times. Dogs are naturally eager to please and she will learn if you are consistent and patient.

Q: *We love to wrestle with Johnson, our four-year-old Boxer, but he does not know when to stop. He gets rough and sometimes bites pretty hard. How can we tone it down a little?*

A: When puppies are small and still with their litter mates, they learn some important lessons, one of which is not to play too rough. It's part of their socialization. If a pup bites too hard on a litter mate, he will yelp and stop playing, and the game ends. If a puppy bites too hard on his mother, she will give a sharp correction with a growl and a grab with her mouth to the back of the pup's neck.

So when your adult dog plays with other dogs, he understands not to play too hard. However, dogs have thick coats and people have delicate skin, so it's best to teach your dog that it is never OK to even *mouth* people. Certainly never teach your dog to "go for your arm" especially if it's padded by heavy clothing. You will only be teaching him that he can bite harder before you yell. Then one day he'll bite that hard on your bare arm.

When Johnson mouths or bites you, give him a sharp *no* and a tug on his collar. DO NOT HIT HIM. When he tries again, repeat *no* and the tug. If he tries a third time, turn your back to him and walk away, don't play anymore. He will learn that if he mouths you, the game ends (he doesn't want that).

Instead of wrestling, try some fetching games, or keep away. Just make sure that you tell him, *"OK, enough,"* and call him to you when you're through playing so that he understands the difference between playtime and coming when you call.

Q: *Our dog, Ralph, jumps up on every person that comes in our front door. How can we stop him from doing that?*

A: Jumping up is another one of those behaviors that is easy to correct when the dog is a little puppy, before it ever becomes a problem. It is a problem almost always contributed to by the owner.

When puppies are so small and cute, owners tend to actually encourage their jumping up. It seems so harmless when the pup is small, and owners are pleased that their puppy is glad to see them. Some owners let their adult dogs jump up on them when they're wearing jeans and a sweatshirt, but then get angry when the dog jumps on their white silk jumpsuit or on visitors. So let's be fair here. Your dog doesn't understand the difference. Rule number one is: *no jumping up*, EVER.

To fix the problem, you have to be consistent. Everybody in the family has to understand the rule. When the dog jumps up, you give him a sharp *no* and knock him off balance. With a large dog you can bring your knee up as he jumps so that he hits himself in the chest with your knee. With a small dog, place your foot under his belly and move your leg to the side. This will throw him to the side, and he'll lose his balance. He will be momentarily surprised, and then he'll jump right back up. Repeat the process: *no*, and knock him off balance. After three or four tries, he'll pause to check you out. Praise him. Rule number two is: *no petting until all four feet are on the ground*. Be consistent. It will take probably up to ten sessions to make the lesson stick.

When visitors come over, put a leash on Ralph before you open the door. As he jumps for your company, say, *"No,"* and pull strongly back and to the side, again to knock him off balance. Repeat as long as he keeps trying to jump. When he momentarily keeps all paws on the floor, have your visitor pet him. If he starts to jump again, repeat the procedure.

Q: *Our family owns a beautiful Irish Setter who is a wonderful pet, except we can't keep her off the furniture. She is two years old and has been getting on the furniture since she was a puppy. Now that she's so big, I'd like her to stay off.*

A: This is another problem where the sins we commit when our dogs are puppies come back to haunt us once they are adults. When you get a new puppy you should decide right then if you want her on the furniture once she is full grown. My suggestion is that you don't let dogs on the furniture at all. Remember, dogs see no difference in getting on the couch with muddy paws versus clean ones. Instead, get her her own bed, maybe two or three, so she can have one in each of the rooms you use the most. If the rule from puppyhood is: *no getting on the furniture*, then she won't ever consider it a possibility as she grows up.

To fix the problem, start by getting your Irish Setter her own bed. It can be a bed you buy at the pet shop or an old blanket. Whatever, it will be hers. Place the bed in a corner of the room where you spend the most time, or the room where she gets on the furniture most. Make a big deal about it. Crawl around on it on your hands and knees and talk in a high excited voice. Basically, convince her this is something really interesting. She'll come check it out. Get her to lie down on it, and praise her lavishly. Praise her anytime she lies on her bed, whether of her own accord or because you encouraged her to.

Treat the couch or other furniture she gets on with an enzyme odor remover to remove her smell. Then spray several towels with pet-repellent spray and place them on the furniture where she usually lies. You will need to respray the towels every day and leave them in place for probably at least two weeks. If you ever catch her on the furniture again, sound *very disappointed* in her and say, *"No, bad dog, off!"* Then lead her over to her bed, have her lie down on it, and praise her. Take her bed into your room at night so she can sleep in your room (not on your bed).

Q: *We love to have our Rottweiler out in the front yard with us on the weekends, but he will chase cars, joggers and even kids on bikes. How can we break him of this habit?*

A: That is a bad habit. Not only could a child panic and ride in front of a car, your dog could get hit by a car. He may even bite one of these times. He is, after all, acting on a predator–prey instinct when he chases.

If your dog has not been obedience trained, do so first thing. While obedience training is important for all dogs, it is absolutely essential for large, aggressive breeds such as Rottweilers, German Shepherds and Dobermans.

Then, when your dog is in the yard with you, attach a long line to his collar. (You can either buy one at a pet shop or make your own out of a twenty-five-foot length of soft cotton rope, with a snap attached to one end. The rope should be strong, but light enough that your dog will forget he has it on.)

Keep hold of one end, and let your dog wander freely about your yard. When you see an unsuspecting car, jogger or child approaching, tell your dog to stay. If he takes off in chase, give a loud, sharp *no!* If he doesn't stop (and he won't at first), let him run a ways from you, then pull back strongly as he nears the end of the rope. The impact should knock him backward, for best effect. Then call him to you, as if you can't imagine what happened to him. If he doesn't come, reel him in with your line. When he gets to you, PRAISE HIM. This is very important. The last thing that happened was that he came to you, and he should be praised for doing so (even if you had to help with the line). Don't punish him now. The line correction was his reprimand. After several sessions, he will start to understand that chasing will not be tolerated.

A side note to this: No dog should be allowed off leash in an unenclosed area until you are certain he is well trained enough for you to control him at all times. This is essential, not only for the safety of others, but for your dog's safety as well. He could easily chase a squirrel right into the path of a car.

Q: *We have a beautiful Doberman called Athena. When we are at the park and she gets very far from us, she won't come when we call her. How can we get her to come on command?*

A: Dobermans are very intelligent dogs and highly trainable. They are so intelligent though, that they sometimes decide they are "alpha dog," or the leader, if their owner is not quite firm and consistent.

Athena needs to go back to basics with her obedience training. It is important that you not let her off leash in an unenclosed area until she is very reliable with all her commands. She has discovered that she doesn't have to mind you if she is out of your reach.

Review all her obedience work on leash until she is very obedient with her heel, sit, down, stay and come. Then take her to the park and attach a long line to her training collar. Release her from her *heel* command with *OK* and encourage her to go explore. Let her wander five to ten feet from you and then say, "Athena, come." Give her a couple of moments to respond, and if she does, praise her, *a lot*. If she doesn't come, give a sharp pull on the line and reel her in. For best effect, try to knock her a little off balance with your first pull. When she gets to you, praise her like crazy, as if she had come running of her own accord. Let her wander again, and repeat. Always give her a moment or two to respond before you yank the line. When she starts coming to you consistently at five to ten feet, gradually increase the distance until you are using the entire twenty-five to thirty feet of line.

All this good work can be totally ruined by a couple of very common mistakes. If she ever does not come to you when you call, DO NOT punish her when she finally comes. Coming to you MUST ALWAYS be a totally positive experience. Never call her to you to punish her if she has done something bad. If you must reprimand her for something, go get her and bring her to the scene of the crime to reprimand her.

Q: *Our Dachshund, named Rascal, likes to visit the neighbors. Many times we come home and he is nowhere to be found. How can we keep him at home?*

A: This is a prime example of a bad behavior blamed on the dog that is, in reality, totally the fault of the owner. It is unrealistic to expect that Rascal should know to stay home on his property if there is nothing to keep him from wandering off. Although there are dogs who do live on properties without fences and never leave their property, these are rare cases. It is not a realistic expectation of your dog.

For Rascal's safety and well-being he needs to be in a fenced yard or in the house when you are not with him. Running loose he could be hit by a car, be poisoned, be badly injured in a dog fight or get lost or stolen. It is also inconsiderate to your neighbors to let Rascal run loose. He can potentially dig up your neighbors' flowers, defecate in their yards, spread garbage about and cause dog fights with leashed dogs on walks with their owners. Most irresponsibly, if not neutered, he may end up fathering unwanted puppies.

If you have a large property of half an acre or more, you might consider an "invisible fence." A wire is buried at the circumference of your property, and your dog wears a special collar which delivers a very small, but uncomfortable shock when he gets within ten feet of the edge of the property. Thus he is trained to stay within the confines of his property. However you do it, keeping Rascal home is *your* responsibility as a pet owner.

Q: *We took our Cocker Spaniel, Rex, to obedience school when he was a year old but now he just doesn't remember any of it!*
   How old is your dog?
   Four!

A: Obedience, like high school Spanish, doesn't stay with you for life if you don't keep using it. It must be reviewed and practiced almost every day. Consistency is one of the most important factors in successful training. Not only should you continue to practice heeling, sit–stays, down–stays, etc., you should incorporate them into your daily interactions with your dog.

- Take your dog for a walk each evening, and make sure he heels and does his automatic sits when you stop. The exercise will be good for both of you, and I promise he will look forward to it as the favorite part of his day.
- Make Rex sit and stay before you give him his dinner. Set it down and don't let him go to it until you release him with an "OK" command.
- Before you let Rex outside, have him sit at the door and wait until you give him the "OK" command before going out.
- Put Rex on a down–stay in the corner of the room while the family has dinner. The prolonged down–stay (up to thirty minutes) is a wonderful way to establish self control in a dog and to reenforce that you are in charge (in a positive way). Don't forget to release Rex from the down–stay with the "OK" command when you finish dinner. A stay must always have a start and a finish.
- When you give Rex a dog biscuit or other treat, make him do something for it. Make him sit, or down, or shake, anything, as long as he obeys a command to get his treat.

Since it's been three years since you've done any obedience training with Rex, you may want to go back to a good obedience class for a refresher course for both Rex and you. Once you establish obedience as a way of life for you and Rex, you will find he will listen to you and be under your control at all times. You'll probably take him more places, and you'll certainly enjoy him more.

Q: *My wife and I are taking our Brittany Spaniel, Webster, to obedience classes, but Webster and I are not doing too well when we practice. No matter how loud I shout at him, I have to tell him to sit six or seven times before he does it. Do you think he's dumb or just hard of hearing?*

A: Actually, I don't think he's either. I have to tell you that *you* are the problem, not Webster. I'm glad you're taking your dog to obedience class, and I hope that you've found a good class where the instructor can give everyone some individual attention. If so, I'm sure he or she will really help you with your training techniques.

There are some very simple, but vitally important principles of training. One of these is: *Don't repeat a command.* Webster heard you the first time. By repeating the command until he decides to sit, you've taught him that you didn't really mean it the first time. He thinks you're not *really* serious until the sixth or seventh time. If Webster doesn't sit the first time you tell him, then immediately give him a leash correction and say a sharp, *"No."* Don't repeat the command, but make him sit. Then praise him once he does (even if you had to help him sit). Have your instructor watch your leash correction to make sure you are doing it correctly. It won't be long until he is sitting the first time you tell him to.

You also mentioned shouting your commands. It is not necessary, or desirable to use a loud voice when giving a dog commands. Certainly you don't want to shout. You want to teach your dog to listen to you. Speak to him in a clear voice of normal conversational volume. Once Webster has learned a command, you can even practice whispering the command to encourage him to really focus on you and listen.

Q: *Dr. Jim, my husband and I want to obedience train our eight-month-old Rottweiler, Ben. There is a place in our town that will kennel Ben for four weeks and train him for us, but I hate for him to be away from us for a month. Do you think this would be OK, or should we go to an obedience class. We're only considering the first place because we've never trained a dog before. Are there any other options?*

A: There are typically three different options when you start to look for an obedience trainer: group obedience lessons, private obedience lessons or board and training kennels. All these options can be appropriate for someone who has never trained a dog before. Which option is best depends on your situation.

I prefer group obedience training for almost all dogs. These classes are typically available through obedience clubs, pet stores or grooming shops, city recreation departments, community colleges or breed clubs. In a group class, one or two instructors teach a group of owners and their dogs. It's a good socialization experience for your dog, getting him exposed to different people and other dogs. He'll learn to pay attention and mind you, even around the distractions the other dogs and their owners provide. Most owners enjoy the camaraderie of the other owners, and you will learn a lot by watching the other owners with their dogs (a lot of what you want to do and *don't* want to do!). An added plus is that this is typically the least expensive training option.

In a private training situation, one instructor works individually with one owner and dog. The trainer may come to the owner's house, or the lessons may take place at the trainer's home or a local park. There are a couple advantages to private training. You have the instructor's undivided attention, and the trainer can adapt the training to any specific needs you might have. Private training works well for people who have transportation difficulties in getting their dog to a group class or who have physical disabilities that would make participation in a group class difficult. In the case of a very aggressive dog or one that the owner just cannot physically control, I suggest private training. Such a dog would be dangerous and disruptive in a group situation. Private training is usually considerably more expensive than group lessons, and you don't get the support and motivation of the other owners in a group. Your dog also doesn't get the socialization benefits or the chance to learn to mind in spite of distractions.

The last option is the type you mention, where the dog is kenneled and trained at the instructor's facility. This is by far the most expensive of the options. The biggest problem with this method is that the dog is being trained while the owner is not. A professional can train a dog much quicker than the owner can, but if the owner isn't taught how to follow up with practice sessions, then the dog will forget everything he learned once he goes home. In all types of obedience training, the biggest need is to train the owner. A good board and train facility will include regular lessons with the owner all through the training process with followup sessions after the dog goes home. So, even with this type of training, there must be a commitment on the owner's part to attend all the lessons, learn how to handle the dog and to practice on a regular basis once the dog goes home. This is my least favorite option. When a trainer trains your dog for you, rather than having an instructor teach you how to train your own dog, you lose the special bonding that occurs between dog and trainer. Your dog is going to look up to and respect the one that trains him. It's really best if that's you.

Q: *I have a six-month-old, mixed-breed puppy. How do I go about finding a good obedience trainer?*

A: First you need to decide which type of training option will work best for you. Then take your time in finding a good trainer, and don't let anyone pressure you into making a decision. There is no licensing or regulating of dog trainers in the U.S. Anyone can call himself a "dog trainer," so be cautious.

Ask for references from your veterinarian, breeder, breed club or pet store. Call and talk to each trainer you are considering and ask them about their experience, education and training philosophies. Ask them how long they've been training in your community, to give you an idea of their stability in the area. Ask them if there are any books they suggest you read. It's a good idea to check out and scan any suggested reading. The type of books a trainer suggests can tell you a lot about her style. If you read anything that sounds harsh or cruel to you, avoid this trainer completely. While you want to chose a trainer who is confident, beware of anyone who comes across as macho, arrogant or pushy. These personality traits are not compatible with good training.

Look for a trainer who uses positive reinforcement with a minimal use of force. Before you sign up for any classes or training, ask to observe some classes or training sessions. If you see anything that makes you uncomfortable, keep looking for another trainer. In group classes, make sure the group is not so big that the instructor has lost control of the group or that some people are lost in the crowd and don't get enough attention. See if everyone gets some amount of individual attention, especially if they're having problems. Make sure the trainer has a happy, enthusiastic attitude towards both dogs *and* owners.

Q: *How long should I work with my dog when I am practicing her obedience work?*

A: Dogs, especially puppies, cannot concentrate for long periods of time. You will undo a great deal of training by working at training sessions for too long. Fifteen minutes twice a day is enough for any dog over six months old. Younger pups can endure even less time—probably no more than five minutes at a time.

Q: *My wife and I are taking our family dog to obedience classes. Is it OK if she takes him to class sometimes and I take him sometimes, or does it need to be the same person each time?*

A: For consistency, it is best if one person in the family actually does the training. However, everyone in the family should know the commands and give them consistently when necessary. In fact, I recommend having a family meeting and going over all the steps of training, including the proper commands and signals. This way, everyone in the dog's environment is "speaking" the same language.

Q: *I'm trying to train my six-month-old Dalmatian, Cinder. I get kind of frustrated with it sometimes, I'm just not sure I'm doing it right. Can you help me?*

A: Training should be a positive experience for both you and your dog. If you let expectancy get in the way, and become disappointed about your dog's progress, the process can be negative. Training dogs, or any animal, takes time. Some things he'll catch on to very quickly, others will take time, patience and persistence. Understanding a few basic principles will help.

- Realize that your dog has no basis for automatically knowing what you expect of him. He must be taught using consistent signals: rewards in the form of praise and food treats; and corrections in the form of quick jerks on the leash and verbal reprimands.
- In order to begin on a positive note and to make training fun, play with your dog for a few minutes both before and after each session. When work begins, however, be serious and let him know you mean business.
- Always begin a new lesson in a distraction-free area.
- Be consistent. Use the same word and the same hand signal each time you give a command. Use a short word such as sit, come, down. Your dog learns to recognize the sound of the word, not its meaning. I've seen many people give commands like, "OK, now get away from there and come over here and sit down," or "I told you to sit, now I mean it!" The dog doesn't understand these long sentences, he only hears noise. A simple command, followed by a signal as to what you expect from him, followed by praise for proper performance is how he will learn.
- Use your dog's name before each command to get his attention. Dogs key in on their name. This gets their attention and makes them expect a command. Speak firmly, but do not yell.
- Let your dog master one skill before trying to teach him another. Training is like building an inverted pyramid. The dog must accomplish basic skills and establish learning patterns. Once that's established, dogs can learn an amazing amount.
- Most importantly, you must not lose patience or become irritated. If you feel yourself starting to lose patience, end the session at once, but never on a bad note. Make the dog complete whatever you have commanded, even if he doesn't do it well. Praise him anyway, then play with him for a few minutes. *Every* session should end on a good note.

Training should be a fun, positive experience for both you and your dog. Done correctly, it does more than make your dog a joy to live with, it forms a strong bond between you.

Q: *I just started an obedience class with my seven-month-old Boston Terrier. The instructor told everyone in the class to go out and buy a "German pinch collar" before the next class. I'm not real comfortable with that. I don't want to do anything harsh to my puppy. She is very sweet and sensitive. What do you think?*

A: I think you're right to be concerned. Although, different dogs need different measures to get their attention and to be able to control them, in my opinion, a German pinch collar is *rarely* needed. Certainly a trainer should *never* recommend its use on a young puppy. On some very large, energetic dogs with long hair, a regular chain training collar just doesn't provide enough control for some smaller owners. The prongs of the pinch collar can penetrate the long haircoat and put some pressure on the neck. (The collar should be adjusted so that there is no tightening, or "choking" action to the collar.) In these cases, I think a German pinch collar is useful, *if* used carefully under the supervision of a *good* trainer. Initial obedience training should *never* be started with a German pinch collar. It is a more severe tool to be used to deal with more severe problems. Rarely, would I recommend the use of one on a short-haired dog.

Any trainer who would tell a whole class of puppy owners to go out and buy pinch collars is *not* a good trainer. These trainers tend to be lazy and depend more on the use of force than on sound training principles. Overaggressive training measures like these can be very damaging, especially to sensitive little dogs like your Boston Terrier. Definitely find a different trainer.

Q: *I'm in the process of obedience training my eight-month-old Springer Spaniel. What is your opinion of using treats as a reward? Also, how should I correct her when she won't mind a command?*

A: Treats are very useful in training, but don't make a practice of giving your dog a treat every time she performs well. Reward her with a treat occasionally, but always with kind words and petting. Treats are primarily used to get a young puppy's attention during early training. Later in life, dogs will perform very well just for your praise.

Never punish your dog physically. This will serve only to destroy her trust in you. Physical punishment is not necessary in training and the dog will only learn you are to be feared and that you represent a negative thing in her life. If a reprimand or punishment is needed, use a stern tone of voice and sharp jerk on the leash to let her know she has done wrong.

Q: *We have a two-year-old Beagle cross. We listen to your show and you've convinced us how important it is to obedience train our dog. Can we teach our dog obedience from a book, or do you think we should actually go to a class?*

A: While it is possible to learn to obedience train your dog just by reading books, I don't suggest it for people who have never trained a dog before. There are just some physical moves, such as effective leash corrections, that you need an instructor to help you learn and perfect. There are also many common mistakes and pitfalls that an instructor will notice you getting into, and can help you correct, before you cause yourself a big problem.

I recommend working with an obedience instructor, preferably in a class situation, if at all possible. You will benefit from your instructor's expertise, your dog will benefit from learning to work around the distraction of other dogs, and you will learn a lot by observing the other members of your class.

I *do* recommend that you supplement your obedience classes by reading a couple of good books on obedience training. Once you have been in the class and started your training, they will make more sense to you and will help you refine your understanding and technique.

CHAPTER 13

Barking, Escaping, Out-of-Control Dogs and Coprophagia

"Dr. Jim," the sweet little elderly woman's voice came in over the phone line. . . . "My precious little Muffin barks constantly. What can I do?"

"Well, Mabel, what is she barking at?"

"Anything, but mostly a tree!"

"A tree?"

"Yes, she just barks and barks at this tree."

"Well, is there a squirrel in the tree?"

"No," she said quietly.

"Are leaves falling from the tree?"

"No."

"Are there birds in the tree?"

"No," she said calmly.

"Are you sure she's barking at this tree, maybe it's something else."

"No, it's the tree, she just barks and barks at this damn tree until I just want to ring her little neck!"

Almost all dog owners describe some behavior problems with their dogs. These range from minor annoyances that the owner may choose to overlook, to destructive or dangerous behaviors that may lead the owner to get rid of the dog, or even to sweet little old ladies turning into not so sweet little old ladies.

Behavior problems are the number-one reason why dogs are euthanized. Most dogs relinquished by their owners to shelters or humane societies are given up because of behavior problems. That's shocking, sad and unnecessary. Almost all behavior problems can be prevented if a puppy is raised correctly. Most adult behavior problems are correctable if the owner is willing to spend some time and effort to do it. As a matter of fact, most behavior problems are caused or contributed to by the owner, yet it is the dog who may end up paying the ultimate price.

While there is a great deal of joy to be had from owning a dog, there is also a great deal of responsibility to ownership. So, if your dog has a behavior problem, make up your mind to invest some time, effort and energy to correct it. Your effort will pay off in years of wonderful interaction with your dog.

Coprophagy is a technical word that means "eating feces." I get a lot of calls on talk radio from thoroughly disgusted owners who have discovered that their dog is eating feces, either its own, the cat's or another dog's. It's one of the more unpleasant things dogs will do.

Q: *It is so disgusting! My puppy eats her own stools. I just about died when I saw it. Why does she do that? How can I make her stop?*

A: Few things that dogs do alarm and disgust their owners more than coprophagy, or eating feces. It is especially common in young puppies. When pups are very small, before they are weaned, their mother consumes all their waste. It is a natural maternal instinct. Dogs in the wild must keep the den clean to avoid attracting predators to the den, where the pups are.

Young pups often experiment with tasting stools and may eat them. As a pup gets older, eating feces may indicate a nutritional problem. If a large amount of undigested protein or fats come through in the stool, the pup may smell this and be attracted to eat it. My experience is that most of the time it is *not* a nutritional problem, but rather an introverted behavior problem or simply a carry-over from puppyhood.

You'll want to correct the problem as soon as you notice it. Your pup can reinfest himself with worms by eating his own stools and may pick up new parasites by eating the stools of other dogs. The best approach is to keep all feces picked up every day. When you take your puppy out for walks, keep him on a leash. If he stops to investigate the droppings of other dogs, give him a leash correction and tell him, *"No."* If your dog never has the chance to be near the stool, he can't investigate it.

You should also make sure you have your puppy on a high-quality dog food that is highly digestible. I recommend a top, premium-brand food formulated for puppies.

As you begin to train your pup in basic obedience, you can simply stop the behavior by consistent corrections and he will learn the behavior is not acceptable.

Q: *Our four-year-old Scottie, James, has started eating his stools. We've just noticed this since my wife went back to work. She used to be home with him most of the day. Could this have anything to do with it? What can we do to break him of it?*

A: Yes, James' new habit could very well have to do with his change in routine. Coprophagy, feces eating, is often related to boredom. Dogs who spend a lot of time alone in a back yard with nothing to do sometimes start eating their stools.

However, I'd have your veterinarian check James to rule out any health problems since this problem started just recently. Fat in the stool from a pancreatic or intestinal disease could cause this. Make sure you have James on a good, high-quality dog food that is highly digestible. I recommend you put him on a premium brand such as Hill's Science Diet, Iams or Nature's Recipe.

It is very possible that James' new habit is related to boredom now that he is spending more time alone. Make sure James is getting enough exercise. He should get daily exercise of at least thirty minutes, such as a walk or playing fetch. Let him spend as much time as possible with you once you get home. I'd get him some new and interesting toys and leave two or three with him in the back yard every day. Rotate toys every four or five days to keep him interested. Most importantly, make sure you pick up all feces daily, or more often if you can. That's the best prevention.

You can also try some aversion conditioning by treating a couple of stools with hot cayenne pepper or Bitter Apple and then leaving them for James to eat. Make sure you pick up all untreated stools. Pick up the treated stools after a day and keep all stools picked up for a week, then leave a couple of treated stools out again. After getting a couple of tastes of hot pepper, most dogs will break the stool-eating habit.

Another trick I like is to put MSG (the meat tenderizer and flavor enhancer) on the dog's food for two to three weeks. A tablespoon sprinkled over the food will impart a very bitter taste to the stool and will deter this behavior.

Q: *Our Basset Hound, Corky, barks and barks and barks. I've never had a dog that barks so much. Why does she do that?*

A: Excessive barking is a common complaint among dog owners. The first thing you need to understand is that *barking is normal for dogs*. It's how they communicate with their people and with other dogs. A problem arises when the amount of time the dog spends barking becomes excessive to you (or to your neighbors).

> *Dogs bark for two main reasons:*
> 1. They "alarm bark" to warn of intruders to their territory. This will usually be other dogs or unfamiliar people, but may also include cats, birds and squirrels.
> 2. Dogs bark out of loneliness, boredom, anxiety or stress.

Q: *I have a two-year-old Australian Shepherd named Buddy. Buddy seems to bark at everything and nothing at all. What can we do to stop him?*

A: If your dog seems to be barking excessively, the first thing you need to do is determine *why* he is barking. When Buddy barks when you're home, go and investigate what he seems to be barking at. Is he outside where he can hear people talking or children playing? Is he inside an apartment where he can frequently see and hear people walking by and talking?

If you can determine what Buddy is barking at, you may be able to decrease the stimulus or move Buddy away from it. If you live next door to a school yard and Buddy can hear kids yelling and playing all day, you might want to let him stay in the house, where there is less noise. If Buddy seems to bark at any unfamiliar sound, try leaving a radio playing while you're gone. Tune it to a talk station so that Buddy gets a constant background of conversation. That will make him less reactive to hearing people's voices.

Sometimes a dog that is behind a high, solid wood fence will bark at every noise he hears because he can't see what's causing the noise. It often helps to cut small windows on each wall of the fence so that the dog can see out. Cut small openings about 6" x 12" and cover them with a fine wire mesh. That way your dog can see out but remains protected behind your fence.

The most common reason why dogs bark excessively, however, is out of boredom, loneliness, anxiety and stress. You may be leaving Buddy alone too often and for too long. Let Buddy be with you as much as possible. When you are home, Buddy should be in the house with you. At night, he should sleep in your bedroom, but not in your bed. He should have his own bed, beside yours. While you sleep you can be spending eight hours of good bonding time that doesn't cost you a thing, and it's another eight hours where Buddy has companionship and won't be lonely.

Lack of exercise and mental stimulation can lead to excessive barking out of boredom and anxiety. Make sure Buddy gets daily opportunity to exercise. That doesn't mean putting him in the back yard. Dogs don't exercise themselves. You need to get out with him and walk, or play fetch, or something. Practice Buddy's obedience commands or do some agility work. If he hasn't been obedience trained, do it. Dogs need mental stimulation in order to be happy and avoid boredom. Teaching him something new is the best mental stimulation you can give him.

Q: *Our neighbor went to her vet for advice about her dog's constant barking. He wanted to cut out its vocal cords. I think that sounds cruel. What do you think?*

A: I think it sounds cruel too. I was first introduced to veterinary medicine in the 1960s. Even then cutting a dog's vocal cords was considered "old" procedure and barbaric by many veterinarians. I can't believe that thirty years later the suggestion still comes up. Ventriculocordectomy, or removal of the vocal cords is *not* a modern procedure. It's a procedure that was sometimes done years ago, but even then was routinely done only on dogs used in experimental laboratories, to decrease the noise levels in the labs. A dog who is deprived of his ability to bark cannot warn of danger, cry out if he is in pain or communicate normally with other dogs. It is an abnormal state that can be highly stressful to the dog. Many people who've been around "cordectomized" dogs say the sound they make after the surgery is worse than before.

This is not a procedure I would ever recommend for a family pet. The veterinarian your neighbor went to is probably either a very "old school" vet or is not educated about behavioral modification techniques to decrease excessive barking. There are some veterinarians who do not recommend this procedure, but feel obligated to perform it when a client insists upon it. These doctors may have a hard time standing up to their clients and recommending behavioral therapies rather than resorting to such an extreme procedure.

Q: *My husband and I have a three-year-old Doberman, Misty. Misty only seems to bark when she hears or sees people or other dogs go by our house. I'm glad she alerts us to strangers, but I wish she wouldn't bark so long. How can we get her to stop a little sooner?*

A: One of the benefits of having a dog is having them alert you to the presence of intruders by "alarm barking," but it can irritating if the "alarm" goes on and on for ten minutes. Different breeds have different tendencies toward barking. Some breeds, especially some hounds, just love to bark. German Shepherds, Dobermans and Rottweilers seldom bark just to hear themselves bark. They are good alarm barkers, however. What you need to do is get control of Misty's barking without discouraging her from alerting you to intruders.

A lot of owners just start yelling, "No," and "Shut Up," as soon as the dog starts barking, even though they have no idea what the dog is barking at. You don't want to discourage your dog from performing its protective duties. When Misty barks, get up and go see what she is barking at. Once you have seen and are satisfied there is no need for her to keep barking, PRAISE HER ("Good girl, Misty.") and then say, *"Enough."*

If she continues to bark, slip your hand under her collar and give it a jerk and say, *"No, enough."* As soon as she's quiet, even for a few seconds, PRAISE HER! ("Good girl, Misty, good girl.") If she starts barking again, reprimand her again. When she's quiet again, don't forget to praise her. In this way, by your praising the behavior you want and reprimanding the behavior you don't want, Misty will learn what it is you expect of her. Consistency is vital here, as in any training.

Q: *Our neighbors are complaining that our Beagle, Jack, barks constantly while we are gone. How do we do anything about his barking when we're not there?*

A: "Owner-absent" problems, or those that occur when the owner is not present, are the most difficult to cure. First you need to make sure Jack is getting plenty of exercise and interaction with you. A tired dog is a happy (and quiet) dog. He should be getting daily exercise and should get to spend as much time as possible with you. Make a commitment to get Jack out for a thirty-minute walk every evening. Then, let him spend the rest of the evening, and night, in the house with the family. Dogs are, by their very nature, social creatures. In the wild, dogs live in packs and are seldom alone. Loneliness is a major reason why dogs bark. Barking helps relieve their anxiety at having been left alone and gives them something to do. Boredom is the other big reason why dogs bark excessively.

Look at the situation from Jack's point of view. It is very boring (and lonely) to spend the majority of your time, all alone, with nothing new or interesting to do, looking at the same fence and back yard every day. If you are going to have a social animal, like a dog, for a pet, you owe it to him to spend as much as your time with him as possible. Let him be in the house with you when you're home. If your dog must spend a lot of time alone, consider getting him another dog as a companion. Two dogs keep each other company and form their own little "pack," and so are less lonely and bored.

So, first, make sure you're not leaving Jack alone too often and too long. Then, try leaving a radio playing for Jack during the day, tuned to a talk radio station, if possible, so that he can hear human voices. Give him some new and interesting toys to play with, maybe hang a strong rope from a tree or the fence for him to pull on. Keep departures low key. Don't make a big deal out of leaving, but give Jack a new chew bone just before you leave for the day to give him something to do.

If Jack's barking continues once you have done all these things, you may need to do some behavior-modification training to break Jack's habit of barking when you're gone.

Q: *Can you explain what you mean by behavior-modification training to stop excessive barking. I think our dog needs that too!*

A: Of course. What you do is set up some training sessions. Do all your normal "preleaving" behaviors, such as putting on your coat, getting your car keys, etc. Leave the house, but stay nearby where you can hear if Jack starts barking. The best sort of reprimand for barking is "remote punishment." In other words, one your dog doesn't associate with you.

Try using a loud noise such as hitting metal garbage can lids together or a blast from an air horn. Squirts of water from a garden hose, using a long-range spray nozzle can be very effective. Whatever type of "punishment" you use, the goal is to startle Jack into stopping his barking, even briefly. The reprimand should be applied immediately after Jack starts barking and should stop immediately when Jack stops barking. Don't keep making noise or spraying water after he stops barking.

Then you must reward any quiet behavior. This is real important. Once Jack has been quiet for five minutes, return to the house and heap praise on him, as well as giving him a small food treat. Continue to have one to three training sessions each day, gradually increasing the time up to one to two hours. You will have to continue to monitor Jack during the entire training session, so that you can remotely reprimand any barking (with noise or water) and praise quiet behavior. After several days, you should notice that Jack will remain quiet for longer and longer periods of time and that he will happily anticipate your return because he knows he'll get praise and a food treat. He will learn that quiet behavior gets him rewards.

Q: *I have a ten-year-old Poodle, Sir Lawrence. In the last year he has started barking whenever I put him outside while I am in the house. He doesn't seem to bark when he knows I'm gone, just when he knows I'm in the house. He spends most of the time in the house with me and stays in at night, but there are times I need to be able to put him outside without him barking. What can I do?*

A: It sounds like Larry has just gotten a bit spoiled and is demanding attention all the time. It doesn't seem to help much in these situations to go outside and scold him when he barks. Since he's looking for attention, even bad attention usually seems better than no attention and this tends to make the problem worse.

"Remote punishment" seems to work the best. This is means punishment that Larry does not associate with you. Either a loud noise, such as an air horn or banging two metal trash can lids together or a spray of water from a garden hose with a long-range spray attachment seems to work very well. The idea is to startle Larry and interrupt his barking. You'll need to set up some training sessions and probably need to get a friend or family member to help.

Put Larry outside while you stay in the house. Have your helper monitor Larry's barking from the other side of your fence where he can hear Larry, but where Larry can't see him. When Larry starts to bark, your helper should "punish" by either making a loud noise or spraying Larry with water. As soon as Larry stops barking, stop the "punishment." If he starts to bark again, repeat the "punishment." If Larry stays quiet for five minutes, let him in, praise him and give him a food treat. You can do one to three of these little training sessions a day, gradually increasing the amount of quiet time Larry must give before being let in and praised. Eventually get the time up to one to two hours. It won't take many days before he starts to figure out that he gets rewarded for quiet behavior.

As with any training, consistency is vital. You'll have to make a committed effort to "punish" each time Larry barks when you put him outside during this training period. If he gets punished sometimes and not others, it won't work.

Q: *Our family's Miniature Schnauzer dashes out the front door every chance she gets. It can take an hour or more to catch her. No matter how much we spank her when she finally comes back, she just doesn't learn not to run off. What can we do?*

A: I get frequent calls on talk radio having to do with dogs escaping, or running away. This question is a perfect example of an owner-created problem. That's right, your family has created the problem, not your Schnauzer!

Your Schnauzer should be obedience trained, every dog should be. How else do you expect to have any control? An obedience-trained dog knows the meaning of sit–stay, in which case you can have her sit and stay in the house while you bring groceries in from the car. An obedience trained dog waits for an OK before going out the door. An obedience-trained dog knows the meaning of come, both on and off leash, and obeys that command immediately.

So, by not training your dog, you have created a dog that you really have no control over. That's the first mistake.

You have also taught your dog NOT to come to you by punishing her when she finally does. Look at it from you're dog's standpoint. You keep yelling at her to come, but when she finally does, what do you do? You spank her. Would that make you want to come? She's no dummy, she's going to avoid coming to you as long as she can.

Coming to you needs to always be a positive experience for your dog. Even if you've had to chase her, if she finally comes to you, PRAISE HER!

You have to reward the behavior that you want, and you want her to come to you, so praise her whenever she does (no matter how mad you are).

Many owners unintentionally teach their dogs *not* to come when called in just the same way you have. Here are some points to remember:

- Coming to you must *always* be a POSITIVE experience for your dog.
- If your dog is not reliably off-leash trained, then don't put yourself in a situation where you call her to you and can't enforce it. Work more with the come command on leash and on a long line (see Chapter 12) until your dog is reliable with the come command.
- NEVER call your dog to you to punish her. If you must reprimand your dog, go get her. Don't call her to you.
- Don't call your dog to you for negative tasks like giving pills, taking baths, etc. Go get her instead.
- *Always* praise her and pet her when she comes to you.

Q: *My wife and I have a five-month-old Bichon Frise puppy, Scarlet. We have a large property and sometimes I can't get Scarlet to come to me. We end up playing "catch me" all over the property. Now she's figured out she doesn't have to come when I call her. Help!*

A: This is a common occurrence as puppies enter the more independent fourth and fifth months. The little puppy that used to shadow your every step is suddenly feeling very independent and starts to make a game of not coming to you. Not only can this be very aggravating, it can be dangerous for your puppy and can become a major obedience problem if not corrected. The first thing to do is to never let your puppy be off leash in an unenclosed area. She could easily dash into a street and be hit by a car.

If you get into a situation where your puppy is loose and is running from you when you try to catch her, don't chase her. Instead, try running the opposite direction and see if you can get *her* to chase *you*. When she gets close to you, quickly grab her collar.

Another trick that works well is to stop and look intently at something on the ground, like you've just found some really interesting treasure. Get close to the ground and talk quietly and excitedly like you've found a baby bird or something. Your puppy's curiosity will probably get the best of her and she'll come over to investigate. Be careful not to try to grab her too soon, she might get away and then she'll be on to you. Keep up your little act until she comes right over to where you are looking, then carefully grab her collar.

Don't forget to PRAISE HER once you get hold of her. I know she didn't technically come to you, but praise her anyway. Never punish her at this point, no matter how angry you are or how long it took you to get her. Remember that coming to you must ALWAYS be a positive experience if you want to teach her to come when called.

Q: *My husband and I have a six-year-old German Shepherd named Kelly. We've always meant to have Kelly obedience trained but never have. She's very sweet and would never intentionally hurt anyone, but she's just totally out of control. I can't let her in the house because she just goes crazy running around and knocking things over. She still nips our hands when we try to pet her. I'm ashamed to say she's spent most of her life in the back yard alone because she jumps up on us when we go outside. I'm thinking about trying to give her to someone who knows more about dogs. What do you think?*

A: Poor Kelly. She sounds like a basically sweet and affectionate dog that was never given a chance to be a real part of the family because you didn't train her. I wouldn't give her away, I'd have her obedience trained by a professional who will also work with you and your husband. It won't take a good professional very long to train Kelly, but he'll also need to teach you and your husband so you can continue to practice good obedience with Kelly at home.

Kelly has had a pretty isolated and lonely life so far, but at six (middle age for a Shepherd) you are the only family she knows. Get her obedience trained immediately, then let her be a part of your family. Take family walks in the evenings, including Kelly. Let her be inside the house with you when you're home. Give her a bed of her own next to your bed and let her sleep in your bedroom at night. This is a great way to increase the bond with your dog. She'll be so much happier and she'll be good company and protection for your family.

Because of your lack of experience in training, and because Kelly is such a big, out of control dog, I would suggest either a private trainer or a good board and train situation for Kelly (see Chapter 12), rather than group obedience classes. If you choose a board and train situation, make sure they provide lessons with the owners all through the training process as well as follow-up lessons once Kelly goes home. It won't do you any good to have Kelly trained if you and your husband are not taught how to continue the training at home.

Please do this right away. You will get so much enjoyment out of Kelly once she is trained and able to be a real part of your family. Good luck!

CHAPTER 14

Destructive Behaviors

"I know my dog hates me!"

"Oh? Why do you think that?"

"Because when I'm gone on a business trip, my dog gets up on my bed and either chews up my pillows or messes all over them. He hates me I tell you!"

"No, he does not hate you. Dogs are not capable of that kind of cognitive and revengeful thought. They are very sensitive to changes in their routine and environment, however, and changes in established routine will make them anxious. Anxiety is displaced by chewing, and severe anxiety is many times displaced by abnormal urination or defecation. The fact that it is on your pillow should be comforting to you. He is seeking you out in his very serious time of emotional need!"

"Yeah, right!"

It is very common for dog owners to believe that their dogs purposely destroy things, by chewing or digging, out of spite. I'll assure you right now, dogs don't think up ways to aggravate you or "get back at you." Chewing and digging are both normal doggie activities. Dogs like to do these things, they're fun. Trained correctly from puppyhood, a dog learns where and how these activities are acceptable. Chewing, digging and barking are also ways in which dogs relieve stress from anxiety or boredom. They may also be used to get attention. Just like kids, dogs who don't get enough attention will do anything to get it, even if it's the negative attention of being scolded.

Punishing your dog for chewing or digging does little but make the problem worse and make your dog afraid of you. Instead, you need to correct the *underlying problem* that caused the destructive behavior. Most of the time, these behaviors are caused by loneliness, boredom, not enough exercise, health or nutritional problems or lack of training.

Q: *My four-month-old, Beagle-mix puppy is destroying my house! She chews on the furniture, on my shoes, even on the baseboards and walls. How can I make her stop?*

A: Your puppy is teething. Teething typically occurs from about four to six months of age, depending on the breed. During this time, puppies *must* chew. Your job is to make sure your puppy learns to chew on only approved objects. She doesn't automatically know which objects are approved and which aren't, you have to teach her.

Puppies that are teething should be given a variety of approved chew toys, some hard, some soft. I recommend Nylabone, treated natural bones, rope toys, stuffed toys covered with canvas or artificial sheepskin and hard rubber toys like the Kong. Your puppy may have a dozen toys, but don't leave them all out at once or she'll start to think that everything in her environment is a chew toy. Leave two or three out at a time and rotate them with new toys every couple of days.

When you can supervise your puppy, let her be out with you in the house, but keep your eye on her all the time. If she starts to chew on something "unapproved," clap your hands loudly to startle her and say, *"No!"* Then walk over to her and give her a chew toy. PRAISE HER for chewing on the chew toy. That's how she learns what she can and can't chew on, by verbal reprimands for chewing on the wrong things and praise for chewing on the right things. Simple.

DON'T HIT HER OR IN ANY WAY PUNISH HER for chewing, just clap your hands and tell her, *"No!"* Physical punishment will only serve to make her afraid of you and will destroy the bond you are trying to build.

Q: *We've heard you talk so much about kennel training a puppy for housebreaking. Can the kennel be used to stop chewing also?*

A: You bet! When you can't supervise your puppy, she should be in her "doggie room," her kennel. Kennel training is the best way to prevent behavior problems like chewing. When she is in her kennel, make sure she always has a couple of her chew toys with her. (For more information on kennel training, see Chapter 11.)

Not only can she not destroy your shoes, baseboards and furniture when she's in her kennel, she'll feel more secure in her little "doggie den" while you're gone and so will have less anxiety. When she's out of her kennel, watch her carefully and you'll be able to interrupt (and redirect) any unapproved chewing before she does any damage. It also helps to treat any places she has chewed with a bad tasting substance, like Bitter Apple, or Chew Stop. You can find several types of these sprays at your pet shop. That way, she gets a negative reinforcement if she chews on these things. You'll have to respray the area every couple of days.

Q: *How old does a puppy have to be before you can trust it not to chew things up?*

A: By about six months of age, most puppies who have been kennel trained are reliably trained enough to be left in the house unattended. Start by leaving your puppy out of her kennel and loose in the house while you leave for only five minutes. If she has been good in your absence, praise her when you return. Gradually increase the length of time you leave her alone. If she does any "unapproved chewing" while you're gone, go back to your kennel training and try again in a couple of weeks. *Don't punish her for any unapproved chewing she did while you were gone.* She won't understand why she is being punished, and it will only increase her anxiety the next time she is left alone. Remember, dogs chew to relieve anxiety, so by punishing her you will probably make the problem worse.

Q: *I have a three-year-old yellow Lab named Buddy. Buddy is a wonderful dog except when I have to leave him alone. If I leave him inside, he chews up magazines, shoes, even my furniture. If I leave him outside, he digs up plants and chews on my trees. He doesn't do any of these things when I'm home. What's wrong with him?*

A: Buddy is suffering from "separation anxiety." He gets very anxious and stressed when he is separated from you, his "pack."

Dogs relieve stress and anxiety by barking, chewing and digging, a lot like people relieve stress by pacing, chewing their fingernails or smoking. It won't be helpful to punish Buddy for his chewing or digging when you return. Since you didn't catch him in the act, he won't know why you are punishing him. Punishment will also increase his anxiety about your being gone. It won't make any sense to Buddy.

Most of the time, destructive behaviors are caused by loneliness, boredom, not enough exercise and poor training. Labradors are very energetic dogs with a need for a lot of exercise. Remember, Labradors were bred to hunt—swimming and retrieving game. They need daily opportunities to run and play off all that energy or they'll have to expend it some other way, like digging and chewing. They are also very intelligent dogs, capable of being trained to a very high degree (they are one of the breeds trained to be Seeing Eye Dogs). If not trained, seldom taken anywhere new or taught anything new, these dogs get bored. They are also very sociable and need companionship or they get very lonely.

Q: OK, how do I go about curing Buddy's separation anxiety?
A: In order to fix the problem, you have to fix the underlying cause for his digging and chewing.

1. Make sure Buddy gets daily exercise. That does *not* mean putting him out in the back yard. Dogs don't exercise themselves. It means putting him on a leash and taking him for a thirty-minute walk, taking him to the park and playing fetch, or finding a pond and letting him retrieve sticks you throw in the water. A tired dog is a happy dog and will probably just sleep while you are gone.

2. Teach Buddy something. If he hasn't been obedience trained, do it. Take an obedience class with Buddy. Dogs love to learn new things; it keeps them alert and interested. Try doing some agility work with Buddy. There is probably an agility club in your area. Ask your veterinarian, groomer or pet shop. A dog that is learning new things isn't bored and is less likely to look for ways to entertain himself.

3. Make sure Buddy always has some chew toys so that he can

relieve his need to chew on his own toys instead of your things. Get him several different kinds, some hard chew toys like Nylabones, sterilized cow femur bones, and hard rubber toys, and some soft toys like a canvas-covered retrieving dummy, large knotted rope or a sheepskin-covered stuffed toy. You can find all these at your pet shop. Don't leave all his toys out at once. Leave two or three out at any time, and rotate the toys every four or five days to keep him interested. Stay away from rawhide toys, many dogs actually eat these and end up in the emergency clinic with intestinal blockages.

4. Let Buddy spend as much time as possible with you. Don't leave him alone too often or for too long. When you're home, let him be in the house with you and let him sleep in your bedroom at night. That eight-hour period while you're asleep can be bonding time that doesn't cost you a thing, but it's eight hours when Buddy has companionship and isn't lonely. (Make sure he has his own bed and does not sleep on yours, that can contribute to other behavior problems.) Dogs are, by the very nature, social animals with a need for companionship. You are now Buddy's "pack." Let him be with you when he can, and he will accept your absences as part of the routine.

5. Don't make a big deal out of leaving or coming home. Many owners unintentionally contribute to the problem by getting the dog highly excited with a big emotional good-bye. Then they go, leaving the dog in a state of excitement with no way to work it off except to bark, chew or dig. Make your departures and arrivals very low-key. Don't emotionally reassure your dog that you'll be back. He doesn't know what your words mean, but your tone of voice and mannerisms will tell him that there's something he should be worried about. Be cool about leaving.

6. Use a kennel to confinement retrain Buddy when you are gone until he has become comfortable with your absences.

Q: *My wife and I have a dog that also chews things up when we're gone. What do you mean by confinement retraining using a kennel?*

A: "Kennel training" is absolutely, and without doubt, the best way to train a young puppy. (See Chapter 11 for more information on kennel training.) It is also the best way to correct destructive behavior problems and housebreaking problems in the adult dog.

By a "kennel," I mean a dog kennel, either a metal wire kennel or a Fiberglas airline-type kennel. I personally like and recommend the wire type. They are open and airy and when the dog is in the kennel, he feels more a part of the family and his environment.

You'll have to set up some training sessions. Take your dog out to let him urinate and defecate, and then put him in his kennel with a couple of chew toys. Do all your usual leaving behaviors such as putting on your coats, getting your car keys, etc. Be happy but low-key about your departure. Leave the house and return in about ten minutes. Be casual about your arrival back home as well. You want your dog to learn that your leaving is no big deal, you'll be back. Ignore him for a few minutes after you come home, then greet him quietly and let him out of his kennel. Praise him quietly, and give him a little treat.

Continue these sessions, gradually increasing the time you leave him in his kennel. Also, vary the times, an hour one time, ten minutes the next, so that he learns that you will come and go on different schedules and it's still no big deal. Within about two weeks, you should be able to leave him in his kennel for up to eight hours while you're at work. Don't leave him in the kennel more than eight hours a day. He's not supposed to live there, he's supposed to live with you. Let him be loose in the house with you when you're home.

Eventually, you should be able to start leaving him loose in the house with his kennel door open so he can go in and sleep when he wants to. Kennel train him for at least four to six weeks before you try this.

Again, you'll need to set up training sessions and leave him out alone for only five to ten minutes at first, praising him *quietly* upon your return if he's been good. If he chews while you're gone, DON'T PUNISH HIM, just go back to your kennel training and try again in a couple of weeks.

Gradually increase the time you leave him loose in the house until eventually you can leave him in the house eight hours while you are at work and he'll be good. Remember to always provide some chew toys and leave his kennel open so he can go in and out as he pleases.

Q: *My husband and I have a 1+-year-old Springer Spaniel, Samson. He's very good when we're gone, except he chews on our landscape lights. He never chews on anything else. He has chew toys in the yard. What can we do?*

A: When a dog has focused on one or two particular objects to chew on, it usually helps for you to make those objects unattractive. Try spraying your landscape lights with a chew-stop spray such as Bitter Apple. You can find several different types of these sprays at your pet shop. You'll probably need to spray them every day until Samson's habit is broken. I would also get some pet-repellent granules and sprinkle them around the base of each light. Pet-repellent granules are usually available at pet stores and lawn and garden stores.

Q: *My wife and I have three dogs, a Bichon Frise, a Yorkshire Terrier and a Rottweiler. Our problem is the Rottweiler. She is just about a year old and she loves "gardening." She doesn't really dig up our bushes, she just takes them in her mouth and pulls them up, roots and all!*

A: The good news is, your Rottweiler will probably outgrow this once she hits about two years old. She's really still a puppy right now. In the meantime, use some aversion conditioning. Sprinkle dog-repellent granules around the bases of the bushes. If Bitter Apple or Repel isn't strong enough, ask your pharmacist for some alum powder. Mix a little of this powder with water to make a paste. Then spread this on some of her future gardening projects. The extreme bitter taste of alum will stop her for good!

You can also run a small electric fence around your bushes. There are even solar-powered fences you can buy. Once your Rottweiler hits the fence once or twice, she'll leave the bushes alone and you can probably turn the fence off and just leave the wire up to remind her.

Don't let your Rottweiler watch you when you garden, especially when you replace these bushes. Dogs love to mimic our activity, and seeing you dig in the yard will often cause your dog to start digging too.

Make sure your Rottweiler gets lots of exercise. A tired dog is a happy dog and will probably just sleep most of the day while you're gone.

Q: *Our family has two Dachshunds, Debit and Credit. They love to dig. As a matter of fact, they've just about rearranged our entire yard. Can you help us?*

A: There is a strong tendency toward digging in certain breeds. All the terrier breeds are notorious for digging. Dachshunds were actually bred to dig after badgers in their dens, so you have two dogs who were "bred to dig."

Dogs dig for several reasons: because it's fun, to escape, to bury a bone, to dig up a bone, to dig a cool hole when its hot, and unspayed females will dig "nests" when in heat.

If the digging is restricted to a certain area, you can try using the aversive conditioning measures such as pet repellent, mouse traps turned upside down, or electric fences.

If the digging is random and widespread, you might consider making your dogs an "approved digging spot." Make an area at least 4' x 4' and fill it with dirt and sand. Encourage your dogs to dig there by playing digging games with them. Get out there and start digging with your hands and encourage them to join you. You can even bury a bone or their favorite toy and let them find it by digging. It shouldn't take much encouragement for them to jump right in there and dig. Then use the aversive measures on the other spots in the yard where they dig or make them their own "dog yard," including their digging spot. Good luck!

CHAPTER 15

Biting, Aggression and Fear Reactions

"Dr. Jim, we have got to do something about Alex. He is so afraid of thunder he is literally hurting himself and destroying our house trying to get away from the sound!"

"How is he hurting himself?"

"So far he has chewed through the side panel on a plastic travel kennel and the metal grating in the little window, cutting his mouth up something fierce! Then he chewed through our washroom door where we keep him during storms. Finally, two days ago he chewed through a wall!"

"A wall?"

"Yes, he chewed through the dry wall on both sides of the wall and got into the garage and tore up everything! What can we do?"

Fear reactions are a common problem in dogs. Sometimes the fear is so great that the dog causes damage or even injures itself trying to escape the fearful situation. Since we can't sit down and explain to a dog that thunder or firecracker noises won't hurt him, or that other dogs aren't going to eat him, we have to help him over his fear by gradually getting him accustomed to the fearful thing. This process is called desensitization. This can take some time and certainly takes a lot of effort on the part of the owner, but it does work well. It can make the difference in saving a dog–owner relationship.

Another technique used to help solve severe fear reactions is counter-conditioning. In this approach, when the fearful stimulus is applied and the dog is about to be fearful, the owner acts jolly and happy, even playing a favorite game with the dog, to elicit a different, possibly happy or playful reaction from the dog. Over time, the formerly fearful stimulus will have less of a fearful effect on the dog and he will associate it with positive things—he might even go look for his ball for a game.

Aggression is a frequent problem in dogs and one that most owners find difficult to handle. Most of the time, the owner has unintentionally contributed to the problem by incorrect training, failure to socialize the dog, spoiling or coddling the dog. Aggression problems can almost always be prevented by good socialization and obedience training.

Aggression problems take several different forms. The most common are:

1. Fear or shyness aggression; 2. Pain-induced aggression; 3. Territorial aggression; 4. Intermale aggression; 5. Dominance-status aggression; 6. Predatory aggression and 7. Trained aggression.

Whatever the type, problems with aggression should be dealt with immediately. Don't wait, thinking the problem will go away or get better on its own. Aggression rarely decreases left alone, it usually gets worse. Most owners should seek the assistance of a good professional dog trainer as soon as possible. In cases of aggression, I recommend a private trainer who can work with your dog on an individual basis to evaluate and attempt to cure the problem. (An aggressive dog would be a danger in a group obedience class, and its aggression problem couldn't be dealt with on an individual basis.)

Q: *My husband and I have a three-year-old Irish Setter, Scarlet. We recently moved to the West, and it seems common to have afternoon thunderstorms here. Scarlet is terrified during these storms. During the last one, she actually broke a glass window and injured herself. I try to comfort her when I'm here during a storm, but it doesn't seem to help. What are we going to do?*

A: Scarlet is having a severe fear reaction to thunderstorms. Because she didn't grow up where thunderstorms are common, she didn't get used to them as a puppy. Puppies usually adapt to loud noises such as gunshots and thunderstorms more easily than do adult dogs.

The treatment requires getting the dog used to the sound of thunderstorms through desensitization. It will take some time and effort commitment on your part to help Scarlet get over this. The first thing you need to do is stop reassuring and comforting her when she is fearful. It's a natural reaction, but it only makes the problem worse. When you pet and reassure a dog when it is acting fearful, you accomplish two things: 1. you praise and therefore reinforce the fearful behavior and 2. you confirm in the dog's mind that she is right to be afraid. Instead, assume a happy, carefree attitude. Ignore any fearful behavior and praise only happy, nonfearful behavior. I often recommend people simply act jolly and a little silly so that the dog will get the signal that there is nothing to be afraid of, *and* in fact, it's time to play.

You will need to set up some training sessions. Buy a tape of thunderstorm sound effects. Play it once on full volume to see if it causes Scarlet's fearful behavior. You'll need to find a recording that reproduces her fear. Then start your training sessions by playing the tape at the lowest possible volume, so low that it doesn't cause any fear reaction in Scarlet. While you're playing the tape, play a favorite game with Scarlet, maybe fetching a favorite toy and give her lots of praise. Give her a small, tasty treat every minute. The session should last about ten minutes. Do two to three sessions a day. For best results, it helps during this time to avoid giving Scarlet any affection except during the training sessions.

With each session, gradually increase the volume. Continue to maintain a happy, carefree attitude. Ignore any fearful behavior on Scarlet's part. DON'T REASSURE OR PET HER WHEN SHE DISPLAYS ANY FEARFUL BEHAVIOR. She should only get attention and praise when she is calm and nonfearful. Continue to give her a really tasty treat about once a minute. Pick something she really likes, such as little bits of cheese or hot dog. If at any time she exhibits a fear reaction, ignore the behavior and end the session. Go back to a lower volume setting at the next session. Increase the volume very gradually. Eventually, you should be able to play the recording on a high volume without setting off her fear reaction.

By getting Scarlet accustomed to these sounds on a gradual basis while providing affection and treats, you will desensitize her to the sound and make her associate thunderstorms with good things, treats and praise from you.

Q: *My wife and I are going to be getting a new Pomeranian puppy soon. We lost our last Pomeranian to old age about a year ago. She was a wonderful dog but was terrified of other dogs. Is that typical of Pomeranians? I'd like to avoid that problem with our new dog.*

A: No, it's not typical of any particular breed of dog to be fearful of other dogs. This type of fear reaction is usually caused by the puppy not having contact with other dogs during the crucial socialization period from six weeks old to twelve weeks old. During this time in your puppy's development, it's really important to get her out and let her experience new things, play with other dogs, and be handled by other people. Puppies who don't get these experiences during this time in their development often end up shy and afraid.

Take your new puppy to a puppy socialization class when she is about eight to ten weeks old. You can find out about classes from local obedience clubs, your veterinarian, groomer or pet shop. These are not obedience classes and should be very play oriented. The puppies in the class should get an opportunity to play with each other, and all the puppies should get handled by all the other owners in the class. This is the first really important thing you can do to ensure your puppy grows to be a happy, confident dog.

Take your puppy lots of places with you. The more she sees and experiences during this time, the better. Be careful to see that these are positive experiences. The period from nine weeks to twelve weeks is a "fear imprinting" period. Bad experiences during this period may stay with your dog forever. That doesn't mean you should keep her locked up at home during this time, just remember this and don't choose this time for her *first* exposure to loud noises, trip to the vet, etc. She should have already been to the vet for first shots when she was six or seven weeks old.

One other thing, owners of small dogs often cause their dogs to be fearful of other dogs by grabbing them up and reassuring them every time a large dog comes into view. It's a natural reaction I suppose. Those small-breed puppies are *so* little and other dogs seem *so* big. However, if you do this, you are teaching your dog that she has something to fear from any big dog. Fearful, shy dogs are not happy dogs, just like fearful, shy people aren't happy. So, don't coddle or reassure your dog when you see another dog. Don't reinforce fearful behavior by petting or reassuring your dog when she acts scared. Ignore any fearful behavior and praise happy, confident behavior around other dogs.

Q: *Our Poodle, Pierre, gets just frantic whenever he is left alone. He just goes into a frenzy, tearing papers, digging at the door, chewing cushions, anything. Otherwise he is a wonderful pet. My dad has about had it with him. He spanks him and puts him outside when we come home and find such a big mess. That doesn't seem to be helping. What can we do?*

A: Pierre is suffering separation anxiety, or a fear of separation from his "pack," his family. You have to understand that dogs are very social creatures. In the wild, dogs are seldom alone, and when they are, it can even be life threatening. When a pup in the wild gets separated from the pack, he will howl and bark to let the pack know where he is and that it is an emergency!

Because your dog can't understand human words, you can't tell him you'll be back soon, the way you can tell a child. The longer his family is gone, the worse his anxiety gets. Dogs only know that we'll return when we leave, by our going through a lot of repetitions of leaving and then returning.

Since this is a fear and anxiety problem, it doesn't help to punish the destructive behavior Pierre does in your absence. Punishment only increases his anxiety about separations and about your returning. It only makes the problem worse.

To get Pierre used to being alone, set up short training sessions where he is left alone for no more than ten minutes. His anxiety probably doesn't get bad until you've been gone for at least fifteen minutes. Here's what you do:

- Do two to three short training sessions a day where you leave Pierre alone in the house for ten minutes.
- Make sure you do all the things you usually do when you leave, such as turn out the lights, put on your coats, grab your car keys, etc.

- Don't make a big deal about leaving, be low-key about it, but give Pierre a chew bone just before you leave.
- Return in ten minutes. Be calm and causal about your return as well, but do praise Pierre if he's been good and offer him a treat.
- Don't punish any destructive behavior, just ignore it, but shorten the time you are gone for the next session.
- *Gradually* increase the length of time you are gone. Go from ten minutes to fifteen minutes, to thirty minutes, to forty-five minutes, to one hour. Alternate the times so that Pierre gets used to you being gone for short or long times and realizes that you always return. Always praise him for having been good and offer him a treat. Eventually, you will be able to leave Pierre in the house for about eight hours while you are all gone during the day. Don't leave him inside longer than eight hours, he'll need to be able to go outside to urinate and defecate.
- Don't leave Pierre alone in the house all day until you've completed the training sessions. Leave him outside in the yard, take him with you or take him to a friend's house until his training is complete.

It may be helpful to kennel train Pierre if he continues to have problems during his training sessions. (See Chapter 14 on destructive behaviors for more details on how to kennel train.)

Q: *Our two-year-old Pekinese bit my brother yesterday. He had never met our dog and she was scared to go to him, so I picked her up and handed her to him. She obviously didn't want to go to him, but I didn't expect her to bite him. Why do you think she did that?*

A: This is an example of fear or shyness aggression. This type of aggression always occurs when the dog is fearful and would escape if it could. This is the most common type of aggression and occurs as often in females as in males.

Usually these dogs were not well socialized as puppies and are rarely taken anywhere outside the home, except to the groomer or veterinarian. So, these dogs have had little positive experience with strangers or new situations and so are fearful of them. Most of these dogs have not been obedience trained. Obedience training gives the owner control over the dog in all situations and gives the dog confidence that the owner is its leader. Obedience trained dogs look to their owners for direction in new situations and so are more confident.

To prevent further occurrences, start obedience training with your Pekinese right away. Not only will this make her more confident, it will signal to her that you are her leader (that you are alpha dog). Start some training sessions to gradually and carefully expose your Pekinese to new people and situations. Plan these carefully to assure they will be positive experiences for your dog.

Here are some important points in socializing a fearful dog:
- Never pet or reassure your dog when she acts fearful. You will be unintentionally praising her fearful behavior. Instead, adopt a happy, playful attitude. Your dog will look to you for clues about how she should feel about a new situation.
- You will use praise and treats (something tasty like bits of cheese or hot dog) to reward calm and happy behavior. Sit with your dog in a room and have your brother (or a friend your dog doesn't know) come just to the door of the room. If your dog remains happy and calm, showing no fearful reaction, then praise her and give her a treat. Withhold any attention or treats if your dog displays any fearful or aggressive behavior. Repeat having your brother appear at the door about ten times, always rewarding happy behavior. That will make up one training session.
- In the next training session, have your brother approach a little closer, continuing to praise and reward happy behavior. Gradually, in subsequent training sessions, have your brother approach closer and closer. Eventually, have your brother be the one to reward your dog's happy behavior with praise and treats.
- Once you've gotten past the problem with your brother, have different friends approach your dog in the same way. These sessions should progress faster than the first.

In the future, don't force your dog into a situation she is obviously fearful of. Don't unintentionally reward fearful behavior by reassuring or coaxing a fearful dog. Always assume a confident, happy attitude and your dog will take her cue from you and assume everything is OK.

Q: *My wife and I have a eleven-year-old Golden Retriever. Our grandchildren were over today and one child kind of "sat down" on our dog's hindquarters. She spun around and snapped at him. We've never seen her act aggressively. What do you think is going on?*

A: Your old dog may be suffering from some hip arthritis and probably had quite a bit of pain when your grandchild sat on her. This is an example of pain-induced aggression. It is the only way your dog has to tell you that what has happened caused her a lot of discomfort. Luckily, she didn't actually bite, as is the case in well-socialized dogs. It was just a warning.

Have your veterinarian check your dog for possible painful hips or back. He may have you treat her with aspirin or other antiinflammatory medication.

Explain to your grandchildren that your dog is getting older and should only be played with gently. Teach them never to put their weight on her anywhere, not to pull on her or poke at her, and to be careful not to wake her suddenly.

Other typical instances of pain-induced aggression occur when a dog has been injured, especially hit by a car. Be very careful in handling an injured dog. The pain can cause him to bite even his owner. After an injury heals, the dog may well learn to warn-bite or bark just to remind you or anyone else that it hurts!

Q: *My one-year-old Doberman, Duchess, is friendly to strangers when we are away from home but gets very vicious if anyone comes near the house. She won't let the mailman up to the door, and she won't let repairmen in the house. What can I do?*

A: Duchess is displaying territorial aggression. Dogs have a natural instinct to protect their territory. Territorial aggression isn't all bad. After all, one of the nice things about dogs is their tendency to protect their homes and their people. In fact, houses with dogs are less of a target for crime, and that makes this a plus. However, you need to be able to control Duchess and let her know when enough is enough.

Duchess definitely needs to be well obedience trained. While important for all dogs, it is absolutely essential with large, aggressive breeds such as Dobermans, Rottweilers, German Shepherds and Akitas. Once Duchess is well obedience trained, you will have good control of her, both verbally and with hand signals.

When someone comes to the house that you want to let in, tell Duchess, *"OK, enough!"* to stop her barking and aggressive behavior. Put her on a sit–stay or down–stay. If she continues to bark or growl, tell her a sharp, *"No!"* and give her a sharp leash correction. (Leave a short leash hanging from her training collar during these training sessions until she is reliable.)

If she charges, chases or bites, she will need a severe and immediate verbal and physical correction. Bark a loud, *"Noooo!"* and roll her over on her back, grabbing her by the scruff of her neck on both sides of her head. Shake her by the scruff, glare right into her eyes and growl a deep, low, *"I said Nooo!"* Let her turn back over and immediately put her in a down stay. The down is a submissive posture, and this reinforces to Duchess that you are in control. *This is a very severe reprimand,* called an alpha roll-over. It is similar to the reprimand an alpha wolf would deliver to a *severely* misbehaving pack member. *The alpha roll-over should never be used lightly, only for very severe misbehaviors such as aggression.*

If you don't feel you can carry off such an assertive reprimand, get immediate help from a professional trainer. Large, aggressive breed dogs need strong leaders if they are to be well behaved. It is very easy for them to decide that they are the leader if their owner is very passive or a little afraid of them. That can have disastrous results.

Q: *I like to take my dog, Blackie, to the park and let him off leash to play Frisbee. He minds pretty well and gets along OK with female dogs, but he fights every male dog we encounter. We're becoming very unpopular at the park. Can you help us?*

A: It is not uncommon for unneutered male dogs to fight with other males. The good news is that neutering your dog will probably cure this problem. Neutering won't make him less protective of you or your home. (For other good news about neutering, see Chapter 5.)

Intermale aggression is related to testosterone secretion. Unneutered males can have some pretty serious fights, causing severe injuries. If your dog is unneutered, keep him on leash when you're at the park. It is not fair to other dog owners to have your aggressive dog intrude upon their outing and start a fight. Call your animal hospital today and make that appointment!

Q: *We have two male dogs, a three-year-old Labrador and a two-year-old Springer Spaniel. They're both neutered. They used to get along fine, but lately they've been fighting, and our Lab has even gotten badly hurt. We're keeping the Lab inside with us in the evening now and making the Spaniel stay outside. They don't fight when we're gone, only when we're home. Help!*

A: Dogs who live together establish a peaceful living arrangement by establishing a hierarchy (kind of a pecking order). One dog is the most dominant dog, and each other dog falls somewhere in order beneath him. As long as this order is firmly established, every dog lives by it and everyone gets along just fine. Problems occur when there is confusion about which dog is dominant over the other. Then fighting breaks out, as the dominant dog tries to establish order. This is called dominance-status aggression.

We, as owners, sometimes unintentionally mess up the hierarchy by naturally favoring the "underdog." We feel sorry for him and give him special favors such as feeding him first, petting him first, and letting him spend more time inside with us. By doing this, we are granting him favors that should, by "dog law," go to the dominant dog. That way, we actually cause the fighting, because the dominant dog must constantly reestablish his dominant position.

So, instead, treat your Springer Spaniel as dominant dog. Feed him first, greet him first when you come home. Let him in or out the door before the Labrador. Don't grant your Labrador special favors you don't give the Springer, such as coming in the house with you. Don't punish the Springer for fighting, instead reprimand the Labrador. Let the Springer choose the favorite sleeping spot or toy.

I know this goes against all our natural tendencies. We want to protect the underdog and punish the aggressor. However, we must respect the natural law by which dogs live together. You will actually be helping establish the peace and contributing to the increased happiness of both dogs by following these rules.

Q: *Our family dog is very aggressive toward cats and other small animals. He is a Labrador–Doberman cross about two years old. He almost caught a cat in our neighbor's yard yesterday. The neighbor's little girl was just hysterical, and now our neighbors are upset. We are obviously going to have to do something about this. How do we break him of this?*

A: This is a predatory aggression, based on the carnivore nature of dogs. In the wild, dogs are predators, of course. So this is a natural reaction. It is not, however, acceptable behavior and must be corrected as quickly as possible. Predatory aggression can become very severe. Once a dog catches and kills an animal, it is almost impossible to break. This type of aggression should be immediately and severely punished.

There are several points I want to make about correcting this problem, but the first is this. Your dog was obviously loose and not under your control when this happened. That is both irresponsible and dangerous. Not only could someone have lost a precious pet because of your dog, he himself could have been hurt. He could have easily chased the cat right into the street and have been hit by a car. Not to mention that someone is liable to shoot him the next time he goes after their pet.

A second point is this. Owners often contribute to this type of behavior by playing "sic 'em" games with the dog every time they see a cat or squirrel. The dog is actually being encouraged and praised for being aggressive.

You need to obedience train your dog. There is no way to be in control of your dog at all times without proper training. Make sure your dog is on a leash when he is out of your yard. Then reprimand any aggressive behavior toward other animals. If your dog barks or growls at a cat, tell him, *no*, and give him a sharp leash correction. If he lunges or tries to chases, bark a sharp, *no*, and pull back as hard as you can just as he hits the end of his leash. For greatest effect, you want to knock him off balance. Then put him in a down position. This is a position of submission and establishes your control over him.

It would be a good idea to set up some long-line training sessions with your dog. Let him be in the front yard with you. Attach a lightweight, but strong rope to his choke chain, about fifteen to twenty feet long. Let him wander freely about the yard as far as the rope will let him go. (You keep good hold of the other end.) If he sees another animal and takes off in chase, yell, *"No!"* If he doesn't stop, brace yourself and give a big pull backward just as he hits the end of the rope. He will hopefully get yanked off his feet and wonder, "What happened?" Call him to you. If he doesn't come, reel him into you with the rope. When he gets to you, PRAISE HIM. His reprimand was the leash correction. You want to praise him for coming to you, even if you had to help him with the rope. After two to three sessions with the long line, he'll start to respect that "no."

Q: *My wife and I had our one-year-old German Shepherd trained at a place that boards dogs and trains them. She did real well with her training, and we're very happy with her. Now the trainers are trying to talk us into having her "protection trained" What do you think?*

A: I'd like you to seriously give second thought to any ideas about protection training. First ask yourself some questions. Why do you want your dog protection trained? Do you know anything about protection training and how its done? Have you ever seen any dogs that were protection trained?

Consider if your dog needs this kind of training and if you really need a dog trained to attack. Most dogs, especially aggressive breeds like German Shepherds, are naturally protective of their home and family. They usually naturally bark to warn you of strangers. That is all that is usually required to make an intruder decide to go elsewhere. Most dogs will also naturally protect their owners without any special training.

Protection training typically requires agitating the dog to the point where he feels he must attack. You'll be putting your dog under a great deal of stress with this type of training. Some dogs can't handle this stress and become unstable or difficult to control. Some dogs become too aggressive and can't be trusted around strangers.

My guess is that your dog will protect you and your family just fine without putting her through that kind of stress. I suggest you don't do it.

PART IV

Fleas, Ticks
and Worms

CHAPTER 16

"Miracle" Cures
and the Four Steps
of *Real* Flea Control

"Dr. Jim, does ginger root get rid of worms?"

"You know, Mary, there are many old wives' tales about various foods and medicines either causing worms or getting rid of worms. Personally, I believe you should stick with proven safe medicines to treat worms in pets. But I will say, if a little garlic, brewer's yeast or even ginger root isn't going to harm them anyway, why not give it a try. Sometimes there is truth in those old wives' tales."

"Well, how will I know if it will harm her?"

"After you give just a little, just be sure she doesn't throw it up!"

"Oh no, Dr. Jim, you don't understand. I don't feed it to her, I rub it on her forehead!"

It is true, there are many old stories passed along from generation to generation about simple foods, herbs and household products having incredible effects on certain medical conditions. I will tell you here and now, that if any of these things worked as well as the story tellers say, they would be bottled, packaged and advertised as an existing cure.

Q: *I've been told that garlic and brewer's yeast will cure flea problems and kill worms. Is that right?*

A: Some common things may very well have some effects. For

example, garlic powder does seem to stimulate finicky eaters to eat better. In fact, the pet-food manufacturers use this trick to convince dogs to eat the ground corn in their pet food. But I do not believe that garlic, by itself, will cure fleas. There may be some very slight repelling effect, and it may help in very light infestations. But I do not recommend you rely solely on this ingredient to solve a flea problem.

Brewer's yeast is another ingredient often touted as being "the flea cure." In this case, there are manufacturer's producing commercially available products you can buy for your dog. However, you will notice that *nowhere* on the label does it say "for the control of fleas!" That's because they can't prove it.

I have learned that as long as a product causes no harm and the pet owner is also using other, more well-proven methods of parasite control, the placebo effect of the magical ingredient may be worth some peace of mind.

However, there are some new flea-control products that *can* cause harm.

Q: *My brother goes to a vet in west Texas and he gives him some drops in a bottle to put on his dog for fleas. He says it's cattle dip. It seems to work really well. Where can I get some?*

A: I suggest you forget that idea. Your brother is getting a chemical called Spoton, illegally I might add, from this vet. Spoton is a very concentrated, highly toxic organophosphate chemical that was formulated so that only very small amounts could be poured on to the backs of *cattle* to rid them of parasites. It is not made for dogs, licensed for dogs, tested on dogs or concentrated for dogs and, therefore, *should not* be used on dogs.

If your brother's dog were to have a reaction, or heaven forbid die, from the chemical—and some have—he could have a legal action against the vet.

I had a lady call me from Florida not long ago whose veterinarian had used this chemical on her dog in the clinic and sent her home. Doctors have incorrectly thought this would be a safer way to control the toxic substance. On the way home, she stopped at a store and briefly left her two children in the car with the dog. When she returned the youngest girl was having a severe reaction to the small amount of the chemical that had vaporized in the closed car. Now that's toxic!

Stick with the more traditional methods of flea control.

Q: *My daughter does not believe in using chemicals. She doesn't want to use any harsh chemicals for her dog's flea problem, but he is itching constantly from fleas. She gives him lots of garlic and brewer's yeast. Is there anything she can use like this that is effective?*

A: I believe the key is the severity of the flea problem. For very mild flea infestations many people successfully use garlic, brewer's yeast and even small scarves soaked in eucalyptus and pennyroyal tied around the dog's neck.

While these dogs smell pretty funny (and I'm sure their doggie friends talk about them behind their backs), these things do no harm. However, they also don't do much good in controlling anything but the most occasional flea. An occasional bath in regular shampoo would be just as effective.

It sounds like your daughter has a moderate to severe flea problem and a whole health food store full of organic goodies probably won't help. She will need to undertake the four-step flea control program (outlined in this chapter) to get an initial knock-down of the flea population. Then, once the problem is somewhat under control, she can continue all the nonchemical methods of repelling fleas.

The nonchemical, nontoxic methods that I like, and that are proven to be effective, are the use of diatomaceous earth in the yard and sodium borate dusted into the carpet. Frequent baths and the yeast and garlic are certainly fine. I know many people who control a mild to moderate flea problem using the proper application of these things.

Q: *I bought an ultrasonic flea collar. I can't tell if it is doing any good. Do these things really work?*

A: Every ultrasonic device I've seen and tested for flea control does not work. I've tried them, friends have tried them, clients have tried them and universities have tried them and no one will say they work.

I can tell you that after six years of talk radio, I have spoken with no one who has called this show to say how well they work. I have spoken with about five manufacturers about their products. They all *say* their device works and have varying explanations as to how they think it works. *None* will send me any proof, university test or controlled studies done by an independent source. It's a totally unproved gimmick.

I, like you, would like to believe it works. I would like us to have a nonchemical method of true flea control. However, mild levels of ultrasonic sound waves produced by a small ceramic speaker aimed at right angles to the dog's neck just do not work.

I also know there are many clear frauds out there. I talked to a senior citizen, living on a fixed income, who spent $69 for one of these. When it "quit working" she sent it to me thinking I could help her. I opened it up and found it to be a plastic shell, housing a metal slug glued to the inside. Clearly a fraud.

Q: *I've always heard that you could feed a dog hardwood ash for worms. Do you think that works?*

A: For as many people there are in the world, there are probably that many "cures" for worms. Just about the time I think I've heard it all, someone will call with another.

No! Please don't feed your dog hardwood ash. I'm not even sure what that is, but I am sure I don't want you feeding it to your dog. It could contain toxins and harmful chemical irritants. It could constipate your dog and perhaps make him vomit for days. Please don't.

Why not visit your local veterinary clinic and ask for a deworming pill? If you know your doctor well and he knows your pets, he may prescribe something simple without seeing the dog if the symptoms you describe are obvious, like visible tapeworm segments.

If the doctor is not real familiar with you and your pet, or the symptoms are unclear, he will probably need to see your dog first. Veterinarians do not give any kind of medication for conditions that are not well diagnosed.

Q: *My mother bought an ultrasonic unit that sets on a bookshelf. It's suppose to rid the house of rats, mice, insects and fleas. Do they work?*

A: I am somewhat of an authority in the use of ultrasonic sound and pest control. In the early '80s I ran Bio-Acoustical Laboratories in Dallas. We studied various ultrasonic devices for manufacturers. We were specifically trying to decide if they worked, and if so, on what species of rodents and insects. We tested rats, mice, roaches, houseflies and fleas. I defended my studies to the Federal Trade Commission and was quoted in *Business Week* and other national business publications.

The results of months of testing, thousands of dollars of equipment, video taping and hours of crunching numbers were inconclusive. I can say that rats and mice seem to prefer an area without constant saturation of high levels of ultrasonic sound waves. However, after a while they can "ignore" the sound and show back up again. (We think they go range deaf and therefore can no longer hear in those high frequency ranges.)

With insects, the results were even more inconclusive. We used very high levels of sound in some of these tests and concentrated it right at populations of fleas and roaches. I can say I believe there is *some* effect, but I don't know what that is, how to maximize it or if it's safe to pets and children. Until a major company pours a lot of money into research and development and produces a well-tested, safe product, I would not waste my money on one.

Q: *I was in one of these pet superstores the other day and bought some worm medicine for my dog. It is supposed to be all natural. I haven't given it yet and heard you on the air today, so I thought I'd see what you think.*

A: I really don't like to see pet stores sell medications. First of all, they do not have access to the latest veterinary drugs and medications. These products are strictly controlled by the FDA and the pharmaceutical manufacturers. Many times what pet stores can sell are older preparations that no longer have much demand by veterinarians.

Pet store sales people aren't qualified to give you recommended use, dosage, side effects and so on. That's what your veterinarian is for. At times, pet-store staff may give very wrong, very dangerous information. I actually had a girl working in a pet store tell me not to put a flea collar on my cat because "cats have a hormone, and therefore, the flea collar can kill them." She said it with such conviction she would have made a believer out of someone who didn't know any better.

My best advice to you is to ask your veterinarian. If he or she says something is effective and can be purchased in a pet store, then certainly buy it there to save some money. I strongly support pet stores and the role they play in helping us get food and supplies at good prices, but they are not qualified to give medical advice.

As far as "all natural" cures, some work and I am all for them. Most, however, have only marginal effectiveness and I have been mostly disappointed using such things. My suggestion is, get your vet on the phone and read him the ingredients on the bottle you bought. The doctor will tell you if it will work and if it is safe to give your pooch. He may tell you to come in and get some "real" medicine.

Q: *Doc, we used to give our dogs motor oil and Tabasco sauce to keep 'em clean of worms. Is that OK?*

A: Those were either very tough dogs, or very short-lived. Motor oil contains many ingredients that will irritate stomach and intestinal tissues as well as other compounds, that in sufficient amounts, will poison your dog. Tabasco sauce will, no doubt, upset their stomach. In fact, that may be where this idea originated. Many old medical "cures" for intestinal worms were chemicals that did nothing but make the stomach and intestines very upset and actually kicked out a few worms by mechanical action (when the dog vomited). We now know that this does no good whatsoever because if even a few worms are left in the body, they can still cause damage.

Keep the old farm cures in your file of golden memories and away from today's dogs.

REAL FLEA CONTROL—THE FOUR-STEP PROCESS

Q: *Could you go over what you think is an effective flea-control program we can do at home?*

A: Remember, a flea problem is an *environment* problem, not a dog problem. For every adult flea you see, there are literally thousands of immature stages of the flea's life cycle in your carpet, furniture, cracks and crevices. Traditional flea-control measures, and even many of the tried and true old wives' tales, concentrate on killing the *adult* flea and have *no effect* on the many other life stages.

If you only concentrate your flea-control methods on killing the adults, you will NEVER get rid of fleas. For every adult you kill, there are hundreds of eggs, larvae, pupae and preadults waiting for the chance to be the next in line.

You must understand the stages of the flea's life cycle and the timing and environmental factors that affect this life cycle, as well as the products that control each level of this life cycle, before you can effectively control fleas.

It helps if you can do these things yourself, because even a professional pest-control operator, who may have properly applied chemical in your pet's environment, cannot be there to treat your dog every time he returns from the park and walks in with a few fleas. You are there, to constantly stand vigil against these pervasive pests, and that's how you get a handle on the flea problem. It's not that hard, it just takes a little knowledge, a few trips to the pet store or animal clinic and persistence.

It takes just a quick look at the flea's life cycle to see why control must be on several levels. The four stages of a flea's life cycle are: Egg, Larvae, Pupae and Adult.

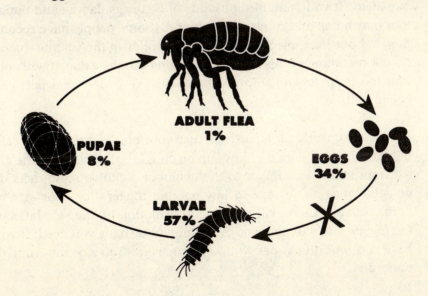

ADULT FLEA
1%

PUPAE
8%

EGGS
34%

LARVAE
57%

It may be easier to think of this life cycle as a pyramid with one adult flea at the top of the pyramid, ten to twenty pupae on the next level, fifty to sixty larvae one step below and finally hundreds of eggs at the base.

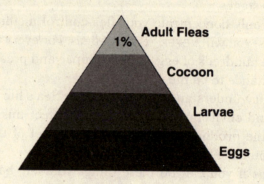

By looking at this pyramid, it's easy to see why killing adult fleas only is *not* flea control.

Step 1: Treating the Indoor Environment

Vacuum   The battle begins with a very thorough vacuuming. Use the crack and crevice tool and get in all the corners. Even vacuum hardwood and tile floors. Be sure to immediately throw the vacuum bag away. It will contain thousands of flea eggs, larvae and pupae that may hatch and reinfest your home. (Some people have recommended putting a piece of leftover flea collar in the vacuum bag. I do not recommend this as the air rushing out the exhaust will contain too much chemical and some sensitive people and pets can become ill.)

Fog   Next cover your aquarium, turn your air conditioner off, ceiling fans off, turn couch pillows up on end, take the bird and the cat to Grandma's, send Rover to the neighbor's and you and the kids go see a movie! Be sure to buy enough foggers for your size of home. Usually there will be some information on the side label of the fogger that will help you determine how many you need. If you have any questions, ask your veterinarian! You do not want to underdo it!

Point the fogger away from you and set it off. Carefully set the fogger on the floor in the middle of the room and get out. One by one set them off and exit the room.

You may want to spot-treat a few areas where the fog can't reach and especially where your pet sleeps or other heavy pet activity areas. For this purpose you will find "premise sprays" that are like foggers but allow you to point the fogger can down and spot-treat areas.

Most foggers contain an only an adulticide (agent that kills adult fleas). This means they will only kill adult fleas. Immature preadults, larvae, pupae and eggs are not affected. Some of the newer foggers also contain an IGR or insect growth regulator. This non-toxic compound works at the larvae level and prevents development of one stage to another. It is safe and has a residual effect. The IGR will prevent developing immature stages of fleas in your carpet for up to 210 days! However, adult fleas can develop from dormant preadults or they can catch a piggyback ride into your house on you or your pets and reinfest your home a few weeks later.

Therefore, you do not have to reapply the IGR-containing foggers each time you fog. I suggest you apply the IGRs twice a year (spring and fall). In between times, when you are seeing adult fleas, simply use an adulticide-only fogger.

Some people report a worse flea problem after using the IGR foggers. This is due to something called population dynamics. Somehow a population of fleas "knows" it's been hit hard. All the young fleas (called preadults) that have been dormant will "sense" this and suddenly emerge. (They were not affected by the adulticide or the IGR.) When they emerge, they are hungry and their only goal in life is to get a blood meal (from you or your pet) and then begin reproducing. Don't worry about this. It only occurs in severe infestation problems, and if it happens, simply refog your house with adulticide-only foggers in about two weeks.

Step 2: Treating the Outdoor Environment

Mow and Edge Mow and edge the yard very well. Fleas and ticks love tall grass. It is the perfect breeding ground and serves as a constant source of reinfestation for your environment.

Spray Once you have a neat yard, use a yard- and kennel-type spray and follow the label directions exactly! Some sprays require you to wet the lawn first, then apply the chemical, then wet the lawn again. Others need to be applied with a special applicator on a special setting. These chemicals are safe, but many of them are still toxic chemicals, so read carefully and don't use the product in any other way. Dursban is still the chemical of choice, although that changes from time to time. Your veterinarian will know the chemical your area has the best luck with.

When you're through, wash out your equipment very well, wash your hands and change your clothes if they have become wet in the process. Keep your pets off the lawn for about twenty-four hours or at least until it has dried. Take care in how you dispose of the left-over bottles and cartons. You do not want pets or kids getting into these containers.

Although this is currently under study, unfortunately there are no IGRs for outdoor use now. Sunlight breaks down the delicate compound very quickly. Therefore you will have to spray your yard as I've described every three or four weeks, depending on the extent of your flea problem.

STEP 3: TREATING THE DOG

There are literally hundreds of products with which to bathe, dip, powder, spray, comb and brush fleas away. Some work better than others. It is impossible for me to recommend the exact product for your situation. I can, however, recommend you buy carefully. Purchase well-recognized brands and only products designed for your type of pet. Again, the best place for advice on this is your pet's doctor.

Bathe and Dip Begin with a good bath. If your pet shudders at the first sight and sound of a bath, you may want to undertake a little careful training so that a bath is fun and not scary to your little friend (see Chapter 8).

Use a mild pet shampoo that contains some flea-killing or -repelling ingredients. Such common and safe ingredients are pyrethrums and d-Limonene. In the case of a mild flea infestation, this may be all that is needed. With puppies and kittens this is all I recommend.

In the case of moderate or severe infestations, you will now need to dip your pet. Again using a dip designed for your dog, cat, pup or kitten, sponge the dilute chemical on the wet pet. Let the chemical stand on the pet for just a few minutes, then gently pat dry with a towel. Let the pet air dry the rest of the way.

Flea Collars   The next day or two, place a flea collar on the pet. Yes, flea collars *do work!* They have been given a bad rap because too many people buy a flea collar *only*, put it on the pet and expect to never see a flea again. You can see from our discussion of the flea's life cycle that this will not work. Flea collars are very well designed, researched and tested. They are effective when used as a part of this overall flea-control program. Please include it in your arsenal!

Some special flea collars now contain IGR compounds, and this is a real plus. Flea eggs that contact the collar will be unable to hatch, and in this way you are treating the environment by decreasing the viable flea egg count in your carpet.

Whatever type of collar you use, take it out of the inner package and let it air out for twenty-four hours before putting it on the dog. This allows the initial high concentration of chemical to dissipate a little. Put it on the dog and trim off the excess. I've used the excess flea collar piece in my garage in hard to reach places where pests are a problem. But, as I've mentioned, *don't* use it in your vacuum-cleaner bag.

On-Pet Sprays   Use sprays on your pet on an as-needed basis. For example, when you see a flea and it is between bath time, give your pet a few sprays of a mild on-pet spray. I usually give my dog a few squirts of the spray before we head out for a walk or to the park. Then when we get back I give him a quick check, and if I see any fleas, I give him a few more squirts.

Don't overdo this spraying and don't rely on the spray alone, just as you should not rely on flea collars alone. Also, *do not soak* your pet with these sprays. Remember a few years back when Hartz

Mountain released Blockade? The reason they voluntarily pulled the product after several dogs and cats died was not because the product was dangerous. It was because people were literally *soaking* their pets in the stuff! Hartz simply rereleased the product the next season with a string-attached instruction booklet cautioning users on its proper application. To my knowledge, there have been no more reports of problems.

Some spray-on products now contain the IGRs. This is great! Now the eggs laid on the pet are coated with the IGR even before they hit your carpet. They have no chance of developing into adult fleas.

You may have noticed that IGR foggers work at the larval stage and the IGR on-pet sprays prevent the egg from developing. That is because the concentration of IGR required to work at the egg level is much higher and it is not practical to apply it at this level via foggers. But on the pet, the higher concentration is highly effective in actually coating the flea eggs laid on the pet. When they roll off into the environment they are already treated and will not hatch. *That* is flea control. I highly recommend the use of these IGR-containing products.

STEP 4: PREVENTION

After you have done a good job of killing adult fleas and have applied the IGRs in your home, have mowed and sprayed your yard and have bathed and dipped your dog, you need to undertake a few preventive steps.

Dusting your pets sleeping area with a good flea powder is a good idea. The use of the on-pet sprays before a walk in the park is good prevention, and the use of insect growth regulators (IGRs) is today's most advanced way to prevent a problem with fleas in the future.

Prevention also involves the use of sodium borate compounds in the carpet. These naturally occurring chemicals are safe for children and pets and last in your carpet for almost a year! They are dusted on, brushed in and do not leave a residue. They work at the larval stage, much like the IGRs and I recommend their use, especially for people sensitive to chemicals or for those not wanting to use any toxic chemicals in the house.

Other Tricks   One of the organic gardening tricks to control fleas does have merit. Diatomaceous earth, or DE, is mother nature's insecticide. It is made up of microscopic razor-like particles that damage the protective waxy coating of insects that come in contact with them. The insect then dehydrates and dies. Many people have used DE very successfully in their yards. It is approved by the USDA as an ingredient in animal feeds for insect control and is very safe as long as you take precautions not to breath it in. Because of this possible problem, I'm not real enthusiastic about its use on your dog. But if you were careful and treated only the back three-quarters of the dog, you should have no problem.

Buy the kind of DE used in organic gardening (rather than the type used in swimming-pool filters) and apply it as a dust all over your yard about once every couple of weeks.

One day while driving along I was listening to a famous organic gardening expert on talk radio give some glowing testimonies about DE. He said you must be careful not to overdo it in a broadcast application because it can actually knock out all your friendly insects. Good point! Also, when DE is wet, it has no effect because, again, those little razor edges aren't going to have their effect of cutting the waxy coating all insects have. However, when it dries out, it becomes effective again. Therefore if you were using DE on a fire ant mound, for example, you would not want to water it in.

In summary, this is the most concise, complete and no nonsense approach to flea control you'll find. Follow these directions carefully, using steps 1 to 4. Use organic and nontoxic methods where you can, and hopefully you will have a spring, summer and fall without the pesky problems of fleas and ticks. *Get hopping!*

> *Did You Know?*
> - The average life span of an adult flea is about six weeks.
> - An untreated pet can support a colony of 60–100 fleas.
> - A female flea lays an average of 20 eggs per day—that's nearly 900 eggs in six weeks.
> - If your pet is home to 60 fleas, it could yield 54,000 eggs in just six weeks.

Q: *We have recently heard about spraying "bugs" in your yard for flea control. What's that all about?*

A: In the past we have had only strong chemicals to spray in the yard to control fleas there. Unfortunately, IGR's don't work in sunlight. However, now there is an environmentally safe and effective flea fighter that goes after fleas in the yard.

Microscopic flea-eating nematodes, which are beneficial bugs, can be sprayed onto your yard. This product immediately goes to work by seeking out flea larvae and destroying them. They don't harm people, pets or beneficial insects. Children and pets can play in a yard that's just been sprayed. One application works for up to four weeks.

After all the fleas are gone, the nematodes die off and biodegrade. This product is the latest thing and is now commercially available from feed stores and pet stores.

University studies have shown a 100% mortality of immature fleas after this application. It is a great idea that works well and I recommend it.

CHAPTER 17

Ticks, Mange, Mites and Lice

"Marge, from Sarasota Florida, you're next up. . . . "

"Dr. Jim, I read last week, in Dear Abby, that children can get pinworms by letting a dog lick their face. Our dog, Midnight, only occasionally licks my daughter's face. Should I be worried?"

"Marge, Dear Abby is a great place for advice about love and life, but not about pet care. It would take Dear Abby about eight years of college to become Dr. Abby, then she could offer veterinary advice.

No, children do not get pinworms from a dog lick, in fact, dogs cannot get pinworms at all. Pinworms are a parasite of people, horses and mice, but not dogs and cats. Therefore, your daughter cannot get them from Midnight!"

Sometimes I have to remind myself there are other parasites besides fleas. Ticks, mites and lice are occasional visitors to the exterior of our dog friends. Each represents its own challenge in terms of diagnosis, treatment and control.

Q: *My father always used to put spent motor oil in our dog's ears to control ear mites. Have you ever heard of this?*

A: Yes, I've heard of this but I would never recommend it. This will in fact get rid of ear mites, and it will also make your dog look and smell awful, not to mention cause possible chemical irritation of very delicate anatomical parts.

This old farm cure is based on the fact that almost any oily substance will kill ear mites. The oily texture closes off the breathing holes on the mites and eventually kills them. However, today you can buy a small bottle of Tresaderm or Cerumite at the animal hospital. These medications have a gentle oil base, mixed with a mild insecticide. This will take care of ear mites in short order.

Q: *I've used Cerumite, but my puppies still have ear mites.*
A: You have to use these medications *exactly* by label instructions or not all the mites will be killed and the infestation will return. You will also have to treat every puppy in the litter because mites are very contagious.

It is common for me to hear that ear mites have returned. Like the flea, you need to know a little about their life cycle in order to effectively kill a mite population. Adult mites are the culprits of the irritation caused to the sensitive ear tissues. They are easily killed with oily substances mixed with a little insecticide—like Cerumite. However, that preparation does nothing to the nymphs that are also present in the ear canal. In the short time of only ten days, these nymphs grow to become whole populations of adult mites and begin the irritation all over again. Therefore, with any ear-mite preparation you must treat for seven days, wait about seven to ten days, then retreat again for seven days. Only then will you kill the two levels, adult mites and their reinforcements.

I am always amazed when dog owners leave a veterinary hospital, ear mite medicine in hand, and do not know that.

In cases where Cerumite does not work, I have had good results with a product called Tresaderm. You may want to ask your veterinarian about this medication.

Q: *We have ticks this year. We have never had ticks before, and they are driving my wife crazy. Help!*
A: Ticks are member of the spider family and, therefore, are a little more on the creepy and crawly side than fleas. This is not to mention the diseases they carry, Lyme disease being the most highly publicized.

Controlling ticks is just like controlling fleas. You have to treat the pet, the yard and if your problem is severe, the house. Luckily, ticks generally stay in the yard or on your pet. Occasionally, if the population is high and your pet is infested, they will become a problem in the house.

Review Chapter 16 on the control of fleas. Just about all the chemicals and application methods used to control fleas, also apply to ticks. There are no IGRs for ticks, however, so your control will be based strictly on the adults. Their life cycle is slower in development and, therefore, you can get good control by controlling the adults as they emerge and become a problem.

I like to use chemicals with more of a residual effect for ticks. Diazinon granules sprinkled in the yard work well. Years ago many people used Sevin Dust. However, most now report it has lost most of its effectiveness. Dursban also kills ticks, is less toxic than Diazinon but is not put up in the long acting formulas like other chemicals. If you live near a grassy or wooded area, your problem will be more intense because these are perfect breeding grounds for ticks. If you can, cut all tall grass in a twenty-foot-wide swath around your property. Treat with your chemicals into that area.

On the pet, I recommend dipping the dog every week to ten days if the problem is bad. If not severe, you can separate dips by two to three weeks. Spray him well with a good flea and tick spray before going to the park, hiking or playing anywhere there is tall grass.

Q: *What do I do when I find a tick on my dog? Do you think it's OK to pull it off?*

A: It is OK to pull the tick off, but you must do it correctly. Get a pair of tweezers, and gently and steadily pull on the tick. This gives you the best chance he will release his mouth parts and come all the way out. I suggest you place removed ticks in a jar with a small amount of dilute dip chemical in it to kill the ticks.

If you do break off mouth parts in your dog's skin, it will usually only cause a mild irritation for a while. However, some of these can become more severely inflamed and make a real red, sore spot. You can use some topical ointment to help in these cases.

Q: My father always told us to light a match, blow it out and put that on the tick to make him back out!

A: I suppose if you were *real* good and your dog were *real* still this would work, but I do not recommend it, because somebody is liable to get burned in the process. If you don't want to use tweezers and pull the tick out carefully, just use a little bit of dilute dip chemical on a cotton swab and treat the tick individually. It will either back out then, or in a few days. It may even die in place and can then be easily removed with tweezers or brushing.

Q: We've heard a lot about Lyme disease in people, and we take precautions when hiking and so forth. Our dog goes with us all the time. Is he at risk?

A: Yes he is! Dogs can get Lyme disease just like people can, and the symptoms and secondary complications are the same. Because dogs are covered with fur, you may not see the initial red, target-shaped inflammation around the tick bite. Then the disease will progress to a stage where the dog will run a fever, be lethargic and may even act like it hurts to walk. Most veterinarians see dogs with Lyme disease at this point. Vigorous antibiotic and supportive therapy is needed to keep dogs from having more serious complications.

I suggest you look your dog over very carefully during your outings and dip him every time you come back. Roll him over and check carefully between his toes, under his belly, in his flanks, behind and in his ears. Those are favorite hiding places for ticks.

The best thing you can to is to have your dog vaccinated against Lyme disease. Call your veterinarian and see if they have the vaccine. It is inexpensive preventive medicine, and you'll have greater peace of mind on your hiking trips.

Q: We just got a new puppy, and we noticed a bald spot over his right eye. Our vet says it's red mange and it may take six weeks to treat! What's red mange? It sounds bad.

A: Red mange does sound very bad, and in some cases can be. It is more appropriately known as demodectic mange. It is caused by the *Demodex canis* mange mite that burrows deep in the layers of the skin. This mite is actually an inhabitant of normal skin in dogs and even in humans. Therefore, it is not the presence of these mites that causes mange. It is the overrun of the mite population in certain locations that causes the hair to fall out and the skin to become very inflamed. We feel this is caused by a failure of the dog's immune system to keep the mites in check, allowing the mites to overrun an area of skin. Some of these dogs can get so bad as to have spots all over their body. This generalized mange can even be life-threatening!

Most cases of mild localized mange are successfully treated with the use of ordinary drugs and advice from your veterinarian. When the pup matures, and so does his immune system, the spots will probably go away. However, the cases of generalized mange can be so severe as to make dogs completely hairless and completely miserable. Even though this disease does not cause itching, the serious inflammation caused by the mites makes the dog very uncomfortable. I've seen generalized cases so severe that the dog was put to sleep because it was the most humane thing to do. I've seen others that, with persistent treatment over a period of six months, recovered to be completely normal.

Q: *Our dog just got back from a friend's place in the country, and he is covered with little tiny gray ticks. I mean covered. There must be thousands on him! What do we do?*

A: I would suggest you take the dog to your veterinarian for a strong dip. You can do this yourself, but I think it would be easier on you and the dog if a veterinarian or a professional groomer did the job. After a day or two when all the ticks have died and released their grip, you can give him a good grooming and get most of the dead ticks out of his hair coat.

Next time he visits the country, dip him just before he goes and put a new flea collar on him.

Q: *Our dog Sammy began walking funny and finally acted like he couldn't get up on his back legs. Our vet thinks he has tick paralysis. Can you tell us what that is?*

A: Tick paralysis is not common, but can be severe. There are two types of ticks in North America that carry a neurotoxin in their saliva. This neurotoxin blocks impulses in the long nerves that serve the legs. The engorged female tick has usually been attached to the dog for about five to nine days before you will see any signs. Sammy's funny walk was actually what is known as ataxia and is the first sign he has this disease. The toxin can spread and actually cause paralysis and even stop his ability to breath!

Treatment involves the removal of the tick, and the symptoms will disappear within two days. There is no antitoxin available. You must be sure to remove all ticks because the symptoms I've described can be caused by just one tick. Check his head and neck, ear canals, flanks, toes and under his tail. Give him a good dip and treat your yard thoroughly as well.

CHAPTER 18

Heartworms
and Intestinal Worms

"Doc, do dogs get worms from eating chocolate?"
"Do dogs get worms from eating white bread?"
"Do dogs get worms from store-bought dog food?"
"Do dogs get worms from eating popcorn?"
"Do dogs get worms from eating (you may fill in the blank)?"
The answer is yes, if (whatever) has worm eggs on it! But that is the only way.
Worms are caused by worm eggs, and generally worm eggs infect a dog's body by the oral route. The most common way dogs get worms is from fecal–oral contamination. Poor environmental conditions contribute to this, but many dogs, even those in great conditions, can get worms.

One of the most common ways puppies get worms is scientifically known as transcolostrially, or through mother's first milk. If the mother dog has roundworms at the time of her pregnancy, the puppies can get them via the milk. Also, transplacental, or through the birth sac, is a known mode of worm infestation.

It is estimated that up to 70% of all puppies in many parts of the country have roundworms because of this subtle, yet common method of transmission.

Other intestinal worms, like hookworms, whipworms and tapeworms, are also very common and must be properly diagnosed and treated by a veterinarian.

Heartworm disease is quite different from these other parasite infestations. This worm actually lives and multiplies in the chambers of the heart and large vessels. Therefore, as you can imagine, it causes a great deal of secondary medical problems. It is the most serious of the parasitic diseases.

Q: *I think our dog has worms. Can you tell me what medicine to buy at the pet store to cure them?*

A: There are many different types of worms. Roundworms, whipworms, hookworms and tapeworms are the most common. Each of these parasites requires a different medication to rid the dog's body of the infestation. I suspect you do not know which your dog has because that requires a laboratory test. Therefore, if I told you to get XYZ medication and your dog had ABC worms you would have wasted money and time.

Unless you know what the worm type is, and exactly what medication to give for that type, don't medicate your own pets. Call your veterinarian and let her exercise her professional advice. The test is simple, fast and inexpensive. It will tell you and your doctor what you are dealing with and exactly what you have to do to get rid of it.

Far too many pet stores sell worm medicines and haven't a clue about what advice to send out the door with you. They are doing you a disservice.

Q: *Dr. Jim, our dog, Heidi, died last year. We have a new puppy named Oscar. We found some of Heidi's old heartworm pills, and we went ahead and started Oscar on them. Is that OK?*

A: That is definitely *not* OK! You have run the risk of a serious reaction with Oscar. Please don't give him anymore and get to your veterinarian on Monday to have him tested for heartworm.

You see, heartworm pills are preventive medications. They work by building up a level of medication in the dog's system so that if the dog is bitten by an infective mosquito, the heartworm larvae will not develop in his system.

If a dog already has an active heartworm infection and heartworm preventive medication is administered, it may react with the microfilaria in the bloodstream and cause a shocklike reaction. I have seen this happen several times. Also, if Oscar had a mild or early infestation of worms in the heart and you gave him the pills before having him tested, it could cause what is known as an occult infection. This is where the dog has adult worms but no microfilaria or baby worms circulating in the bloodstream. This would mean that Oscar could have heartworm disease but no way to prove it on the blood test.

The medicine you have on the shelf may also be out of date and therefore not effective either. Get to the vet on Monday and have him test Oscar for heartworm disease. If he is negative, go ahead and resume the preventive pills at that time, but check the expiration on the bottle of old pills.

Q: *We have heard that the new once a month heartworm pills cannot be given to Collies. Is that true?*

A: When the initial research was done on Ivermectin, there were some strange reactions in the sight hounds, the Collie-type breeds. However, this was at a dose much higher than is currently being used in the new once-a-month medications. Heartgard 30 has been tested extensively and is safe for use in all dogs, even pregnant females and breeding animals. However, as is always the case, follow the recommendations of the doctor who prescribes the medication and if any strange symptoms occur, give him a call. I would not hesitate to give Heartgard 30 to a Collie. But many Collie owners and breeders feel safer giving Filaribits, the once-a-day preventive.

Q: *Our vet just told us that our dog, Scruffy, has heartworms. The treatment sounds kind of scary. Can you explain it to us?*

A: Treating heartworms is a bit scary. It begins with a complete physical exam and even some blood work to see if Scruffy can withstand the rather rigorous treatment. If everything checks out well, Scruffy will be hospitalized and given twice-daily injections of a carefully measured medication that will kill the adult worms in the heart. Some dogs become quite ill during this treatment and there are secondary complications.

After three days of this, the dog is sent home for recovery. He must have strictly enforced rest for two months! Many doctors even require confinement in a kennel, and the only exercise the dog gets is for elimination. This is very important because the adult worms have now slipped over into the lungs. The lungs secrete enzymes to break these foriegn objects down. The delicate lung tissue suffers some damage during this process, as well. If a dog were to exert too much effort, he could collapse in respiratory failure.

After this critical phase, the dog is then treated to rid its body of the microfilaria, or baby heartworms, circulating in the blood. Once this is done, the dog is considered treated and then, and only then, put on heartworm preventive medications.

As you can see, this is a difficult treatment and risky for the dog. In the case of heartworm, the best treatment isn't treatment at all—it's prevention.

Q: *We have moved from Chicago to Ft. Meyers, Florida. In Illinois we did not have to give heartworm preventive during the winter months, but down here the vet told us we have to give the pills all year round. Why is that?*

A: In very cold climates, where mosquitoes are not a year-round problem, many veterinarians have their clients give the heartworm preventive only during mosquito season. This saves money and is more convenient for you. However, before the dog can be placed back on the medication, it must be retested to be sure active infection has not occurred during the off period.

In the southern states, mosquitoes are active in the winter months. Because of this, transmission of heartworm disease can occur year round and, therefore, it is best to keep these dogs on heartworm preventive medications year round.

Q: *I can't believe it. I just saw the most disgusting thing! Little white worms crawling on my Mimi's rear end! What is that? Should I take her to the emergency clinic?*

A: Take a deep breath . . . Mimi simply has tapeworms. No big deal. You do want to get rid of them, however, and that, too, is easy. First get Mimi treated at the vet's office. Then he will want to follow up with her in about three weeks.

However, I can tell you that this is a sure sign you have a flea problem. Tapeworms can come from only one place—ingesting a flea. Dogs ingest a flea when it is biting them, and they chew at the flea. The flea then is digested in the dog's stomach, and a tapeworm head is revealed.

This tapeworm head attaches to the dog's small intestinal wall and begins to grow. This is a segmented worm, and as it gets longer, the segments will break off and come out of the dog. That is what you see. They do move and wiggle while they are fresh, and it *is* pretty disgusting. You or your family are not in any danger, but I would suggest you get your flea problem under control. (Review Chapter 16.)

Q: *I think my dog has ringworms. There are small patches of no hair on his side. How can I cure these?*

A: It is unfortunate that ringworm was ever called that. *Ringworm is not a worm. It is a fungus.* I guess because it forms a ring of hair loss in animals and a red inflamed ring on human skin, it got labeled ring "worm." The fungal spores that cause ringworm are found in dirt and, once a spot develops on a person or animal, are freely transmitted mechanically. It is only moderately contagious, requiring a great deal of contact on soft, thin-skinned areas of the body. For example, the head and neck of children is a common spot because kids will carry a cat around their neck. The face is another spot where ringworm is transmitted from an infected cat who sleeps on the same pillow you sleep on at night.

Successful treatment usually involves the local application of antifungal ointments. If it is more widespread, the dog (or human) may be put on systemic antifungal medications, like Griseofulvin, for a month. I usually also bathe the dog in antifungal shampoos weekly for a month.

Q: *We just saw our dog in the front yard eating grub worms! Will that hurt him? Will he get worms from that?*

A: Parasites are fairly species specific organisms. In other words, if a worm likes a dog, it will usually not infest a horse, and so forth. This is especially true for plant parasites, like grub worms. So the good news is, your dog cannot get "worms" from eating grub worms.

Q: *We brought our new Welsh Corgi puppy home from the breeder today, and she threw up worms! We were shocked! What are these, and what do we do?*

A: Most likely what you saw were roundworms. It is not uncommon for young puppies to have roundworms. When an infestation is high, these worms, which normally live in the small intestine, can migrate up into the stomach. This causes such an irritation that it will make the dog vomit and out will come some of the worms.

Only in very rare cases do such worm infestations cause serious or life-threatening problems, but because this is a sign of a higher infestation level, I would get the pup to a veterinary hospital immediately and get her treated.

Although technically it is not an emergency, because it is Saturday afternoon and most veterinary clinics are closed, I would take her to the animal emergency clinic. This will get her some immediate treatment and allow you this evening and Sunday to watch her for any secondary problems. She will probably pass a large number of these long, slender, white, "spaghettilike" worms after the treatment. So be prepared!

PART V

NUTRITION
AND EXERCISE

CHAPTER 19

All About Food

"We've put together a food that our dog likes so well we'd like to sell it!" the caller said proudly.

"What is it?"

"We start out with Purina Chow, and mix in a little boiled egg, some garlic salt, green peas and some chopped-up SPAM. That's our secret ingredient. How would we go about selling this? We may even advertise on your show!"

"I appreciate your confidence, but first of all I think the kind folks at Purina would be giving you a call about using their food as a base for a different formula to be sold for a profit."

"All right, we won't tell anybody that, what else?"

"Well, secondly, you've listed several ingredients that will spoil when packaged"

"Well OK, we'll freeze it. What else?"

"Finally, your formula itself is not good. It is too high in fat, protein and salt, plus all the added ingredients you've put in there are throwing off the initial balance of the primary food."

"Boy, you're just full of good news aren't you, Doc!"

"My best advice is to find another line of part-time work and let the PhDs formulate pet foods, and the MBAs market it!"

The pet-food business has really changed in the last decade. Increased competition has made everyone do a better job of formulating their foods and educating their customers. The trend in improvement was initiated by Dr. Mark Morris who developed Hill's pet foods in the 1970s. Hill's began selling very high quality foods through veterinary offices. As Hill's began educating veterinary clients about nutrition and the diseases caused by poor nutrition, more and more people bought their food from veterinarians.

Today we have many companies such as Iams, Nature's Recipe, Natural Life, Fromm, Protocol, Nutro and many others which all make a superior pet food, back it up with lots of research and sell it through pet stores and veterinary clinics.

Superior pet-food brands now account for about 20% of pet-food sales. Ten years ago specialty brands were less than 5%! So far supermarket sales of the standard brands is down 10% in the last ten years. The net effect of this boom in specialty pet food has been improved nutrition for our pets. For years, the leading killers of our pets have been heart disease, liver disease and cancer, the top three diseases caused by poor nutrition.

Because of the erosion of grocery-brand pet-food sales, the major grocery-store brands such as Purina, Kal-Kan and Quaker have undergone some serious reformulating. Every one of them has now created premium brands of their own. Good for them! It's about time. I believe that our pets will live longer and healthier because of it, and now you have a choice. It is no longer a choice between quality food for $45 dollar a bag or poor quality grocery-store food. You now have a range of foods to choose from that allow you to spend a little more and get better nutrition for your pet at either the pet store or grocery store.

Of all the things we do for our pets, feeding them is one of the most rewarding ways we can "give back to them." However, everything we put inside them affects their health, their resistance to disease and their longevity.

Q: *We can't afford those expensive brands of foods at the pet store. What can we buy at the grocery store that will be OK for our six-month-old retriever pup?*

A: Good question. I can understand how the price of the super-premium brands sold at pet stores and veterinary clinics can be out of budget, especially with a big dog. Most dogs that are very young will do well on most any brand. They are healthy and their organs are pretty resilient to nutritional insult in the short term.

It is your dog's long-term health that concerns me. If right now you cannot afford one of the super-premium brands, I'd suggest one of the grocery-store premium brands like O.N.E., Expert Diet, Cycle Puppy or Alpo. These brands have all been reformulated and are much improved. They will provide your puppy excellent nutrition as long as he is healthy. As your dog gets older, I'd suggest switching to a formula for older dogs. Expert and Cycle both have senior formulas and of course, all the super-premium brands at pet stores do as well. For senior dogs I highly recommend a pet-store premium diet!

Q: *We feed a grocery-store canned food to our pug, Bugsey. He has bad breath all the time. Do you think it's the food?*

A: It could be the food, it could also be dental tartar and gum disease caused by the exclusively soft food diet. Because he doesn't eat any type of dry food, Bugsey is not getting any rough form of abrasion on his teeth. The soft food may be accumulating on his teeth and the decaying food particles causing the bad odor. Try mixing a good quality dry food with just a small amount of the canned food and see if he'll eat it just as well. If so, he will be getting good nutrition and the abrasive action of crunching on dry dog food will help the bad-breath problem.

I suggest you first have your veterinarian look at his mouth to make sure there are no badly infected areas of gum tissue. He may also want to do a dental prophy and send you home with a doggie toothbrush kit.

Q: *I've seen both pet-store foods and grocery-store foods that brag that they are "all natural" and "free from added preservatives." Is this really important or is this just marketing?*

A: It is mostly marketing, but there is some scientific basis in feeding a food free of preservatives. However, most of these pet-food companies are playing a name game trick on you. By saying they have "no added preservatives" they are not saying there are *no* preservatives in the food. *They* don't add them, but the preservatives have already been added to the raw ingredients before being purchased by the company! Pretty tricky isn't it?

Preservatives are necessary in all pet food. If they didn't have preservatives of some kind, they would spoil on the shelf in a matter of days or even hours. Many so-called "all natural" foods use vitamin E or vitamin C as a preservative.

Some preservatives have been tagged as the cause of problems in people and pets. The goal is to find preservatives that can be used in very small amounts and cause no side effects. Today, most pet food companies use ethoxyquin, which has been found to be quite safe.

Q: *We saw an article in a dog magazine about a pet-food preservative called ethoxy . . . something. The breeder who wrote the article said we should all boycott foods with this chemical in it because it is killing our dogs. Do you know what this is and how dangerous it is?*

A: The desire for an all-natural pet food has caused every preservative added to be a target of scrutiny and often unfounded accusations.

Every few years, in circles of dog breeders around the country, someone will have a litter with medical problems then place the blame on a compound called ethoxyquin.

This is an additive to almost all pet foods, and some human food, that helps prevent the oxidation of fats. This gives the food a longer shelf life, prevents the formation of dangerous toxins in foods and makes the food taste better. There is even some evidence that the chemical has some anticancer properties. Gee, what more do you want from a preservative?

Ethoxyquin has been tested and retested and has been found to be safe time and time again. It has been successfully used in pet food for over thirty years. Even the "all natural," "no preservatives added" foods have it, in which cases it has been added to the basic ingredients before the manufacturer formulates the food.

It is used at a level of .001 ounce per average daily ration. It prevents the use of other preservatives such as BHA and BHT, which would have to be used in substantially higher amounts, which would, of course, add to the cost of pet food. The most researched and highly formulated premium brands of pet food contain this compound because of its many benefits.

There have been no scientific studies or investigations done or cited to support the claim that ethoxyquin causes any problems.

Q: *We buy large, bulk quantities of dog food at our farm store. It's not a brand anyone has ever heard of. Do you think it's OK?*

A: Seventy percent of all farm stores carry pet food. Convenience is a factor. It's easy for owners to pick up dog food while they are buying food for their livestock. It saves another trip to the pet store.

Most of the feed stores I've been in, lately, carry some of the premium brands as well as some private-label brands such as the one you have been buying. I suggest you stick with a premium brand that you know is of higher quality.

There are large dog-food manufacturers who do nothing but private-label dog foods for anyone who wants to pay for a private label. It is probably the exact same food in every different private label bag. While healthy dogs can do OK on this type of food for many years, your dog's best chances for a long and robust life are with the highest-quality nutrition. I'd stick with the top name premium brands, no matter where they are sold.

Q: *After listening to your show, we looked at our dog-food bag and read the ingredients. We were surprised to find corn, wheat, barley and many other grain and plant materials. Aren't dogs meat eaters?*

A: Yes they are. Although dogs will do fine when fed plant proteins, I think we see fewer problems in dogs fed meat-based foods. Pet foods are generally a by-product of large corporations who have their main interests in grain products. Pet foods are a way to turn a highly available resource into a profit center.

This means that grain hulls, peanut shells and wheat middlings are used to make pet food. As it turns out, a little wheat or corn is a good source of nutrients, even for carnivorous animals like dogs and cats.

The fact is that many times pets *cannot* tolerate these leftover grains. Food allergies, gastrointestinal disorders, kidney disease, cancer and other serious diseases can be directly linked to the "junk" in pet foods. Again, I recommend buying the best brand of food you can afford. Premium brands of food, available from pet stores and veterinary clinics have meat-based protein sources. Stay away from bargain brands, obscure brands, private-label brands and generic brands.

Q: *Which pet-food brand should I buy?*

A: The answer is simple. Buy any super-premium brand which your pet likes and tolerates well. Stick with it, do not switch from brand to brand just for the sake of change. If your pet has very soft stool, diarrhea or gas with a particular brand, switch to another, preferably one containing a different protein source. If your veterinarian has a medical reason he wants your pet on a particular brand, definitely follow the doctor's advice. Kidney disease, food allergy and heart disease are all excellent reasons to switch to prescription or hypoallergenic diets.

Q: *Our dog is getting old. We've fed her standard grocery-store brands most of her life. Should we change her food now, because of her age?*

A: Absolutely! As a dog goes through life, many things happen. She is exposed to many toxins, chemicals and allergens in her food. An older dog needs special nutrition to "go easy" on its kidneys, immune system and intestinal tract. Geriatric dogs should get the highest-quality food, made for older dogs, that you can buy.

These senior diets are made with more restricted, although adequate levels of protein and phosphorous with moderate levels of salt. They may have a slightly higher amount of fat so that the dog can get its calories from fat instead of protein, which could stress delicate kidney tissue. The reduced sodium will lower blood pressure and therefore decrease stress on the heart muscle.

Standard grocery-brand dog foods, while fine for young, healthy dogs, are not what your senior citizen should be eating. Put your dog on a high-quality premium dog food formulated for senior dogs. I recommend Hill's Science Diet Canine Senior or Nature's Recipe Senior/Pension Canine Diet.

Q: *We have always mixed two or three brands of food together and our dog eats it just fine. Is that OK?*

A: I'd prefer you did not mix different brands like that. Each brand has its own formula that has been scientifically balanced for a specific protein type, vitamin and mineral mix, and the like. When you mix brands, you throw off the balance of each brand. The result is an unbalanced diet. It's OK to mix canned food with dry food as long as you stay within one manufacturer's brand.

Q: *Our dog eats Hill's Science Diet. We also give him Pet Tab vitamins every day. Are the vitamins necessary?*

A: The answer is *no*. Back in the old days of mediocre grocery-store brands of dog food, dogs *needed* supplemental vitamins because they were not getting fresh sources of vitamins and minerals in the foods and some foods were simply not well balanced. This is also the reason many people put oil or bacon grease on their pet's food, to add a fresh source of fatty acids to the deficient diet.

Premium food diets have more well balanced vitamins and minerals, more digestible fresh oils and fatty acids, and more absorbable protein and carbohydrate sources. Why pay extra to supplement that kind of food? It makes no sense, except in the rare case of some metabolic disease or special skin problem. Many vitamins and minerals that a body cannot utilize are simply flushed out of the body in the urine. You can actually cause disease by overloading the kidney and liver functions with too many metabolites to get rid of.

Q: *My dog eats its own stools! I know he started this when I switched to a generic brand of dog food from our grocery store. When I switched him back to his regular brand, he stopped. Why did he do this?*

A: This is a perfect example of why low-end and generic brands of dog food are no good! Your dog is aware that there is undigested food in his stool, so much so, that he's decided to eat it again. What more proof do you need to know that the generic food is going right through him, without him being able to absorb it into his system.

Stay with a higher-quality dog food, and your dog will be happier and healthier.

Q: *Would canned or dry food be better for my eight-month-old Chihuahua?*

A: As long as you buy one of the premium brands it does not matter. Both forms are formulated to be the same in terms of nutrition, quality and balance. However, the canned food is mostly water and you're paying for that water on a weight basis. Dry food is by far the better bargain.

Also, canned food will be more likely to cause dental tartar problems in your dog's teeth later in life. What I do with my dogs, and recommend to my clients and callers, is a happy medium. I always feed a base of an excellent-quality premium dry food. Then at each feeding, usually twice a day, I simply put a spoonful of canned food on the top and stir it around a little. Sometimes I'll use a little hot water and make a nice gravy. This stimulates their interest in eating. But beware, dogs get hooked on that little bit of canned food and many times will not eat if you run out!

Q: *We've fed our Sheltie, Lady, one of those moist, processed, "hamburgerlike" diets for years. We supplement her diet with table scraps, and she seems to do OK. What's your opinion?*

A: Cellophane-wrapped, artificially colored, heat-treated, pressure-extruded pet foods are about the worst thing you can put into your dog's mouth. It is probably only because of your own good cooking and table scraps that this dog is doing so well. *These foods are a joke.* PLEASE stop feeding your dog these things and get her on some real nutrition. If your dog is middle aged or older, she may have some blood cell or organ system damage from this dietary intake for so long. I'd suggest a good physical examination by your veterinarian. This exam should include a blood work-up and organ function tests. Cats fed these soft moist-type diets, actually develop a disease of the red blood cells.

These foods, if used at all, should be limited to a car trip or hiking trek. In other words, the convenience of the product makes it appealing for those kinds of uses. On such an occasional, short-term basis it is not going to cause your dog any disease problems, except maybe a little pink vomit. So save the cellophane burgers for the hiking trip, and get your dog on a good premium diet.

CHAPTER 20

Obesity, Exercise and Specialty Diets

"How do I know if my dog is too fat? I weigh him every couple of weeks, but I don't think the readings are accurate."
"Why?"
"Well, I can't keep all four of his feet on the scale at one time, so I just add the front end readings to the back end readings!"

Veterinarians estimate that three in every five dogs are overweight. That makes obesity the number one nutritional disease in American pets. Obese pets are more common with owners who are middle aged or older and who are overweight themselves. It is easy to see why this is true. Their less active life style transmits to the dog. Additionally, many owners "love their pets to death" by feeding them far too many table scraps and treats.

Fat dogs are more prone to some rather serious medical problems. Obesity puts extra stress on the dog's heart, aggravates arthritis and other joint problems and increases the risk associated with surgery. Fat dogs have more digestive problems, liver disease, diabetes and even dermatitis than their more trim canine buddies.

Of major concern are senior pets who are also overweight. Their recovery from a medical or surgical problem will be much more difficult. Obesity in these pets can even complicate conditions to the point where the pet does not recover from normally recoverable problems.

More and more diseases seen in modern-day veterinary practice are being treated either primarily with nutrition or with nutrition as an adjunct to traditional medical therapy. Heart failure, kidney disease, liver disease, bladder stones, skeletal diseases and fractures, endocrine imbalances, obesity, allergies, skin disease, bloat, diabetes, diarrhea and even cancer are being completely or partially treated through nutrition.

Q: *How do I know if my dog is overweight? She's a seven-year-old Cocker Spaniel and weighs thirty-five pounds.*

A: Cockers are one of the breeds of dogs that have a tendency to be overweight. Beagles, Cockers, Collies, Dachshunds and Labradors have the highest tendency of all the breeds to be obese.

You know if your dog is overweight by a couple of methods. One is the 20% rule. If your dog is 20% over its ideal weight, then it's considered obese. Cockers should ideally weigh about twenty-five pounds. This means your dog is 40% over its ideal weight, so I'd definitely say your pooch is pudgy.

The second way to tell is the eyeball and fingertip method. You can just look at some dogs and tell. Dogs should not have an hourglass figure, but if they bulge at the abdomen, they're probably overweight.

The best method is to simply feel their ribs with your fingertips. You should be able to feel the ribs easily. If all you feel is fat, the dog is obese. If you can easily count the ribs by running your fingertips along the rib cage, your dog is probably just right.

Q: *If we need to reduce our dog's weight, how do we do that? She is much too convincing with those eyes at the dinner table!*

A: Start by not letting her beg at the dinner table. Put her in another room, in her kennel or on a down–stay in the corner of the room so she will not get one tidbit of people food. Also be careful about giving treats.

Each dog biscuit has fifty to one hundred calories. Try breaking the biscuit up into several pieces and only giving one piece at a time, or give the dog vegetables or fruit, such as carrots, apples or oranges.

Next you must remember that reducing weight involves two key elements: 1. *reducing the amount of calories* she takes in and 2. making her *burn more calories* than she takes in—*every day.*

Find a high-quality, low-calorie pet food that she will eat. I recommend Hill's Prescription Diet r/d, Alpo Lite or Cycle Lite. These foods are high in indigestible fiber so that the dog feels more full when she eats. The fat and carbohydrate content of these foods are low. This decreases the overall calories. Feed about 20% less than the amount that you are feeding now, and feed it in two to three feedings over the day.

Once her weight is down to a more reasonable level, you can switch to Hill's Prescription Diet w/d, which is moderately restricted in the amounts of fats and carbohydrates and has a higher than normal fiber level. This food is designed to be a long-term diet and will help keep the weight off once you've accomplished your goal. You could go back to regular diets, but you will have to restrict the amounts by 20% to 30%.

You will also need to exercise her daily. All dogs need regular exercise to maintain optimum health and to prevent health problems.

Q: *We have a seven-year-old Westie that is overweight. We've been told that feeding her hamburger and rice would reduce her weight. I've done this for some time and she doesn't seem to be losing weight. What else can I do?*

A: I don't know where you heard that hamburger meat and rice was a reducing diet—it is not. It is a bland diet used for dogs with sensitive digestive systems and for temporary treatment of gastritis. It is probably too high in carbohydrates to be a reducing diet. Also, you did not mention how *much* of it you were feeding. The best reducing diet in the world won't work if you feed too much of it.

I'd suggest a commercial reducing diet, either a prescription diet from your veterinary office, or one of the reduced-calorie foods from the pet store or grocery store. Feed about 10% to 20% less of it two to three times per day. Take the dog for twice-a-day walks and stick with this regime for at least sixty days. It will take that long for you to see improvement.

Q: *We have a six-year-old German Shepherd named Zena. She weighs 140 pounds. Our vet has her on a restricted diet and wants us to exercise her twice a day. What would be a good schedule for this exercise?*

A: I would definitely start slowly with this dog because of her age and weight. If you do not take it easy on her, you could end up with serious secondary orthopedic problems.

Begin by walking in the neighborhood at an easy pace for ten minutes, several times a day. Over a period of a month, increase the time of each walk and decrease the number of walks until you are taking two thirty-minute walks a day.

Once she has lost some weight and is healthier, you can begin to pick up the pace of your walks. Think of her as an overweight, sixty-five-year-old lady. Be careful and work up slowly.

Avoid any type of jumping or leaping activity, such as Frisbee catching. She could sustain joint injuries due to the stress of her added weight on her middle-aged joints. An easy game of fetch for ten to fifteen minutes twice a day would also be OK once she has lost that first twenty-five pounds.

Q: *Our veterinarian has our eleven-year-old Labrador, Samantha, on Hill's r/d to lose weight. I always listen to your show and have heard you say that exercise is also necessary for a dog to lose weight. Would it be OK for Samantha to swim?*

A: You're right, Samantha needs to exercise daily as well as being on a reduced-calorie diet. Swimming would be good exercise for Samantha, as long as you follow some precautions.

Remember that at eleven years of age, Samantha is a senior citizen, so take it slowly. Swimming is good overall exercise for the muscular system as well as the cardiovascular system and causes little to no stress on the joints. It is tiring, however, unless a dog is used to it, and many dogs will swim past the point of being tired just to please their owners. So, start slowly and pick only warm days for Sam to swim.

Start with five to ten minutes of swimming twice a day and increase slowly. Watch for signs that she may be getting too tired. Alternate swimming with some nice walks of twenty to thirty minutes at a slow to moderate pace.

Q: *We are trying to reduce our little Sally. She weighs forty pounds and should lose about ten pounds, but she hates all the reducing diets we've tried. Is there anything we can fix for her at home that will work? We'll even cook for her. We love her!*

A: You bet. Here's the recipe for a homemade canine reducing diet:

> ¼, pound very lean ground round or other lean beef
> ½ cup cottage cheese (uncreamed)
> 2 cups drained canned carrots
> 2 cups drained canned green beans
> 1 ½ teaspoons dicalcium phosphate or bone meal

Cook the beef in a skillet, stirring until lightly brown; pour off the fat and cool. Add remaining ingredients and a balanced vitamin/mineral supplement and mix well. Keep it covered and in the refrigerator. This will yield 1¾ pounds, which is the daily ration for a forty-pound dog. (A thirty-pound Sally should get about a pound in several feedings throughout the day.)

Be sure to exercise her daily and be very good about resisting the treats. You'll have to keep her on this diet and exercise schedule for several months before you'll reach your goal. Good luck.

Q: *Our eight-year-old female Beagle has had bladder stones before. We've had her operated on to remove them, but now she has them again. Our veterinarian sent us home with a dog food called s/d. How can food possibly cure a known physical problem like bladder stones?*

A: Very good question. It seems too good to be true, but it is. In the case of struvite-type bladder stones, we can actually feed dogs a special diet called Hill's Prescription Diet s/d and create a urine with an acid pH. This acidic urine helps dissolve the stones, and over time they may go away completely!

In addition to producing an acidic urine, this food has increased levels of salt to make the dog urinate more, thereby helping flushing the bladder. It is also restricted in certain minerals that would contribute to more stone development.

This is a perfect example of how nutrition can literally cure a physical medical problem. This special food has prevented surgery in thousands of dogs. It cannot be used in all cases of bladder stones, just those that are of the struvite makeup. It is not meant to be a long-term diet and is used, therefore, by prescription of your veterinarian only.

Q: *My vet has mentioned the possibility of my dog being allergic to its food. How would I tell if that's true?*

A: Food allergies are much more common than once thought, and true allergies to food are not easy to diagnose. Food allergy causes dermatitis, itching, vomiting and sometimes diarrhea. It is more common in dogs over two years of age, and it is less common than inhaled allergies.

In order to determine if food allergy is responsible for your dog's problems, you must completely avoid feeding your pet anything he has previously been eating. Since most commercial pet foods contain approximately the same ingredients, and most dogs with food allergies have been eating the same diet for some time, just changing the brand of food will not alter the symptoms.

Common ingredients that cause food allergies are beef, milk, chicken, eggs, fish, soy, wheat and corn. These are also common ingredients in many pet foods.

So to determine if your dog is allergic to food you must put the dog on a test diet for at least a month. For dogs, this test diet is four parts of cooked rice with one part lamb. The lamb can be boiled ground lamb, or you can use lamb baby food. Gradually mix small amounts of the test diet with your dog's current diet until your pet is accustomed to the new taste. Then withdraw the old diet.

It's best to feed slightly less than your pet normally eats in a day. If your pet refuses to eat the test diet for several days, or has an upset stomach, you can temporarily go back to the old diet. After the problem subsides, you can try the test diet again. Once the dog is on the test diet, it may take up to twelve weeks for symptoms to disappear. If the dog's symptoms improve, it is likely that the problem is, in fact, a food allergy.

It is not intended for you to feed this test diet to your dog indefinitely. Once her symptoms have subsided, you'll simply begin introducing food ingredients one at a time, one about every two weeks. One by one you add back beef, milk, chicken, cooked egg, etc., until you see the symptoms recur. Then you've found the culprit.

If you have already been feeding your dog a lamb-based dog

food for some time, then you cannot use lamb in your test diet. Rabbit, venison or goat may be substituted for the lamb. Nature's Recipe makes Lamb & Rice Diet, Venison & Rice diet and Rabbit & Rice diet. All are commercially prepared and balanced and so are good choices for long-term management of a food allergy once you've determined the offending ingredient.

Many companies have produced lamb and rice diets which they advertise as hypoallergenic. Actually, lamb is not necessarily hypoallergenic. Lamb can cause allergies if fed over a long period of time just like any other food ingredient. In fact, in Great Britain, where lamb is commonly fed, it is the major cause of food allergy in dogs and cats.

Q: *We are feeding our dog a test diet for food allergies. My husband came home this afternoon and gave him a dog biscuit. Is that going to be a problem?*

A: Yes, you basically have to start over. Even one bite of something else can cause problems, so you will need to start from the beginning again. Make sure that everyone in the house understands the test and cooperates with your efforts. If you have another pet, you either need to feed them separately, or feed them both the test diet only for the duration of the test.

Q: *Working with my vet for the past two months, we've decided my dog is allergic to beef or something. I know I can buy a chicken- or lamb-based food, but what about all the other things in the commercial food—are those going to be problems?*

A: Great question. You are right! Just because a label says lamb and rice does not mean the diet is hypoallergenic! Nature's Recipe pet foods led the way in producing lamb and rice diets. They have been quite successful in educating consumers and in solving thousands of food hypersensitivities. However, I know of several pet food companies who make lamb and rice foods and also include in the mix several offending ingredients. These foods are not hypoallergenic and are simply ploys to ride the lamb and rice popularity.

The fact that you say your pet's doctor has determined your dog to be allergic to beef "or something" tells me you've focused in on a dietary hypersensitivity but have no idea as to the cause—as is most often the case. Therefore, buying a chicken-based food would probably not help you at all. Chicken and chicken by-products are in many pet foods, even those that have beef as their main ingredient. You will have to use a homemade test diet or a commercially prepared test diet.

Q: *We took our dog in for a rash on its stomach a few weeks back. We've returned several times after ointments, shots and tests. Now the doctor has sent us home with rabbit and potato dog food! I have never heard of such a thing. Is this on the level?*

A: It's more than on the level, it's on the leading edge. You have a very up-to-date, knowledgeable doctor. Maybe the only thing he needs is better communications skills so you know exactly what's going on. Here's the deal:

Food allergies and hypersensitivities are more and more common in dogs these days. For years, our dogs have been fed grocery-store brands of foods which contain many offending ingredients. Dogs sensitive to these ingredients show up with everything from upset stomachs to hair loss to rashes.

Surprisingly, it can be caused by a food your pet has been eating for a number of years with no problem. Of course, that is the nature of all types of allergies. There has to be previous exposure to an offending substance for the animal to develop such a antigen–antibody reaction.

This is good news and bad news. The good news is that we know what it is. The bad news is, dogs who are truly allergic to pet food are hard to treat and feed. You must cook for them or find a commercial hypoallergenic diet that is balanced but does not contain the offending substance.

The veterinary profession is literally buzzing about the swell of food-allergy and hypersensitivity cases. Therefore, doctors who attend continuing education seminars are knowledgeable about this problem, its diagnosis and treatment.

The mere fact that your doctor knows about rabbit and potato diets and has gone in that direction after only a few weeks of medical work-up tells me he is on top of this science.

All food proteins are potentially antigenic because they are foreign to the animal's body and to its immune system. Because of this, they have the ability to cause an allergic response. The idea behind feeding your dog lamb and potato, or rabbit and potato or venison and potato or even duck and potato is to minimize the protein sources that have the highest potential of creating the allergic reaction.

While the offending antigens are generally proteins, they can be carbohydrates as well. Potato is a carbohydrate that has not been used in pet foods and therefore has little likelihood to be an offending agent.

Q: *We are trying to diagnose a food allergy in our Westie. As we were leaving the vet's office, he said, kind of in passing, that we should give Charlie only distilled water during the test. Is that important?*

A: Yes. Diagnosing a food allergy or dietary hypersensitivity is difficult, and even the water source should be changed so that you get a fair and accurate test. You could feed a test diet for two months and still see no change because the problem could be a mineral in the water, or even a reaction between your water and the food! So take his advice and be real good about a strict test for at least two months. I know it will be a hassle, but if you diagnose the problem, it will be worth it.

Q: *Dr. Jim, we have an eleven-year-old Irish Setter named Orwell. He is not doing very well. The doctor says he has congestive heart failure and that we can make the most progress by simply feeding him a limited-salt diet. He sold us h/d, but Orwell will not eat it. What can we do?*

A: Try your best to get Orwell liking the h/d. It is the best thing for him right now, and probably for the rest of his life. Salt or sodium will make his blood pressure high and add to the congestive heart problem. A diet of h/d is so highly restricted in sodium it can make an immediate difference in Orwell's blood pressure in a matter of days! Then it can literally extend his life by months to years!

A trick I use is to heat up the food and add a little garlic granules or powder or even real garlic. This will pique his appetite. DO NOT use garlic *salt!* If you have the canned form of h/d, simply cut the firm canned shape into little patties and fry them in a small bit of oil and the garlic. This works on most dogs. No hot dogs, no dog biscuits, no treats because most are loaded with salt!

PART VI

MEDICINE
AND DISEASE

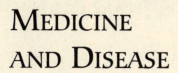

CHAPTER 21

Vaccinations and Preventive Medicine

*"We took our dog in for shots, but the doctor must have
thought he had a problem with his temper."*

"What do you mean?"

*"You know, his temper. But he's always been very nice.
We've never had any problems with him biting anybody!"*

"Did he try to bite the doctor?"

"No!"

*"What makes you think the vet feels he has a temperament
problem?"*

"Cause he said he was given a dis-temper shot!"

Vaccinations for dogs are very, very important. The mix of all the names and abbreviations for these vaccinations are often times confusing. Most dogs need a DHLP-P, CV and RV every year. Many others need BB, LD on top of that! It's no wonder there is confusion and that most pet owners just do what the doctor recommends.

Let's look at the most common questions owners have about these vaccinations and other preventive measures your veterinarian offers. After years of practice and countless thousands of clients' pets, I can honestly say these preventive measures are the most inexpensive insurance you can get.

Q: *We have hunting dogs, and our vet has recommended a new vaccine for Lyme disease. I thought that was mostly up north. Do we need it here in South Carolina?*

A: Absolutely! Lyme disease was once mostly concentrated in the northeastern United States, but now it has been identified in forty-seven states and can be transmitted by more than just the deer tick. There has been a sixteen-fold increase in the incidence of Lyme disease in people since 1982!

For hunting dogs, I would consider it an absolute must because of their unusually high exposure to ticks of all kinds. Lyme disease in dogs is considered to be six to ten times more common than in people. After a dog is bitten by an infected tick, he may develop arthritis, which can lead to rather severe pain and lameness. Infected dogs usually run a fever, lose their appetite and are quite depressed.

After the symptoms are observed, blood tests can confirm the presence of antibodies in the dog's blood. The test is called an IFA test. It is not 100% accurate, therefore many veterinarians will treat dogs that show some of these signs, if they are suspected of being in contact with ticks.

Treatment consists of broad-spectrum antibiotics and is almost 100% effective if the disease is caught early. If allowed to progress too long without treatment, Lyme disease can cause permanent arthritic changes in various joints as well as inflammations and infections of the heart and even the brain.

In your case, not only should you routinely brush your dogs and check them for ticks, you should also routinely treat them with tick-killing sprays and definitely vaccinate them against Lyme disease every year. Remember that tick season reaches a peak between May through October so be especially careful during those months.

Q: *If we live in the country and our dog does not get out of his fenced back yard, do we need the Lyme disease vaccination? How can we prevent Lyme disease?*

A: I would recommend vaccination for any outside dog that has exposure to ticks. To prevent Lyme disease, keep your back yard and the surrounding area mowed down short during the tick months (May through October). Spray your back yard with a Dursban-type insecticide every fourteen days to keep both flea and tick populations down. Check your dog over very well during daily grooming sessions and especially after walks or playing outside of your treated back-yard area. Make sure unwanted animals, including rats and mice, are not making tracks across the area and thereby seeding the area with ticks.

Q: *We live in Denver, and our vet has told us we only need to vaccinate for rabies every three years. I've heard you say it is necessary every year. Why is there a difference?*

A: In some states, where rabies is not a problem, the state has found it safe enough to decrease the rabies vaccination requirement to once every two or three years. Most states, like Texas, where I have practiced for many years, have a once-a-year policy, so that is usually what I say. However, you and your veterinarian are right. Colorado requires rabies vaccinations every three years, and you can rely on your veterinarian to remind you when it's due again.

Q: *We get our dog's rabies vaccination at a "shot clinic" held in a mall parking lot during the summer. I know my vet kind of frowns when I tell him that, but the shots are so much cheaper that way. What's your opinion?*

A: Shot clinics are certainly helpful for people who cannot afford normal veterinary care and preventive vaccinations. If you have many pets and get all their yearly shots at the veterinary office, it may run into hundreds of dollars. At a shot clinic, it may be only twenty dollars per pet. That does mount up to sizable savings! Here's my opinion on this. If you need to save money because of budget or numbers of pets, the shot clinics are fine for actually putting the vaccine in the right spot. However there is one very important sticking point!

When you get your pet vaccinated at a regular veterinary hospital, it's sort of like paying dues to join a little club. As a club member, you can call the doctor anytime, night or day, and ask a question which doesn't cost you anything. You can always know that when you walk in the clinic, the staff will know you and your pet and have kept accurate records on your pet's medical history. At the veterinary clinic, you don't have to wait for hours in the hot sun, and it's much less stressful for you and your pet.

Shot clinics are here today and gone tomorrow. They usually don't keep records on your pet's history and are definitely not around at night, when your pet has a reaction to the vaccine, or a few months from now, when he has an upset stomach at 3 AM. That's when it's valuable to have a relationship with a doctor you can call!

Q: *What shots are really necessary? It seems like every time we go into the clinic, we are told something new.*

A: There is no set answer to this question. Yearly preventive vaccination schedules vary from state to state and in different parts of the country. But generally, this is the routine.

Every year a mature dog (over puppyhood) should receive a distemper, hepatitis and parainfluenza vaccination. Many times the DHP includes an L for leptospirosis vaccination. This is omitted by some veterinarians who know your dog does not have exposure to the *Leptospira* organism. Some doctors have reported inflammatory reactions due to this portion of the vaccine and omit it where it is not absolutely necessary.

Since the early 1980s we have been giving parvovirus vaccinations every year as well. In fact, at first many doctors gave the parvovirus vaccination every six months because the vaccine was new and the disease was so devastating. However, the vaccine is now well proven and yearly is all that is necessary. Rabies is required to be given yearly in most states, but only every two to three years in a few. That's the basics.

The need for other vaccinations such as those for Lyme disease, kennel cough and coronavirus must be evaluated according to each individual dog's history, exposure and environment.

Q: *We are going to put our dog in the kennel next week and were told he will need to have the kennel cough vaccination. I thought that was a part of what we give Oscar every year. I've looked on his slip, and it says parainfluenza—isn't that it?*

A: No, parainfluenza is a different upper respiratory infection for which we vaccinate. Most people do not routinely give kennel cough vaccine unless the dog will have increased exposure to other dogs due to kenneling, traveling or showing. In these cases, your dog will need the vaccine.

By the way, this vaccine is given via nose drops and not by injection, so your dog won't have to endure another needle stick! Nose drops are found to be more effective in getting quick immunity because the virus gains entry through the nose.

I'd like to see you have a good two weeks after the vaccination before you kennel your dog. It sometimes takes that long for a good immunity to build. It is silly for some kennels to vaccinate incoming dogs and then discharge them a few days later, because the vaccine has not had time to become effective. When it does, the dog is already home. Plan in advance when kenneling and get the kennel cough vaccine at least a few weeks before a stay.

Q: *Our dog died of parvo, but he had been vaccinated. Why did this happen and what can we do to prevent this when we get a new dog? We were just devastated!*

A: I am very sorry to hear this. It is never easy to lose a great dog, but it is particularly hard when the death is sudden and unexpected, especially when the cause was a supposedly preventable disease.

Vaccines are tested and retested by their manufacturers. They are chemicals that ask the dog to make antibodies to a particular disease. When that occurs, there is a level of protection. But no vaccine is 100% effective. A dog may have a compromised immune system, it may be unusually stressed at the time of exposure or the exposure itself may be especially strong with a so-called "hot" virus.

If the infection overcomes the dog's immunity, even though it was vaccinated, it will get the disease nonetheless. Parvovirus is such a severe disease that it can kill a very strong dog in a matter of hours.

I can say that even though this has happened to you, it is not normal. Most vaccinated dogs, once challenged with virus, fend off the challenge quite well. Therefore, when you get a new dog, be sure to get all the recommended vaccinations on schedule, and I hope you'll never have to go through this again.

Q: *Our puppy got his DHLP and parvo vaccinations when he was eight weeks old, but we missed his last two scheduled booster shots because of traveling. He is now four months old. What do we need to do?*

A: I'd suggest simply starting over again with the vaccination series. The artificial immunity he received from the first vaccination is now gone, and he is totally susceptible to infection by a number of diseases. Get him into the clinic Monday morning; see if your veterinarian concurs with me on this. It will simply mean a giving him a DHLP/parvo vaccine now, a booster in three weeks and again in another three weeks. You may also go ahead and get the rabies vaccination now, as he is now old enough for that.

Q: *Our dog, Tommy, had a pretty bad reaction to his shots last year. We had to take him back to the vet, who had to treat him for the reaction. It's time for his shots again, and we are afraid of another reaction. What can be done?*

A: Be sure to remind the doctor that Tommy had this reaction. He may want to premedicate with antihistamines before giving the vaccinations this year. The doctor may also want to use a vaccine made by a different manufacturer. He'll want to keep Tommy at the clinic for a few hours to be sure there is no reaction. I've seen cases like this where there have been no other reactions to future shots. I've also had cases that could not be vaccinated again because the reactions were so severe.

Q: *I live alone with my little dog Princess. She's twelve now. We live on the sixteenth floor of a high-rise building, and she's just as healthy as she can be. Do you feel like I could stop giving those yearly shots? She's never exposed to another dog.*

A: In theory, yes, you could stop. She has good immunity from receiving the shots for twelve years, is very healthy and you say she is never exposed to other dogs. But what about the times when you walk her for elimination? What about the times when you have to take her to a kennel or to an animal clinic for illness. At these times she will be exposed to viruses and bacteria that can cause disease. As she gets older, her immune system weakens. This, plus her lack of artificial immunity due to stopping the vaccinations, could catch up with her, and a case of parvo would be deadly to her.

It is very inexpensive insurance, and I highly recommend the yearly vaccinations for all pets. It is also a time when the doctor can give her a very valuable physical examination to pick up on any early senior-type problems.

CHAPTER 22

Orthopedic Problems

"Doc, my dog must be in pain. Every time he walks something clicks. It's loud enough to hear it clear across the room. He doesn't act like it hurts, but it seems like it would. What is that?"

"It's probably a meniscal click from a knee injury."

"No Doc, it's not small at all. Like I told ya, it's loud!"

"No, not minuscule, meniscal. The meniscus is a cartilage in the knee. A torn meniscal cartilage will cause a clicking noise and that may be what you are hearing."

"You're kidding!"

The dog's skeleton is very interesting. Unlike humans, they walk on all four appendages and, therefore, carry less weight on any given leg. I've seen dogs with very painful rear legs walk on their front legs alone. Dogs with severe pain or arthritis in one rear leg will skip (run/walk) and you may never know they are in pain.

Injuries to bones, arthritis or pain occurring in the front legs are more severe because dogs carry 65% of their body weight on the front legs. That is why if an amputation of a leg is required, the prognosis is much better if it is a back leg.

Orthopedic conditions are many times genetically induced, such as hip dysplasia. This condition can be very severe and may even necessitate a dog be put to sleep. Nutrition plays a role in skeletal health and development and even in the management of certain orthopedic disorders.

Q: Our seven-year-old German Shepherd, Athena, has hip dysplasia. We have a friend who is a horse veterinarian. He has told us that there is a horse drug that is good for relieving the pain. Do you know anything about this?

A: Yes, he is probably talking about Adequan. It is a drug used in equine medicine for various orthopedic problems in show horses and race horses. It increases the lubrication effects of the joint fluid in inflamed arthritic joints and that way makes them less painful. Recently, some small animal veterinarians have had great success using it in canine hip dysplasia.

I have used it on several cases, and I can attest to the fact that in mild to moderate cases of hip dysplasia, there was some improvement. In cases that have been going on for some time and have secondary bony changes due the arthritis, the drug will probably not do much to alleviate the pain.

It is expensive and requires several intramuscular injections at first, followed by as-needed maintenance doses. If your dog is in the mild-to-moderate category, I would recommend you try Adequan. Your friend can call the manufacturer and get some help in calculating doses and case histories.

Q: *We have a four-month-old, female Rottweiler that we want to show. She is a wonderful dog but has begun limping on her right front leg. Sometimes it's worse than others. When she's excited and has her attention on something, she acts normal, but when she is relaxed she is definitely lame. What do you think we should do?*

A: I think you should get her to your veterinary hospital and have her examined and X-rayed for a condition known as OCD, or osteochondritis dessicans.

This is a condition seen in fast-growing, adolescent, large-breed dogs (and boys too!). It is caused by the cartilage over the growth plate of the shoulder bone not getting a good blood supply. This can be caused either by a trauma (like jumping) or simply by the growth of the bone outpacing the blood supply. In either case, the cartilage is starved for nutrition and develops a deficit area. Usually this area loosens and a cartilage flap occurs. This means that the joint no longer has a continuous covering of smooth protective cartilage. Movement of the joint then causes pain.

A physical exam and a careful set of X rays will diagnose the problem. It is cured with a surgical procedure that removes the cartilage flap and/or scrapes the deficit area to cause it to heal. The dog is then put in a sling for a few weeks until the healing takes place. After that, the dog is usually quite normal.

Q: *Our veterinarian wants to refer us to a specialist for a total hip replacement because our dog's hip dysplasia is so bad. Our whole family loves Gretchen very much, and we'd do just about anything for her. It will cost about $2,000 per hip. Do you think we should do that?*

A: That depends on your willingness and ability to spend $4,000 on your dog. I know if my dog were in severe pain and that amount of money was the only thing that would correct the problem, I'd find a way to do it. Most hospitals that do very expensive procedures like this, will make arrangements for you to pay it out.

There is the total hip replacement is a major surgery. It requires very special knowledge, special equipment, support staff and the prosthesis (artificial joint) itself. The old hip is literally taken out and replaced with a plastic socket and a metal ball. The dog is totally free from the pain of hip arthritis after surgery, because the arthritic joint is gone.

There is some pain after the surgery due to the incisions through the muscles and movement of muscle tissue in order to get access to the joint. After an initial healing period, these dogs do quite well. By the way, both hips will not be done at the same time. There will probably need to be at least two months between procedures.

My best recommendation is for you to have a family meeting and discuss the expense and the aftercare. Then talk to the specialist and ask all your questions. You will be impressed with the professionalism of such a specialist and with the speed in which Gretchen recovers. Good luck.

Q: *Our dog, Maggie, has arthritis of the lower spine from an old injury. She is now going through allergic skin testing because we think she is allergic to something in the air. We cannot give her steroids because that will mess up the skin test. What kind of pain relievers can we give her?*

A: There are many nonsteroid, anti-inflammatory medications you can use. I would try butazolidin, many times simply called bute. If the pain is not too severe, plain aspirin will help. Ask your veterinarian the proper dosage for the weight of your dog. If she vomits after your give her an aspirin, then you know that the aspirin is upsetting her stomach. In that case you'll need to use something else. Tylenol can be used in dogs (but not in cats). It will not upset your dog's stomach and works as well as, if not better than, aspirin.

I never discount the use of good physical therapy. Hot packs are pain relieving and soothing. I suggest you simply hold her at night when you watch TV and apply hot towels to her back about every fifteen minutes.

Beyond this, you would have to go to a controlled substance, and your veterinarian may prescribe that for her.

Q: *Our nine-year-old Dachshund screams out in pain and stiffens her neck when we try to pick her up. This has been going on for about a month. What is that?*

A: Why have you waited a month on something so serious? I dare say if that were your child, you wouldn't have. This dog probably has a slipped cervical disc and needs immediate treatment. The stiffness in the neck is caused by her guarding her neck movement because any movement causes severe pain!

A doctor can X-ray her neck and tell immediately how many of these discs are affected and how severely. It may require surgery, depending on reactions to neurological exam and response to drugs. Some of these cases simply need steroid anti-inflammatory drugs of a regulated amount for the rest of the dog's life.

Please get her to a doctor as soon as you can. I, myself, had a dog with this condition and know the pain can be quite severe.

Q: *Our dog has broken a rear leg bone and we don't have the money to fix it. Will it heal OK on its own?"*

A: No it won't, but I have seen cases of neglected dogs with fractures heal without surgery or even a splint. Mother nature does wonderful things, but please understand, if you decide not to surgically correct this problem, that the dog will be in constant pain for many months. Any movement of the leg will break down any healing that has taken place, and the process will have to start all over again. She will never walk the same again because of misalignment and shortening of that leg. There may be a large knot form at the healing site. The really down side is that the leg simply may not heal on its own. I have seen dogs come into my clinic with a very chronic broken leg that has never healed. They simply learn they cannot walk on that leg and the pain becomes tolerable with time.

My suggestion would be to scrape together whatever money you can and have the doctor simply splint the leg instead of doing the surgery. This way you have the best chance of getting some acceptable result without undergoing the cost of surgery.

CHAPTER 23

Cancer, Blood Diseases and Immunology

"We took our German Shepherd female in to the vet with a nose bleed, but we are confused."

"What are you confused about?"

"Well, my wife thought it was some sort of nose problem, but the vet took a blood test for some kind of bladder leaking problem."

"Wait a minute—she's a German Shepherd and has a nose bleed and he took a blood sample for a bladder 'leaking' problem?"

"Right!"

"Are you sure the doctor didn't say Ehrlichia?"

"That's it! Her leakia. He said he was checking for her leakiosis!"

"I can understand why you are confused. The term is ehrlichiosis (er-leek-ki-osis). Ehrlichia is a blood parasite that causes dogs to bleed, and one of the first signs is a nose bleed."

"Oh my gosh!"

Some of the saddest calls I've answered on talk radio have to do with wonderful lifetime companion pets that have developed cancer, a serious blood-borne disease or a compromised immune system. These are often times terminal illnesses, and it's hard to hear the despair and heartbreak in people's voices when we talk about these things. I personally have lost three dogs to cancer and immune system failure. It's tough because there is very little that can be done.

For many reasons, some known, some unknown, animals are far more likely to succumb to cancer than people. They are exposed to many chemicals in their environment and the food they eat. They are often exposed more to the sun, and we are just beginning to understand some of the complexities of their immune systems.

Whatever the cause, cancer can take a pet's life just as quickly, or as painfully slowly, as it does in people. Happily, we have chemotherapy, radiation and various surgical procedures that can slow or stop the spread of this deadly invader. We are also fortunate to have the option of a painless death when we find we cannot slow the progression of the cancer.

Q: *Our fourteen-year-old Bassett Hound, Molly, has been diagnosed with lung cancer. She doesn't smoke, but we both do. Do you think that caused it?*

A: I doubt it. Even though the hazards of secondhand smoke are well documented, there are many other causes for the beginning of cancer. Many dogs develop lung cancer and have *never* been around people who smoke. So please don't blame yourself!

During her treatment, however, you and your husband may want to smoke outside so it doesn't irritate those delicate tissues.

If the cancer is small and well defined, or even encapsulated within the lung tissue, your veterinary surgeon can most likely go in and remove most of the affected tissue. Molly will have to be put on many drugs after the operation, maybe even chemotherapy drugs. This depends on what the doctor finds during the surgery.

The outlook for Molly depends on her state of health, how far the cancer has spread and how much of the tumor is removed at the time of surgery. This is no time for inexperience. Be sure your veterinarian and the hospital are experienced in open chest surgery and that they have done these types of cases before. If not, don't be shy about asking for a referral to a veterinary medical center or a veterinary teaching hospital.

Q: *Our fifteen-year-old Boxer has been slowly losing weight and has not been himself for months, maybe even a year. Now he has stopped eating and seems to be wasting away. Our vet has checked him for many things but so far has not come up with an answer. Every time he treats him, he seems to get a little better, but only for a short while. What can we do?*

A: I would immediately have the dog thoroughly checked for a number of things. However, because of the breed and age, I would suspect some form of cancer.

Cancer is one of the more serious causes for pets to stop eating. In fact, in many dogs, anorexia (loss of appetite) is the primary complaint and may be seen without any other signs. For some strange reason, cancer in animals produces chemicals that inhibit the animal's feeding regulators. Also, cancer patients have altered taste sensations that will decrease their appetite.

Boxers have more than their share of cancer problems. It is rare indeed to find a Boxer as old as yours. You have obviously taken very good care of your Boxer because they normally die before their tenth birthday.

Please get him checked for cancer. A series of radiographs of the chest and abdomen and a few more specific blood tests should do the trick. Be advised, however, that sometimes cancer can be elusive and difficult, if not impossible, to diagnose before it's too late.

Q: *We just came back from the veterinary hospital with our Siberian Husky named Master. Our vet has diagnosed him with Rocky Mountain Spotted Fever. We live in Atlanta. That's nowhere near the Rocky Mountains! Does this guy know what he's talking about?*

A: OK, just think of it as Atlanta spotted fever. The true Rocky Mountain Spotted Fever, or RMSF, is caused by a rickettsial infection passed along by a tick. Oddly enough it is seen most often in the southeastern United States and is many times more severe in Master's breed of dog, the Siberian Husky.

Dogs affected by this blood-borne parasite can hide the signs of illness, while others can develop quite a severe syndrome with symptoms being more severe in the spring up to early fall. In general, the illness will last only two weeks or less.

These dogs usually have a fever, may stop eating and many times are just depressed. However, the history of these dogs always includes some exposure to ticks. As this blood parasite sometimes causes rather extensive damage to delicate tissues, you may see everything from cough and nasal discharge all the way to blood in the urine, dizziness and seizures.

Some dogs die from this disease, usually as a result of renal failure or heart attacks.

I assume your doctor put Master on some antibiotics, because that is the treatment of choice. With Siberian Huskies being more prone to severe forms of RMSF, your doctor should be vigorous in his treatment. Because this is a blood parasite, your normal everyday antibiotics won't work. You will need oral tetracyclines or chloramphenicol given for at least two weeks. Dogs that recover from a bout with this disease are immune for about a year.

The only way to prevent RMSF is to totally avoid tick-infested areas. Sometimes that is not possible because it could be your own back yard, so be sure you put into place a regular tick-control program (see Chapter 16). Never remove a tick from your dog with your hands. Use tweezers and wash your hands completely after you are through.

Q: *Our dog has been diagnosed with ehrlichiosis. The vet did explain that it is a blood disease, but I'm afraid beyond that we are pretty much in the dark. Can you tell us if our dog is going to be all right?*

A: Canine ehrlichiosis is caused by a tick-transmitted blood parasite called *Ehrlichia canis*. It is most frequently seen in dogs from the southern states. Signs of this disease are usually quite subtle and range from loss of appetite and transient fever to nose bleed and even neurological signs. If allowed to go untreated for some time, the disease is often fatal.

The organism apparently shuts down the production of blood-clotting cells, and the dogs develop a severe anemia and other blood chemistry abnormalities. The best treatment is oral tetracycline three times a day for at least two weeks. There are other antibiotics that can be used if the dog is sensitive to tetracycline. Dogs in severe status will need blood transfusions and IV therapy, but the outlook is not good. Many of these dogs die from overwhelming infections.

You can prevent this disease with very good tick control, especially dipping your dogs regularly. Again, like I tell everybody, don't remove ticks with your hands, use tweezers and wash your hands thoroughly when you are done.

Q: *Our dog, Baylor, went fishing with us last week here in Weenatche, Washington. We think he must have a upset stomach from eating some of the salmon we caught. He is running a fever, is lethargic and won't eat. Can we give him some Pepto Bismol?*

A: I wouldn't. I would get him to a veterinary hospital and have him checked for salmon poisoning disease. I used to practice in the northwestern U.S. and had never heard of this until I saw a case just like yours that I couldn't diagnose. The established veterinarian I practiced with guided me to a diagnosis of salmon poisoning.

It is a potentially fatal, rickettsial disease of both wild and domesticated dogs. It is limited to just your part of the country. The organism gets into a parasite found in snails, fish and birds. The animal is required for the parasite to complete its life cycle. When Baylor ate the salmon, he probably got some of the fish parasites which have the rickettsial organism in them.

This is a serious disease, and I want you to get to the hospital today. If your clinic is closed already, then get to an emergency clinic. They will know what to do. Failure to diagnose and treat this disease can put Baylor at risk of dying within a few days. I think you have caught it early and you have time for treatment, so get going!

Remember, if you live in the Northwest, do not let your dogs eat raw fish, only cooked fish or fish that has been frozen for at least twenty-four hours.

Q: *We have a six-year-old Boxer named Kylie. He is pretty healthy, however he has been developing small bumps over his back and one on his chest. He even has one over his elbow. What are those?*

A: The lump over his elbow is probably a hygroma. This is a fluid-filled sac that develops over a bony prominence like the elbow from constant irritation and trauma. These hygromas will continue to grow slowly larger until the trauma stops. I'd suggest having the veterinarian look at this spot. The correction will depend on how fluid-filled it is and how big it is. Surgery can be done to literally remove the area, *but* you must make a commitment to give the dog only soft areas to lay down on. Orthopedic dog beds are now a must for this dog, everywhere he sleeps, inside or out!

As for the other lumps, they are probably lipomas. These are tumors of fat cell origin and are usually not malignant. They will grow very slowly in older dogs of various breeds but especially in the Boxer. You can have them removed and get a pretty good short-term correction, but the likelihood is that more will grow. I usually remove them if they are in a part of the body where they are causing some functional problem or if they are getting very large. However, if they are mild to moderate in size, (pea to walnut size) I'd leave them alone. Lipomas are benign and will not cause secondary movement to the lungs or liver as some malignant tumors will.

Q: *Our female Poodle, Buttons, has developed several hard lumps in her breasts. I know how important it is for women to check themselves for breast cancer, and I was pretty surprised today to find these lumps have grown and are now hot. Is this cancer, and what can be done?*

A: It probably is cancer and you need to get her in to your veterinarian first thing Monday morning for evaluation. Mammary tumors are found more often in dogs than any other mammal. They make up almost one-half of all dog cancer problems. Many times they are malignant and can easily move to the lungs and become life-threatening. That's the bad news. The good news is that most are treatable if caught in time.

You see, estrogen, secreted by the ovaries, plays an important role in the development of mammary tumors. If the ovaries are gone early in life, estrogen is not around to stimulate these tumors later in life. Therefore, dogs spayed before their first heat cycle are many, many times less likely to develop breast cancer than their nonspayed friends. So here is a cancer prevention tip for everyone listening—spay your female dogs at five to six months of age and you won't have to worry about this problem.

As for Buttons, there is still more good news. If you have caught this early and there is no movement to the lungs or liver, surgical removal of the breasts can solve the problem. A radical mastectomy can not only remove the tumors, but also hopefully prevent spread of more cancer cells.

The surgeon needs to be experienced and thorough, as this is a major surgical procedure. However, it is a surgery that has an excellent result if done properly and if the cancer is caught early. I would send in a sample of the tumor after surgery to determine what type is was so you can better keep an eye on future lumps. About 50% of all malignant tumors removed from dogs' breasts show up somewhere else in the dog's body later in life.

The most common malignant types of breast cancer are carcinomas and mixed cell origin mammary tumors, both highly malignant. The benign tumors are adenomas and fibroadenomas. Good luck.

Anybody who has a female dog that is not spayed, and is more than about three years of age, should be examining her breasts every month as a part of a good monthly physical examination. You may be able to pick up on these lumps forming very early when they would be very inexpensive to treat.

Q: *Our eight-month-old Great Dane pup has been treated for demodectic mange and ear infections for about two months. The vet has now told us that she feels his immune system may not be functioning right. Have you ever heard of this and what can be done?*

A: The immune system is a complex group of cells and biochemicals that fight off offending substances. It is constantly on alert to fight off viruses, bacteria, protozoa, fungi and any other organism that tries to infiltrate the body. It, like other organ systems, has to mature and become good at what it does. In the very young animal, it is immature and weak at fighting off infections. Therefore we give the young animal artificial immunity via vaccines and mother's milk, until it can fight on its own.

In some cases, the immune system either matures late or functions at a decreased level of efficiency. These animals have more infectious diseases early in their life until they get up to speed.

224 / Medicine and Disease

Animals that have a depressed immune system have more mange, coughs, bouts of diarrhea and more general problems with growing up strong and vital. If the system kicks in at some point, the animal will overcome these things and move on with life. If it does not, it will continue to do poorly and may even succumb to a serious challenge of bacteria or virus.

The immune system has come into more public awareness lately because of AIDS. Both dogs and cats have AIDS-like diseases which compromise the immune system in otherwise healthy animals and make them susceptible to various ailments and diseases, even death.

My guess is that your pup is still working on his immune system and is just a little late in getting it kicked into gear. It is not uncommon at all to see these dogs develop demodectic mange, as we feel this mite is a normal inhabitant of the skin and only causes disease when it can overwhelm the immune system. Ear infections, coughs, digestive upsets can all be seen in dogs that have yet to develop a mature immune system.

If your dog's doctor feels the problem is severe enough, there are immune-system stimulants that can be given. Although usually reserved for cases that are recovering from serious debilitating disease, these drugs may help your dog. You should ask.

Q: *The vet thinks that our little Miniature Schnauzer that we have had for eight years has lupus. We couldn't believe it. What is our hope of getting a cure?*

A: Lupus in dogs is very similar to the lupus we see in humans. It is essentially an immune system gone astray that begins producing antibodies that turn against the immune system. The immune system actually begins attacking itself! It is very strange.

Although we have developed medications that can ease the symptoms of lupus, I'm afraid we are a long way from knowing what exactly causes this reaction and therefore how to treat it.

Current treatment involves the use of drugs that suppress the immune system, because in this disease the immune system is hyperreactive and out of control. Glucocorticoids are used in an initial high dose, tapered down to a maintenance dosage that will alleviate the symptoms. There is another classification of drugs that will do this even more potently. The alkylating agents, like cytoxin and leukeran are the most potent immunosuppressive drugs known. They can be used successfully if your doctor properly monitors the dog's white-blood-cell levels.

I can tell you from experience that the outlook is generally good. Glucocorticoid steroids alone can successfully induce remission in about 60% of cases. So you may never have to go to the more toxic alkylating agents. However, about 5% of the cases of lupus in dogs are very difficult to treat and a satisfactory result from medication may not be seen.

CHAPTER 24

Heart, Stomach and Intestinal Problems

"We've just been told our dog has a PDA. *It's some kind of serious heart disease and we are* MAD *about it. My wife wants to know* WHY *a $500 Poodle puppy has a* PDA!*"*

"Well sir, Poodles are one of the breeds of dogs that has a tendency toward genetic or congenital heart disease. A PDA *is a patent ductus arteriosis or an open vessel from the aorta to the pulmonary artery. It is not that uncommon in Poodles, Collies, Pomeranians, German Shepherds and Shelties."*

"Will she recover?"

"Probably not without surgery."

"Surgery! Forget it, we'll take her back and exchange her for a good one."

Heart disease in dogs can be broken down into two main categories: congenital and acquired. Congenital means the dog was born with the problem. These are usually hereditary defects in the anatomical structure of the heart that lead to heart failure and other secondary medical problems as time goes on. Acquired, as the name implies, is heart disease that happens during the course of the dog's life and is more gradual and subtle until failure or decompensation takes place.

As you can see by our caller here, many people are stunned to find out that an expensive purebred dog would have such a problem. However, it is these popular and often expensive breeds that have the genetic inbreeding that amplifies genetic problem traits.

Like canine vaccinations, congenital heart disease is identified by acronyms like PDA for patent ductus arteriosis, PS for pulmonic stenosis, SAS for subaortic stenosis, VSD for ventricular septal defect, ASD for atrial septal defect and so on. These problems are seen in specific lines and specific breeds of dogs.

If you buy a purebred puppy, you should question the breeder about the pup's lines and ask if any of the parents or litter mates have any heart disease. Many of these problems can be surgically corrected. Even though we veterinarians recommend that these animals be spayed or neutered, because they are usually purebred and expensive breeds, the owners often want the dogs to go on and have other litters. This is a major reason why more litters of affected dogs keep showing up.

Dogs are omnivores. That means they can eat meat or plant materials and do fine, as compared to cats, who are carnivores and need meat to survive. It is a testimony to the toughness of the canine stomach and intestines that they do so well with the awful array of things people feed their dogs.

Many old wives' tales have been passed down through the years about treatments for dogs' ailments. Today, we are much more sophisticated in our approach to disease. Veterinarians use cyto-protective drugs, and histamine receptor antagonists to treat ulcers. They use advanced surgical procedures to correct physical problems and can even biopsy the stomach and intestines for his-tiopathic study through endoscopes, without the dog ever going under a scalpel.

Add to this the improvements in parasite drugs, as well the improvements in dog food and you can see that our dogs today enjoy better gastrointestinal health.

Q: *We took our Keeshond puppy in for his first visit to the vet this morning and were shocked when the doctor told us he had a heart murmur. He said it was a genetic heart problem and he may not make it. We love the little guy very much and want to do what we can. What do you recommend?*

A: Bless your heart. You have already fallen in love with a great lit-tle pup and he has an abnormal heart. That does not necessarily hand him the death sentence. Many congenital heart problems can be corrected surgically allowing the dog to live out a com-pletely normal life.

I would take the pup back to the hospital for a detailed work-up. Once you have an accurate diagnosis of what exactly the defect is, then and only then can you decide if you can practically correct the problem and offer the little guy a normal life.

If it is a PDA, which is the most common form of congenital heart disease, that can be corrected with open-chest surgery. I've done a few of these with excellent results. However, be sure the doctor and hospital have the capabilities and expertise to perform such a delicate surgery.

I do fear, however, that your puppy may have a condition known as a tetralogy of Fallot. This is seen more often in Keeshonds and English Bulldogs. Tetralogy of Fallot is a quadruple whammy of congenital defects, as these dogs have four of them! To correct this condition, you would need the incredible expertise of a veterinary medical teaching hospital at one of the major universities.

I hope is it one of the more easily handled defects and you can correct it. If so be sure to have your pup spayed or neutered and let him live a normal, happy life. Good luck.

Q: *Our German Shepherd was diagnosed with a heart problem when he was just a puppy. It was called subaortic stenosis. He has done pretty well for about fourteen months, and we thought it was not going to be a problem. Lately, however, he has developed a cough and just won't play very long. We are afraid he is losing it. What do we do?*

A: It is not uncommon for dogs with congenital heart disease to compensate for some time. In fact, many dogs, even people, have small defects with a murmur and live perfectly normal lives. However, when the demands of the body become more than what the defective heart can supply, decompensation occurs.

Slowly the heart cannot pump enough blood to supply the body, especially during activity, through the narrowed area just below the aortic valve. This causes a blood pressure backup into the right side of the heart, then into the lungs. This back pressure into the lungs is what causes the cough and is a sign the disease is going into a decompensating phase.

It is time for you and your veterinarian to talk seriously about surgery. This is one of the congenital diseases that can be cured with good surgical procedure. Either your pet's doctor or a special surgeon can do the procedure. If you live anywhere near a veterinary medical teaching hospital at a university, the surgeons there would be excellent sources for the surgical expertise you need.

The surgery involves going into the high pressure aorta with special forceps, passing through the aortic valve and into the narrowed, or stenotic, area. The surgeon then widens the area as well as he can so that the narrowed passageway is no longer restricting normal smooth blood flow through that major outflow tract.

Postoperative care is not terribly difficult. These dogs do well after surgery, and I'd recommend you look into having it done within a few weeks.

Q: *Our nine-year-old Fox Terrier has a heart problem for which our vet has given him digitalis and lasix. He has been on these drugs for a month and seems to be making only slight improvement. What else can we do?*

A: I am amazed at how many calls like this I get, where a dog has congestive heart failure and the doctor does not recommend the two most effective means of relieving the symptoms: low-salt diet and after-loading drugs.

When I was in veterinary school in the seventies, congestive heart disease was treated with digitalis, to increase the strength of the heart's contractions, and lasix, to help the dog get rid of much of the accumulated fluids due to the poor circulation. Just coming on the forefront was the vast improvement made in these cases with low-sodium diets. Hill's Prescription Diet h/d was the only salt-restricted diet available and was a real boon to the treatment of these cases.

Years later I read various technical articles where dogs put on low-salt diets alone did almost as well as those on digitalis and lasix! So merely reducing the sodium intake of the dog, thereby reducing blood pressure, helps dramatically in these cases.

A few years later, veterinarians began using vasodilator drugs to help these cases. These are drugs that decrease the arteriolar and venous blood pressure. Like low sodium in the diet, a decrease in blood pressure can really help these cases. Caprotil and hydralazine are the most commonly used drugs.

Now in the nineties, I continue to be amazed when I hear a veterinarian is still using only the treatments we were taught twenty years ago. A low-salt diet and vasodilators, either alone or in conjunction with digitalis and lasix, are the treatment of choice. Ask your veterinarian about these. If he turns a deaf ear to the suggestion, get out your yellow pages and find a new doctor!

Q: *I've heard you talk about low-salt diets for dogs with heart disease. I had a heart attack myself last fall, and my little Railey also has heart problems. Because I feed him what I eat and I'm on a low-salt diet, I guess what I feed Railey is OK, right?*

A: Wrong! It is true both of you need to be on a low-sodium diet, but it is not true that Railey is "OK" with you feeding him your food. No doubt he is getting less salt than before, however my guess is that his diet is not properly balanced for his long-term health. Often when people feed dogs people food, they give leftover pieces that contain too much fat, salt and a completely unbalanced mix of vitamins and minerals. Railey needs good nutrition besides a restricted sodium intake.

Take my advice! Get Railey one of the special low-salt diets for dogs, and make him eat it. (You will need to get this special prescription dog food through your veterinarian.) You can use garlic powder (not garlic *salt*) and fry the food in a small bit of oil to make it more appealing to him. After all, he is used to eating your good cooking for years. He will live longer with less complications if you will give him special dog food made for canine heart patients!

Q: *Our male Boxer, Sarge, has DCM. Our veterinarian spent a great deal of time with us and did a pretty good job of explaining what it is, but we want more explanation from you. She also used some kind of "idiot" word. We didn't know whether to be offended or if we just misunderstood. Can you fill in the blanks?*

A: Yes. First of all, the "idiot" word is "idiopathic." It means that we, the doctors, not you, the clients, are the idiots. It simply means we don't know the cause of a particular disease. Rather than say, disease of unknown origin, we say "idiopathic disease." Isn't medicine great!

Now, on to DCM. Your veterinarian must be really up to speed on her continuing education. DCM stands for dilated cardiomyopathy. A cardiomyopathy is a problem with the heart muscle that can be either dilated or hypertrophic (excessively thickened). It probably has many causes but many of them we don't know and hence the idiopathic remark. (I try not to use all the twenty-five dollar words, especially not that one!)

As it turns out, Boxers have a high degree of this disease and it is more common in males. Something goes wrong with the heart muscle and it either becomes weak and begins to dilate, or it becomes thickened and less effective in its contractions because of the extra thickness.

In either case, the dog may remain normal looking for many years, but at some point will begin to decompensate, or slowly lose the battle. That is usually when we veterinarians see the dog, and the reason we usually put it on therapy right away. We can do treatments to decrease the dog's symptoms, but that is all. These dogs will usually go on into heart failure and many don't last more than about two years after diagnosis.

The goal behind therapy is to make the heart contract better, stop the abnormal rhythms if they are present and to dilate the blood vessels so there is less blood pressure on the failing heart muscle.

Q: *Our little twelve-year-old Poodle, Raggles, has been healthy all her life until lately when she began coughing almost every day. We feed her a regular grocery-store brand of dog food, and she has a good appetite. What could be wrong?*

A: A cough in an older, otherwise very healthy dog may be an indication of heart problems. I would take Raggles in for a complete and thorough checkup. I have seen many dogs just as you have described with the beginning stages of congestive heart failure.

Don't let the word "failure" scare you. Most of these dogs,

when caught early, can be treated quite successfully with medications and diet and live a normal lifespan and eventually die of some other cause. So I think the prognosis would be good for her if this were the case.

The doctor needs to do a good physical examination, some chest films and an ECG or maybe even an echocardiogram. This will tell the doctor what exactly the heart problem is, how long it has been going on, the type of lung fluid that has accumulated secondary to a heart that is not pumping efficiently enough, and her chances of doing well on medication.

Today we have very good drugs that will help reduce the fluid accumulations in her lungs and abdomen, increase the strength of her heartbeat and decrease the work load on her heart. I think after you get over the initial shock that she has this heart problem, you will be encouraged about the treatment of it.

I can tell you one thing to do right away. Get her off that grocery-store dog food, today! That is not high-quality food and is too high in salt and many other things that are making her body's compensation to this heart problem much more difficult. While your at the vet's office, be sure to ask about Hill's Prescription Diet h/d. That is the food she will need to be on for the rest of her life, with no treats, and no slipups at all. A low-salt diet is *the* most important thing you can do for her. If I had my choice between all the medications and simply a low-salt diet—I would take the diet! That's how important it is, yet many veterinarians ignore this aspect of treatment.

Q: *We have a five-year-old Doberman named Sir George. Last week he "bloated." We thought we were going to lose him. He seems to be doing OK now. We still don't understand exactly what bloat is, and we're afraid he will bloat one day while we are at work and aren't here to take him to the emergency hospital. Is there a way to prevent this problem?*

A: Acute gastric dilation, or "bloat" as it is sometimes called, is a serious gastrointestinal occurrence that can kill a dog in a matter of hours. The mortality rate from bloat is high, over 33%, even in cases that receive fairly immediate treatment. Cases requiring surgery have an even higher mortality rate.

The cause of bloat is unknown. We do know that it occurs almost exclusively in large, deep chested breeds of dogs. Age does not seem to be a factor. Bloat occurs more often in males than in females, by a two to one ratio. Dogs who have bloated before tend to be more at risk to bloat again. There seems to be a slightly decreased chance of survival with each occurrence.

In bloat, the dog's stomach dilates suddenly and excessively. The gas, liquid and solid contents of the stomach are unable to escape either through vomiting or through defecation. This "bloating" of the stomach may cause the stomach to turn over, or rotate. This is a critical situation, closing off the openings at each end of the stomach and causing blood flow to be shut off to parts of the intestine and the spleen. A dog can quickly go into shock and die.

A dog who is in the beginning stage of bloat will act uncomfortable. He may pace and whine, lie down and get back up frequently, and attempt to vomit or defecate without result. Fairly quickly, you will notice his stomach area appearing swollen. Bloat is an emergency situation that requires immediate medical care. If you notice your Doberman displaying any of the early symptoms of bloat, get him immediately to your veterinarian or your animal emergency clinic. Don't wait. The faster they can start treatment, the better chance he has to survive.

While the causes of bloat are not known, we do know some things which seem to contribute to bloat in dogs that may be predisposed.

The incidence of bloat is higher in dogs fed dog food with a very high grain content, so you should put your Doberman on a good premium-brand food with meat, not grain, as its base. Get the most nutrient-dense food you can and stay away from high fiber, bulky foods. I recommend Hill's Science Diet or Nature's Recipe pet foods.

The large buildup of gas in cases of bloat has been hypothesized to be swallowed air. Dogs that eat quickly and gulp their food may swallow large amounts of air in the process. Gas and food buildup may also be made worse by the dog drinking large amounts of water right after eating, and is certainly made worse by strenuous exercise or play soon after eating.

Since your dog has an actual history of bloat, I would recommend that you take a very cautious approach and follow these precautions:

- Feed several small meals a day rather than one large one.
- Feed a high-quality premium food with a meat base.
- Soak your dog's dry food in a little warm water for fifteen minutes before you give it to him. That way the food has swelled *prior* to his consuming it.
- Withhold water for thirty minutes after your dog eats.
- Feed your Doberman in a quiet area away from other pets. If he feels he has competition for his food, he will tend to gulp it down.
- Put a couple of rubber balls in his food dish with his food. If he has to pick around them, he will eat slower. (He may just pick the balls out of the dish, but this is worth a try.)
- No strenuous exercise or play for one hour after he eats.

We also know that bloat has a psychological component, because dogs under stress have a higher incidence of bloat. So, be especially aware and careful during times of stress such as kenneling while you are away and competition for your attention from other pets, especially another dog.

Q: *We give our dog aspirin for arthritis. Occasionally, he vomits after I give him the pill. Today, I saw blood in the vomit. What is going on here?*

A: Your dog seems to have become intolerant to the aspirin. We know that aspirin is irritative to many dogs' (and people's) stomachs. It irritates the gastric lining and causes local irritation, bleeding and even potentially, an ulcer. That is why companies produce enteric coated aspirin, and nonaspirin drugs like Tylenol (acetaminophen) and so forth.

I'd recommend not giving him aspirin for a while and asking your veterinarian to recommend a nonaspirin drug you can give. He may even prescribe some butazolidin for the dog. You may eventually be able give aspirin again but in much smaller doses. However, if the butazolidin or acetaminophen work well, stay with those drugs.

Q: *Our dog has the worst gas problem I believe I have ever experienced. He can flat clear the room, if you know what I mean. What can we do about that?*

A: I do know what you mean. The problem is not your dog, so much, but the food he is eating. Many pet food companies rely on grain as protein sources for their foods because grain is cheaper than meat. These grains contain complex starches that the dog has a hard time digesting. Consequently, the gas develops, and you know the rest.

There are two things you can do for this problem. Pick a different brand of dog food, one that is of high quality (you'll need to pay a little more) and that uses chicken, beef or lamb as protein sources. Now remember when you read the label, almost all pet foods have some grain sources in them. This is not bad. In fact, it is an excellent source of both protein and carbohydrates for dogs. But you will be looking for a food that has less grain and more meat protein. I suggest one of the brands that pet stores carry, such as Hill's Science Diet or Nature's Recipe.

Use the food for a few weeks, and see how your dog reacts. If there is less gas, you have solved the problem and your family and neighbors will thank you for it. However, if the problem persists, it may mean your dog is simply intolerant to even small bits of grain ingredients. In this case you will need to get some CurTail. This is an enzyme supplement you add to your dog's food before he eats it. It will assist him in breaking down these carbohydrates and consequently stop the gas. It is over 90% effective in doing so.

Q: *Today we noticed some blood on our puppy's stool. We were very concerned. She looks OK and eats fine. Should we take her to the vet?*

A: Yes, but it is not an emergency. Take her in Monday morning, and have a fecal examination done for parasites. That would be the most common cause for a small amount of blood in the stool.

When intestines and the colon become irritated, the first reaction is to produce excessive amounts of mucous coating for extra protection. Many times you will see this excess mucoid material on the stool. The next stage of irritation would probably include some erosion of tiny capillaries in the intestinal lining and you would begin to see some blood in the stool. If it is bright red blood, then it comes from the lower intestine or colon. If you see dark black color, this is usually a good indication there is bleeding up high in the tract and the blood excreted has been digested along the route and has become almost black.

There are many things that will cause blood in the stool. The most common are worms, foreign objects working their way through the track, (puppies will ingest many weird things), a change in food, even psychological stress will do it. It is generally not a big deal, but you should have it checked out.

Q: *Our dog is in the hospital. They want to do a gastrotomy on her. She's had an upset stomach for a few days, and we decided to have her looked at. They felt her abdomen, and it is pretty sore. Then they X-rayed her and found several metal parts in her stomach. You know the little screws and nuts that you put a travel kennel together with? Well, that's what she has eaten! (We wondered where those went.) Do you think she should have the surgery?*

A: That depends. The surgery is a pretty straightforward procedure where they will put her under with a general anesthetic, shave her belly, go into her stomach, remove the nuts and bolts and sew her up. However, many things can go wrong during a surgery. She can have a reaction to the anesthetic, she can develop secondary postop infection, there can be leaking from the scar into the stomach, and so on.

I like the conservative approach. I have seen many things move through a dog's stomach and intestines. Mother nature knows how to get rid of these things without our interfering. I would let her try first.

You know she has had a sore stomach for several days so take that into account. If no progress is made, either in her symptoms or in the movement of the nuts and bolts on the X-rays taken in another day or two, then it's time to start talking about going inside her stomach. Good luck!

Q: *Our dog was all of a sudden acting very strange. He would start pawing at his throat and gagging real bad, then would suddenly be just fine. We took him to the vet and he X-rayed Coon Dog, and you know what he found? A screwdriver in his throat! That dog had eaten a screwdriver!*

A: You know just about the time I am amazed at modern medicine, I'm even more amazed at what dogs will do! Is it anywhere near a full moon?

Chapter 25

Injuries
and Environmental Stress

"Doc, I gotta tell ya what my wife does, it's so funny. In the summertime when it's so hot here in South Carolina, she makes doggie tea!"

"OK, I'll ask. What's doggie tea?"

"She will make a pitcher of ice water and add in a little beef broth, just enough to make it look like iced tea. Then she pours some of it in the dog's bowl outside and boy, he just gulps it down!"

"Well, that sounds like a pretty good recipe and a nice treat for your dog on a hot summer day."

"Yea, but one hot summer day, after I was working in the yard, I came in and poured me a big glass of what I thought was people tea—it wasn't."

"What did you think?"

"It wasn't bad. . . . No sir, not bad at all!"

Because our dogs are many times outdoor pets, they are subject to a lot of environmental stresses that can often overwhelm them. Hyperthermia or heatstroke is common in the summertime. Dogs simply can't cool their body like we can and if not given adequate air circulation, cool water and a nice cool place to lie down, they can be stressed beyond what they can tolerate. If this situation goes on for very long, a vicious cycle of panting and increased muscle activity makes their temperature go even higher and heatstroke may be imminent. This can happen in a matter of minutes in dogs left in parked cars.

239

On the other side of the coin, Old Man Winter has taken his share of victims in the cold months. Dogs need an extra source of heat in order to keep warm when the thermometer drops much below thirty degrees. Frostbite can occur in dogs whose extremities are exposed to cold and whose circulation is decreased because of exhaustion or stress. Dogs also need fresh water available all the time, but in cold weather their water is often frozen.

Finally, as the director of a large country emergency animal clinic for several years, I think I've seen just about every kind of injury that can happen to a dog. It is heartrending to see dogs come in the clinic door, yelling in pain from all sorts of injuries—most of which were preventable if people would simply use a little common sense and a leash.

Q: *Dr. Jim, it gets so hot here in south Texas in the summer. I'm worried about my Alaskan Malamute. What can I do to keep him from suffering too much this summer?*

A: Good question. You need to make sure he has access to shade all day long. Remember that shade from a tree in the morning may be totally gone in the afternoon. He also needs good air circulation. If you have a covered porch or similar area, you can place a box fan on the porch where he can lie in front of it. These are fairly inexpensive and can be purchased at discount stores and home centers.

He needs lots of fresh water available all the time. A real good idea is to buy a child's plastic wading pool and fill it with about a foot of water. That way he can get in the water and cool himself off as he likes.

Another option is to put a dog door into your house. That way he can get outside to eliminate while you're gone, but then can get back inside where it's air conditioned. Check out Johnson Pet Doors at pet stores.

Q: *We just came home and our old dog was out in the back yard laying in the sun panting. She was very hot and was not responding to us. Now she is inside with us and seems to be doing a little better. What do we do?*

A: What you do depends on what has happened to her. I can say that if she was very old there may be any number of problems that caused her to not move out of the sun, but the first thing to do is to get her cooled down. She may be suffering heatstroke. Probably the best way to do this is to submerge her body and legs in a tub of cold or iced water, keeping her head out of the water. You can also soak towels in ice water and place them over her body and legs. You'll need to keep soaking and replacing the towels as they lose their cold.

Using a rectal thermometer, I want you to take her temperature every ten minutes. When her rectal temperature has come down to 103° F, stop cooling her. Get her in the car and get her to your veterinarian.

In the meantime, have someone call your veterinarian or animal emergency hospital and let them know what has happened and that you will be bringing her in. You will need to take her in as soon as you can get her body temperature lowered. She could have had a stroke or some injury that made her unable to move out of the sun. The heatstroke must be your first concern though, before we can look into other problems.

Q: *It is really cold this winter, and I have my dogs in a regular wooden doghouse. I went out there the other day, and it is very cold in there. I've tried a few things to make it warmer. Can you give me some tips?*

A: You bet. First, get the house out of the wind as best you can. A flap over the door will help block the wind and decrease the cold. Wood doghouses should be raised off the ground several inches to prevent the wood from becoming wet and soaking the bedding. If the bedding becomes wet, the dog can't possibly stay warm.

Put some old carpet on the floor and tack it down safely. The dog should have some soft, dry bedding in order to stay warm. A fleece dog bed or some blankets placed in the house so the dog can sort of "fluff" his own pillow works well.

A good inexpensive bedding is clean straw. Cover the floor of the doghouse with about six inches of straw. Your dog will arrange it to his liking. Change the straw for clean straw, as needed, if it gets muddy or wet.

Some dogs don't like to be in close quarters with even their best "dog buddy," so each dog should have his own house to prevent one dog from being chased out into the cold. The house should be big enough for the dog to stand up, circle and lie down, but no bigger. A dog's body heat warms his house, so a small dog would have a difficult time warming a big house.

You may want to check out a doghouse called Dogloo. This is an insulated structural foam doghouse that is in the shape of an igloo. It is specially designed to keep warmth inside in the winter and stay cool in the hot summer months. You can find them at pet stores all over the country.

Be very careful about hooking up any kind of electrical heating appliance. I have seen both dog and people houses burn down this way. There are some safe products made especially for this purpose. There is a company in Colorado called Pet Heating Products. They make all sorts of safe heated dog beds, kennel pads and even a water bowl that won't freeze in the coldest winter temperatures. Look for these products in pet stores.

Q: *Dr. Jim, we have recently moved to Minnesota from Texas. This is the first time we've lived in a cold climate. I'm worried about my little dog this winter. Is she in danger of hypothermia?*

A: You certainly want to take some precautions and make sure she has adequate shelter against the cold, especially since she hasn't been acclimated to cold weather, growing up in Texas. However, hypothermia, which results in a significant decrease in body temperature, is rare in a healthy animal that is able to seek shelter. Frostbite of ear tips, tails and foot pads is a bigger danger. Hypothermia generally affects very old or young animals or animals that are caught in a cold environment with no way to get warm.

Make sure your little dog has a good doghouse, protected from the wind. Provide her with a flap over the door and some old blankets or some clean straw inside for a bed. (Check out the Dogloo Dog House.) You can buy special heated kennel pads made for use in doghouses and special heated water bowls so she always has a source of unfrozen water.

A good idea is to put a dog door into your house. That way she can get outside to eliminate while you're gone, but then can get back inside the house where it's warm.

Some small, short-haired breeds of dogs should not be left outside in cold weather, even with a doghouse. Breeds such as the Chihuahua simply cannot tolerate cold temperatures and need to be in the house when it's cold.

Q: *I've heard you mention frostbite. We take our dogs on hikes with us in the snow-covered mountains all the time, and they seem to do fine. How would we know if they were frostbitten, and how would we treat it?*

A: Good question. First of all, your dogs are active and healthy athletes and that is what's keeping them in such good condition on these hikes. However, if you think the conditions are especially cold, and your exposure especially long, then watch them more closely. If their feet, ears or tail seem to hurt after a hike, then you may suspect frostbite. Feel these extremities, and see if they seem to have any sensation. If they appear extremely cold, painful and lack any signs of sensation, then the dog may have a bout of frostbite.

Don't rub these areas in your hands. That will only serve to damage tissues even more. The best thing to do is use warm moist towels wrapped around the affected area. Repeat these packs using warm tap water every fifteen minutes until you can see some signs of circulation returning. You'll see color and feel the warmth as the capillaries begin to open up once again. I will warn you that as this happens and the sensation begins to return, the pain gets worse. You may want to give them an aspirin or Tylenol and keep the areas moist with lotion. Call your veterinarian or animal emergency clinic if the dog appears to be in extreme discomfort. Let your veterinarian check your dog in the next day or two to examine the area for any dead tissue that may require further treatment.

Q: *We've heard antifreeze is toxic to pets. Yesterday I saw my Sheltie licking the floor where I had just drained the radiator putting in new antifreeze. He seems fine today, he's happy and eating well. Should I be worried?*

A: I think you lucked out this time. Thousands of dogs and cats die each year from consuming antifreeze—ethylene glycol. The biggest danger occurs when we flush out the old antifreeze and put in the new. Water containing some antifreeze often collects in small puddles on the ground or garage floor. Luckily, your old radiator water was probably dilute enough that a few licks wasn't enough of a dose of ethylene glycol to cause kidney failure. He would have had to get only about thirty milliliters or one ounce of pure antifreeze to kill him. However, smaller amounts can cause kidney damage and severe illness.

Many people are surprised that dogs will drink antifreeze, but when you realize that antifreeze is attractive in color and it smells and tastes sweet, you can see how a disaster like this might unfold. For both pets and children, antifreeze represents a major household danger and should be handled carefully. Keep antifreeze up out of reach of pets and children. Keep pets out of the area when putting antifreeze in the car or flushing out your radiatior, and clean up any spills very well.

Q: *Our little twelve-week-old puppy just bumped up against the glass fireplace doors and burned herself. It's a small area but she is really crying. What can we treat this with?*

A: I'd first use some cold packs on the area to decrease the immediate heat in the tissues and decrease the severity of the burn. Then I would use some general household antibiotic ointment to keep the skin moist and free from bacterial infection. Finally, if the hair falls out, just treat the skin with some A&E Ointment for a few weeks. This promotes healing and lessens secondary damage to the skin. The hair should grow back in about six weeks. It is because of the hair that the burn is not worse, the hair probably had some insulating effect on the actual skin burn.

Your puppy was in the last few weeks of her fear imprint stage (nine to twelve weeks of age). Therefore, she may show an increased fear reaction to fires and fireplaces. This is good in one respect, she may not go near them again.

Q: *Our dog was hit by a car. He seems badly hurt, what do we do?*

A: About the only thing you can do is to get him to the animal clinic immediately. Be very gentle and place him on a flat board. Be careful not to move any part of him excessively. Just move him gently. He may yelp in pain, and could bite, so be careful. You have to get him onto something sturdy and stiff, so you can carry him to the car and into the hospital.

Have someone call the emergency hospital right now and get on your way. If he is acts as if he might bite, gently tie his muzzle with a strip of old sheet. Loop it around his muzzle, then tie it back behind his ears so he won't hurt you during the trip. If he doesn't seem that scared or in that much pain, simply hold his head and reassure him on the way.

I've seen cases like this where a dog has been hit by a car or had a major fall and has little, if any injury. In other cases there can be collapsed lungs, fractured ribs, spinal injuries, and fractures of the legs and even skull. The veterinarian's first priority will be to see if the dog is in shock and if so to treat that first. Then once vital signs, color and pain have been stabilized he can begin looking for injuries and talk about their correction.

Q: *Our dog has stepped on something that has cut his foot, and he is running frantically around the house leaving little blood spots all over our carpet. What can we do?*

A: First—catch him. Second—check the foot to see where and what is the problem. Third—see if the injury is one you feel comfortable bandaging. If so, get out the first-aid kit and go to it. If not, head to the vet's office before they close.

If you decide to bandage the foot, here are some tips. Foot pads, as well as the skin between the toes, have a great blood supply. A small cut or puncture can bleed profusely. Do your best to wash the area and examine it so you can see what is causing the problem. There could be a piece of glass or something still stuck in the pad. Remove anything obvious and try your best to flush the wound with peroxide. Then use some antibiotic ointment on the area and bandage it up. Use some gauze pads first, and secure them in place with tape. Then use a roll of gauze and wrap the whole area. Finally tape everything securely with the tape and, voilà, you have it.

You should get in to see the doctor within the next day or two so he can look at your job, see if you missed anything and put the dog on antibiotics to take care of possible secondary infection. Good job.

Chapter 26

Itching, Allergies and Skin Disease

"Our white Miniature Poodle scratches all the time. My mother said we could just give him brewer's yeast and use calamine lotion. We did and it hasn't helped. Now he's pink. What do we do?"

"He's pink?"

"Yes, we put the calamine all over him and now he's pink!"

"I'd get a good medicated shampoo from your veterinarian and bathe him every five to seven days."

"We did that, but the stuff is green, and we're afraid of going from a pink Poodle to a green one!"

Itching, scratching dogs make up the lion's share of calls to veterinary clinics nationwide. Fleas are, by far, the major cause of this constant and stressful problem. Many times, clients are convinced that their pets do not have fleas, yet all the evidence points to flea problems.

There are many other causes of itching in dogs. Dogs are very allergic creatures and, when allergic, show both an itching, scratching syndrome as well as human-type allergic symptoms including itchy eyes, runny nose and sneezing. Because dogs scratch so much in response to allergies, these allergies have been termed "hay fever of the skin."

Corticosteroids have been used for years to treat skin disease. They play a very big part in many treatments, even today. However, they have often been overused. Overuse of steroids can create additional problems.

Skin disease is very frustrating for both pet owners and veterinarians. Few skin problems are cut-and-dry. Most require much supportive care and time for things to get better. Many skin diseases never get better and require medications for the life of the dog, just to keep the dog from being miserable. Some veterinarians are now specializing in dermatology for animals. If you can find one of these board certified veterinary dermatologists, they may be able to achieve that extra level of relief and success for your pet's problem.

Q: *Suddenly, our German Shepherd has developed a large red, raw spot on his left thigh where all the hair is gone. It looks terrible. He licks it constantly and it's oozing clear liquid. Whatever is this thing?*

A: It sounds like a hot spot or, more technically called, pyotraumatic dermatitis. "Pyo" means pus or involving bacteria. "Traumatic" means that the dog's licking and chewing has been an important part of the spot's development. "Dermatitis," of course, means inflammation of the skin.

These hot spots can pop up within hours. They are very itchy and the dog's licking and scratching makes them worse. Many times they are set off by flea-bite irritation or allergies. The self-inflicted irritation from the chewing triggers the acute, moist dermatitis.

This syndrome occurs more in the hot and humid summer months and more often in thick, dense-coated breeds of dogs like Labs, Shepherds, Retrievers and St. Bernards.

I've always taken a pretty aggressive treatment approach in these cases for everything but the small hot spots. I recommend tranquilization of the dog and a careful clipping of the thick fur at least one inch out from the border of the spot. I then clean the skin carefully with an antiseptic soap like Betadine. The area will look worse at this point because of the scrubbing, and the spots many times look bigger when you see them after clipping.

I then apply 70% alcohol to the area and quickly and thoroughly dry the spot, followed by use of a good antibiotic–steroid-combination spray like gentamicin and betamethazone. Rarely are shots or pills needed because the topical treatment works so well, but I have used them in severe cases.

Q: *Our dog scratches about half the day and seems pretty normal the other half. We never see fleas on him and have never had a flea problem. We have noticed a kind of rust color comes off him when we rinse him after a bath. Should we be using a different shampoo?*

A: Yes! You should be using *flea* shampoo, and *flea* collars, and *flea* dips, and *flea* foggers, and *flea* outdoor sprays. . . . *You have fleas!*

Many people believe they don't have fleas because they either have never seen them or they don't know what they look like. They are very small and move very fast, so you have to look quickly.

I know you have a bad flea problem because of the rust-colored water. That is flea "dirt," or flea excrement, dissolving in water. The excrement contains digested blood from your dog, and when it is gets wet, it turns red or rust colored.

You probably have seen the flea dirt on your dog and simply thought it was dirt. It actually looks like someone shook pepper on your dog's haircoat. This is positive proof that you have fleas, which are the reason for your dog's half-time job of scratching!

Now, let's talk about flea control (see Chapter 16).

Q: *Our Westie, Marlow, scratches at her rear end. She'll also chew and is now pulling the hair out over her tail area. The hair is turning rust colored there and on her paws. Now she has doggie-pattern baldness on her rump. How can we stop this?*

A: Sounds like your dog has a classic case of ATOPY or allergic inhalant dermatitis. This is very common and is responsible for a great deal of misery as well as many calls to animal clinics every year when pollen counts are high.

It seems that Dalmatians, West Highland White Terriers and Poodles have more than their share of this affliction. It is a true allergy, where the inhaled antigen causes an antigen–antibody reaction in the dog's system and causes the symptoms. Oddly, it's the same process as in human allergies, but with us, the main symptoms are runny nose, red itchy eyes and sneezing. Those symptoms occur in only a very small number of dogs.

By far, most dogs develop itching of the skin. It's worse on the face, the feet, the sides and the rear half of the body. White-haired dogs will develop rust-colored hair on the feet due to the dog's saliva being in constant contact with that area.

Some of these atopic dogs first show these symptoms only during pollen season. Frequent offenders are grass, weed and tree pollens. As time goes on, these dogs may begin to itch year-round if they've added new allergens to the list, like house dust, feathers, molds, wool and even food ingredients.

I know all this sounds complicated—and it is! Unfortunately I don't have a very good solution for you either. You can choose either: A. the cheap and easy, but less desirable way or B. the more expensive and tedious, but proper medical way.

I'll tell you quickly about both.

A. Simply giving the dog injections of long-acting steroids will make the symptoms miraculously go away. Steroids are anti-inflammatory, and the problem with this disease is widespread inflammation. Therefore, treatment with steriods provides immediate improvement. However, the steroids wear off in thirty to sixty days and all the symptoms return.

As you probably know, the long-term use of steroids is not good for people or pets. However, many thousands of pet owners and veterinarians treat these cases in this way.

B. The most preferable treatment involves a financial and time commitment from you. It involves allergy testing Marlow and determining exactly what she is allergic to, then desensitizing her with special antigen shots over the course of six months to one year.

This is exactly what is done in people and is more than 70% effective when done right and combined with other supportive therapy.

Q: *We're desensitizing our dog, who is allergic to house dust, ragweed and fleas. So far so good, but what else can we do to help her with this constant itch?*

A: Good question! Desensitization takes some time, and you can't use steroids during this process, so many severe cases itch very badly during the first few months of the treatment. Here's some supportive therapy you can do to help:

1. Try your best to keep her away from the allergens. For you, this means very good housecleaning and flea control! There's not much you can do about the ragweed. I suggest air-duct cleaning and electrostatic air filters in your house, along with regular, meticulous dusting.
2. Ask your veterinarian to prescribe an antihistamine. Many doctors feel they do little, but I'll try anything for these dogs!
3. Soothing medicated shampoos help, and there are many on the market. I like Dermaplex made by Bioglan Animal Products and Coal Tar Shampoo by Tomlyn Products.
4. Use Omega-three fatty-acid supplements. These fish oils are good for the skin and haircoat, but also have anti-inflammatory properties without the use of steroids. I highly recommend Lipiderm liquid or Liqua-caps.
5. An occasional one-fourth of an aspirin will help as well, if your dog can tolerate it.

Q: *We have a four-year-old Sheltie who has been diagnosed as allergic to fleas. We're giving shots at home that are supposed to help. Our vet does not want to use steroids. To be honest, I'm confused about the shots we're giving. Can you explain this to me?*

A: Sure. You are desensitizing your Sheltie to the allergic reaction it has when a flea bites it. The shots you are giving are flea antigen. You are literally trying to "vaccinate" your dog against the flea's saliva, which is the real culprit. That takes many months to accomplish.

Dermatologists report mixed results with flea antigen, but it does work in some cases. I would continue just as your doctor has prescribed. I would, however, reemphasize to you the importance of strict and absolute flea control. If your dog never sees another flea, he wouldn't break out. In the real world, this is almost impossible, but I would be as strict about it as I could.

You mention your doctor not wanting to use steroids. I agree with his decision. He is trying to follow good medical principles and treat this problem with desensitization. But practically speaking, if your Sheltie's itching became severe, I would use a low-dose, short-acting corticosteroid to ease the constant agony of itching. You may also want to try some topical ointment with steroids on the areas that are especially bad.

Medicated shampoos are helpful. I like Dermaplex, Seleen, Thiomar and even Selsen Blue from the grocery store.

Q: *Our Pug, Charlie, has itched at his sides for years, off and on. Lately he's been really itching at his ears. Why do you think he's changed spots?*

A: It is not unusual for dogs who are allergic to break out in different areas of the body as their allergy progresses and as they become sensitive to new things.

The ears are one of the most delicate skin areas of the body and are a prime target for inflammation. This causes a vicious cycle of itching, scratching and more irritation of the skin. The skin reacts by seeping oils, in which bacteria grow. These can cause a serious, secondary bacterial ear infection in addition to the primary inflammation from the allergy.

Do what you can with your veterinarian to diagnose and treat the allergy. Then I would treat the ears as a separate problem. Use Q-tips and alcohol to clean the ear canals, and use an antibiotic and steroid ointment in the ears daily to stop the cycle of irritation and scratching.

Q: *Our Dalmatian has suddenly broken out with thick red lips. He chews on his plastic food dish, and my wife thought he may have bitten his lip. Now it's infected. Have any ideas?*

A: He may have bitten his lip and caused an infected spot which would cause his lip to become inflamed and sore.

However, if the upper and lower lip on both sides are red, swollen and inflamed, your dog may be showing signs of a localized allergic reaction to the plastic food dish.

I would have your doctor examine the mouth and treat any bite injuries. If he agrees that it may be an allergy to the plastic, then a shot of steroids and a metal or ceramic food dish is the answer.

Q: *Our eight-year-old Irish Setter has had dandruff for many years. We've put her on Iams dog food and have given her Wesson oil as a supplement. Now it's actually getting worse. Can you recommend a course of action?*

A: Irish Setters have a problem with dry skin. It may be a reaction to an allergy or poor nutrition. In your case, I'd switch her to Nature's Recipe Lamb & Rice Diet and supplement with Lipiderm capsules.

The food change will provide her with a new protein and carbohydrate source just in case she has developed a hypersensitivity to the ingredients in the Iams food. In these types of cases, I've had good luck supplementing with a fresh source of fatty acids like Wesson oil. However, since I've learned about the Omega-three fatty acids, I recommend them exclusively.

These fish oils not only provide fatty-acid supplementation, but are proven to have some anti-inflammatory properties as well. I've had a few dogs who were able to get off steroids completely since they started taking Lipiderm. Ask your veterinarian's advice on this.

Q: *Our chubby female has been licking at her "privates" for about two weeks. We didn't think much about it until we saw the spot yesterday. It looked awful! We took her to the vet who said the spot was pyoderma. What's that?*

A: Pyoderma is a very general term meaning bacterial skin infection. It can be superficial or deep, mild or severe, generalized or localized, but it always involves a pretty bad bacterial infection.

Your dog probably has skin-fold pyoderma or vulvar-fold pyoderma. In overweight female dogs, the area around their vulva will often not get cleaned well, and in deep skin folds the crevices never see the light of day. This is the perfect spot for bacteria to set up housekeeping. If left untreated for a while, the bacteria can go wild and actually erode the skin layers, creating an ugly infection that destroys the normal skin structure. These infections are very itchy and smell bad, which makes the dog lick and scratch even more. A vicious cycle ensues, with no end in sight.

The treatment involves simply treating the skin infection and helping the area dry and heal. Severely overweight dogs may need a "fanny tuck" to literally remove those skin folds and prevent this infection from happening again.

Q: *Our precious little shelter dog, Molly, is mostly Cocker Spaniel. She has become scaly and smelly to the point that the house has started to smell like her. What can I do?*

A: It sounds like Molly has seborrhea. This is a chronic skin disease where too much skin oil is secreted from the skin. Most of these dogs develop pretty serious scaliness. Cockers and Springer Spaniels have a predilection to this disease.

Dogs with primary seborrhea develop oiliness of their skin and may also have ear infections. They usually don't itch, which is good, but treatment is a lifetime affair with poor results—so don't expect a cure.

There is a secondary seborrhea condition that shows more scaliness than anything and usually accompanies other ailments, like mange, flea allergy and inhaled allergies.

Dogs with seborrhea become scaly and oily because of excess oil production and excess turnover rate of the skin's epidermis. The skin oil supports Staph bacteria growth, and the bacteria's effect on the oil causes the bad smell.

The goal of treatment is to remove scales and reduce the excess oil on the skin and hair. This is a case where medicated shampoos can really help. Use an antiseborrhea shampoo every three to five days to reduce the odor and scales. There are many of these products on the market, but most contain salicylic acid, tar and sulfur, and hexachlorophene. I like Antiseborrhen Shampoo by Tomlyn.

Steroids are helpful to relieve skin inflammation and some itching that may occur. These drugs are used on a short-term basis only. You can use steroid ointments and lotions for localized help.

Q: *My eight-year-old Miniature Schnauzer, named Pepper, has a lot of bumps all over his back from his neck to his tail. We've tried medicated shampoos, like we've heard you talk about, but so far no improvement. Any suggestions?*

A: Yes. Pepper has Schnauzer bumps. It is pretty common in Miniature Schnauzers. These bumps are actually comedones or blackheads and can become quite widespread. They usually aren't painful and don't cause itching, but a secondary bacterial infection can develop and make the problem worse. When these little bumps break open, they form sharp, crusted projections on the skin. Some people think these dogs have an infestation of fleas, but remember, flea bites itch, Schnauzer bumps do not.

Here's how you treat Schnauzer bumps. I recommend clipping the hair so you can get your treatment right to the skin. You can wipe the area with alcohol every day and shampoo twice a week. Not just any shampoo will work. It needs to be an antiseborrheic shampoo. These usually contain sulfur and salicylic acid. Some brand names are Thiomar, Sebbafon and Sebutone. Ask your veterinarian for a recommendation.

Keep up the alcohol treatments twice a week once you get the bumps under control. You may also want to ask your doctor to check Pepper for hypothyroidism as that is seen in some of these dogs.

Q: *We have a six-year-old Dalmatian that has allergies so bad he's turned golden brown in color and still itches even though we have him on steroids. We've tried everything with this dog and we're at our wit's end!*

A: Your Dalmatian may not be allergic. There is a rare condition seen in this breed only, called Dalmatian bronzing syndrome. It looks very much like allergies but does not respond to steroids, and the dogs literally turn brown or bronze colored.

Scientists do not know what causes this strange problem. We do know enough to help the dog live more comfortably. Before I give you some treatment suggestions, let me also say these dogs often have urinary infections and/or bladder stones, plus demodectic mange and secondary bacterial infections of the skin. The Dalmatian Research Foundation is conducting research to discover the cause and cure.

First, these dogs should be put on a vegetarian diet! I know that sounds strange, but the amino acids in meat-based dog foods make the uric acid secretion into the urine worse. Because of this diet requirement, I recommend a B-complex vitamin supplement. Nature's Recipe has a commercially prepared vegetarian diet I would suggest you try.

Many doctors put these dogs on allopurinol to reduce the production of uric acid. Control of the urine pH is also very important, and your veterinarian will help you with that. You have to also convince the dog to drink 1,500 milliliters, or 1+ quarts, of water per day. You can flavor the water with fish oils, Parmesan cheese or milk to encourage him to drink more.

Reasonable control and comfort for these dogs is possible if you and your veterinarian are willing to strictly adhere to these measures. Good luck!

Q: *Our five-month-old Great Dane puppy, Captain, started getting round red spots on his head. We put some Neosporin on them, but it hasn't helped. Now they are beginning to spread and we've noticed spots on his feet and legs. What will control this?*

A: Well, Neosporin is good stuff, but it won't cure mange. Get Captain into a veterinarian Monday morning and have a skin scraping done. This simple test will probably confirm demodectic mange.

This is a little mite that lives in even normal dog and people skin. For some reason, especially in young dogs, these little mites go haywire and overpopulate an area. They destroy hair follicles and do lots of secondary damage to the microscopic structure of the skin. The body's reaction is a very serious inflammation causing these spots to become very red and hot. In fact, it's often called "red mange."

Your veterinarian will probably prescribe Mitoban dips on a fixed schedule. Some dogs clear up after a couple of treatments. Others take many dips and lots of supportive care.

It is generally felt that young dogs with demodectic mange don't have a mature immune system. Once their immune system matures, the disease will many times spontaneously resolve.

In the meantime, you must treat the mange vigorously because the secondary problems seen with the *Demodex* mite can be so serious as to be life-threatening.

Q: *Chelsea is my twelve-year-old Irish Setter. She's had her share of medical problems and has licked them all, but she can't seem to get rid of two really bad sores. One is on her front leg, where our wrist would be, and the other on her hock. Our vet has tried everything. Do you have any magical cure for this?*

A: I wish I did. These sores sound like lick granulomas which have been frustrating dog owners and veterinarians for centuries.

They usually occur in large dogs. It is thought the spot starts from an initial irritation that begins the licking–itch–licking cycle. The licking keeps the wound from healing and the constant irritation makes the spot thick and red. These spots look like skin cancer, but they are not.

I've noticed many of these dogs don't have a playmate, and therefore boredom likely plays a role in the constant licking. Therefore, diversion with a playmate, either human or animal, may help.

In the early stages, steroids injected under the spot are very helpful. However, the longer the spots have been there, the less effect steroids will have. There are two radical procedures you can use to cure the problem. Speak carefully with your veterinarian about them.

The first one is the use of cobra venom injected into the spot. In most cases, the dog stops licking within twenty-four hours and the results last six months or may be permanent.

In the second procedure, some spots may be surgically removed, depending on the area. I've even known doctors who remove the granuloma and then fill in the deficit with a skin graft.

In the meantime, do your best to keep her from licking it!

Q: *We have a lovable little brown Dachshund, Heidi. Over the past year she's become a pudgy, bald, black Dachshund. She's losing her energy to play, and she's only seven. Shouldn't she be more active?*

A: You've described a textbook case of hypothyroidism. When the thyroid gland does not produce enough thyroid hormone, dogs become overweight and fatigue easily. About half of them develop skin disease typified by a thin, dry haircoat and hair loss. The skin feels cool to the touch and many times these dogs develop secondary seborrhea and ear infections.

Heidi's doctor can run a thyroid-stimulating hormone test to see if her thyroid is working or half asleep. If she is hypothyroid, she can easily be treated by giving her artificial thyroid hormone. The most common drug used is Synthroid. This will stop the progression of the disease and reverse some of the symptoms.

Once she is on Synthroid, it is a life-long medication, and she'll need to be evaluated every six months to monitor her progress.

Q: *Our Collie has developed a real red and raw spot on her nose. We though it might be skin cancer. We called the vet, who said it was Collie nose and we should come in for a tattoo. What's that all about?*

A: Your Collie has Collie nose. It's simply an inflammation of the unpigmented areas of her nose due to lots of sunlight exposure. If left untreated it can develop into skin cancer.

Treatment involves getting the dog some shelter from the sun. I usually use steroids for a few weeks to decrease the sometimes serious inflammation that can occur. I also color the nose with a black felt marking pen to give them a little artificial pigment until they heal. Then, after they are somewhat healed, I will tattoo a solid black nose to solve the problem.

Don't ask the veterinarian to do any little designs on your dog's nose—she won't.

Q: *Our veterinarian biopsied our Poodle today for a potential skin cancer. We are very worried. What are the long-term chances?*

A: Well, I'd have to see her, but if it is not a very malignant cancer and it has not spread, her chances are very good. Skin tumors make up about 35% of all dog cancers. If I had to choose the most survivable type of cancer, it would be a skin tumor.

After your veterinarian gets the lab results back, you will know much more. The doctor will counsel with you about the next treatment steps as well as home care. Good luck.

Q: *Our Boston Terrier, Bugs, was getting thin hair and a little potbelly, so we took him to the vet. She said he has Cushings disease and told us we'd need to come back next week for a whole bunch of tests. She didn't give us any pills for him. Can you give us a second opinion?*

A: Yes. Although I can't see the dog, old Bugs sounds like a case of Cushings disease to me. The reason she didn't send you home with any pills is because this is a complicated disease and she needs to get an accurate diagnosis first before she launches into treatment. Your veterinarian is right on target.

Cushings disease is caused by an oversecretion of the adrenal glands. These glands produce cortisols, which are steroids. Overproduction of steroids from within the body will create the same syndrome we would see if we gave the dog too much steroid by injection. In fact, there are cases of Cushings disease from just that.

The cause of this hypersecretion of cortisol can be either adrenal gland malfunction or an abnormal pituitary gland that overstimulates the adrenal glands. In either case, too much cortisol leads to hair loss on both sides of the body, thinning of the skin and circular patches on the body that become dark and peel. These dogs also drink a lot of water and, therefore, urinate much more than normal. They are depressed and lay around much of the time. They are more susceptible to bacterial infections and they heal poorly.

Treatment depends on the cause. Dogs that show these symptoms due to excessive steroids given them during their life, should taper the steroids down to very low levels or stop receiving steroids completely.

Dogs that have a pituitary tumor or primary adrenal disease will have to undergo Lysodren treatments. This drug selectively decreases the activity of the cells in the adrenal cortex so that it will stop overproducing cortisols. Once an initial treatment is given, the dog will need to be on Lysodren once a week for life.

Many dogs are controlled very well this way and do fine for many years. If the problem is a pituitary tumor that continues to grow, the dog will get worse as the tumor grows and will eventually begin to show neurological signs.

In the meantime you can be using antiseborrheic shampoos to reduce the skin's scaliness and Alpha-Keri rinses to help with the dry skin and hair.

Chapter 27

Diseases Contagious to People

"Doc, I've always heard you could catch diseases by letting a dog lick you in the face. Is that true?"

"Absolutely!"

"Yeah, I thought so. I've told my grandkids to never let a dog lick them in the face 'cause they can catch a disease! I'm glad you agree! What kind of disease can they catch?"

"LOVE."

"What?"

"About all your grandkids are going to catch by letting a dog lick them in the face is Love. And I'd just as soon they have that one!"

"Oh, come on now . . . "

"No, really. Pets are about the best thing that can happen to a child. If taught they should be afraid of them or that they might catch something from them, it takes away from the bond and tremendous benefits children receive from growing up with pets. Children who have pets are less violent and are less likely to join gangs. They are more compassionate and loving toward people and all life. I think a pet is the best thing for a child, licks in the face and all!"

"Land sakes!"

Q: We are having a real outbreak of rabies here in the Northeast. Our dog is vaccinated, but our children play with all the neighbors' dogs as well. What is their risk of coming into contact with rabies?

A: Thankfully, it's very slight. Rabies, while a very serious, usually fatal disease in people and animals, is rare. Every few years there is a spillover of the virus from the wildlife population into the domestic population of animals. This is when we will begin to see cases of dog rabies reported on the evening news.

The likelihood of a dog in your neighborhood having rabies is very remote. So much so, that it is simply not practical, nor good child rearing sense, to prohibit your children from playing with other children and their dogs. Now, stray or feral dogs—*yes!* I would warn your children, in a very positive way, that playing with dogs that are not known to them, or that don't have a collar and tags on is not a good idea and that they should keep away. In fact, give them a reward for bringing to your attention, this type of dog in the neighborhood. This way you can call animal control and have stray dogs picked up and removed from the streets.

Dogs that are owned by your neighbors most likely have their rabies vaccinations, as it is state law across the country. Rabies vaccine is very effective in preventing the disease in case of a challenge. When rabies outbreaks occur, as we are seeing in the Northeast right now, animal control and news departments are usually very good about getting the word out. As a result, we usually see an increase in dog owners getting their dogs vaccinated or bringing their dogs' vaccinations up-to-date.

If your neighborhood borders on a wooded or less developed area where your domestic dogs have free access to wild animals, then the risk is higher. In this case, I would keep all your dogs on a leash or in your back yard and make certain that all stray dogs or wild animals are immediately picked up by animal control.

Remember, if you find a sick or injured bat, raccoon or unknown dog or cat in the neighborhood, let animal control pick it up. Never attempt a rescue or even touch the animal yourself.

Q: *Our daughter has Strep throat and our doctor has her home from school and taking antibiotics. We were surprised to hear him recommend we take our dog to the vet for a throat culture! Could our daughter really get Strep throat from Oscar?*

A: Oscar may not be the original culprit, but he can become infected and pass it back and forth from himself to family members, just as can happen among human family members.

Streptococcal bacteria are normal inhabitants of the mouth of both animals and man. Group A Strep are the most common and the most pathogenic in humans. Animals, however, harbor more of the group G, C and L Strep strains. Group A in animals usually doesn't cause any symptoms, therefore if your daughter has Group A Strep throat and kisses Oscar, he can get it and not show symptoms. He can harbor the bacteria for some time as a normal, non-disease-producing bacteria. Then, when your daughter is better, another kiss can cause the Strep throat again!

This is not very common, but it can occur. That is why in resistant cases, where physicians are stumped as to why they cannot get a particular infection under control, they will often recommend we culture the pet. I can say, after doing many of these, I have only found a few positive cases. So it is a long shot, but possible. A much more likely source of infection is the other children she comes into contact with.

I would not recommend treatment of Oscar unless a throat culture shows he has Group A Strep. If so, remember, he got it from your daughter and may be able to reinfect her. Therefore, he should take his pills along with your daughter!

Q: *Can we get Lyme disease from our dog?*
A: Yes and no. No, in that Lyme disease requires a bite from an infected tick or other blood-sucking parasite. Since your dog is not a blood-sucking parasite, he cannot transmit Lyme disease to you directly.

But yes, he can transmit it to you indirectly. If a tick that is harboring the Lyme disease organism crawls off him on to you, and then bites you, then you have about a fifty-fifty chance of developing Lyme disease.

Q: *I've been struggling with a red spot on my arm for months. I've just treated it at home, and it hasn't spread but it hasn't gotten any better. Today we had our new puppy into the vet's and he showed us where Charlie had ringworm! Could my spot be ringworm?*
A: It could be! Ringworm is a fungus infection. Transmission from animals to man occurs but is not easily accomplished. You can touch a ringworm spot on a dog or cat and not get ringworm. It

requires so-called "intimate" contact. In other words, casual touching contact usually won't transmit the disease. Long-term rubbing onto areas of the body that are thin skinned is the usual mode of transmission.

Let me give you an example. If your puppy lays down to sleep on your old T-shirt all day and then you put that shirt on to go work out in, that could be "intimate contact." This type of more long-term contact, both with the dog to the shirt and with the shirt to you, is what it takes. Children who carry a pet over their shoulders have enough rubbing exposure to areas of delicate skin to transmit ringworm from the pet to their head, neck and face.

Therefore, if you have been holding the puppy in your arms for some time, that could be enough exposure to the ringworm spores to cause infection on your arm.

If you treat these spots, as many people do, with ointments that contain any amount of steroids, the spot will only get worse. However, if you switch to a fungicidal ointment prescribed by your doctor, you should see remission of the spot in a few weeks. Ringworm is a more long-term infection, and therefore you'll have to have patience for the spot to go away.

Be sure to follow your doctor's advice on treating Charlie. If the spot is very localized, you can use a topical antifungal like Tolnaftate. However, if ringworm begins to spread and is present in several spots on Charlie, the doctor will most likely use systemic antifungal medications (oral medications) like Griseofulin.

Q: *We recently saw a television news report about roundworms infecting children and causing problems. We were pretty surprised by that report and want to know how we keep our dog free from these worms and how we can prevent their transmission to our child.*

A: Ascariasis, or infestation with roundworms (ascarids) is common for dogs. In fact, most, if not all puppies have roundworms when they are young. They can get these worms from their mother via the placenta, milk or the oral route. The worm eggs are ingested by the puppy and develop into larvae in their intestine. These larvae penetrate the intestinal wall and migrate through the liver into the lungs. They are coughed up and swallowed again, to end up in the intestines as mature roundworms. This process of larval migration is the cause for much of the disease seen in puppies, in addition to the nutrient-robbing aspect of the adult intestinal worm itself.

Puppies are treated for these worms upon their first few visits to the veterinarian because they are so common. After they are rid of the parasite, they usually don't get another infestation unless they are allowed to be in unsanitary areas where infested dogs have defecated. Many who are reinfested simply fight off the infestation due to their more mature immune systems, and it is not a problem. Occasionally, you will find an adult dog that has become reinfested with roundworms and will need treatment again and again.

As for children, pretty much the same process goes on inside their bodies if they are exposed to roundworm eggs. Children, being children, will eat dirt or grass blades and not wash their hands as often as we would like. Therefore, they are exposed to roundworm eggs often. For most children, like mature dogs, this is not a problem because their immune system fights off the infestation. However, for some, the infestation goes on and they exhibit symptoms of the larvae migrating through the liver, lungs and so on. This syndrome in pediatrics is known as visceral larval migrans or VLM. It is seen more often in lower socioeconomic regions of the country and world.

Here is what you can do to be sure your child never has a problem with this. 1. See your veterinarian and make sure you dog is free from ascarids. 2. Keep the area where children play clean, and pick up any pet waste from sandboxes and play yards. 3. Teach children to wash their hands after playing and especially before eating.

Q: *Our dog scratches a lot, and now even my husband and I are scratching! I've noticed a few little red dots around my waistband. They itch like crazy! Have we caught something?*

A: I'd say you probably have scabies, the so called "itch mite." This little mite is very transmissible from dogs to dogs and from dogs to people. The one major symptom for both dogs and people is pretty intense itching. The mite seems to migrate to panty lines, belt lines and bra strap areas of the body and cause very small red spots.

For the dog, the elbow and the ear tips are favorite places for the mite to inhabit. It will cause hair loss, itching and redness at those areas. When you pet the dog or carry it around with you, you can pick up the mites, which will try to burrow into your skin. They immediately know you are not a dog and will back out. However, their burrow trails make for very itchy red spots for about two weeks.

The good news is that your itching problem will go away by itself and even faster with treatment. As soon as you treat the dog, the problem will be gone altogether. However, if your dog becomes reinfested or you do not properly treat the dog, you may become reinfested as well.

You need to dip your dog with a special dip that will kill the mites. Your veterinarian can recommend one, but I use Ronnel or Kem Dip. Dip the dog once a week for four weeks and then have the doctor reevaluate the dog's progress. If the dog has only small areas that are affected, you can use topical treatments like ointments containing benzyl-benzoate or sulfur. I also usually give these dogs a shot of steroids to help relieve the intense itching they are suffering. Finally, I'd recommend antiseborrheic shampoos every week to help remove the scales and soothe the skin.

As for you and your husband—call your doctor and let him recommend treatment. Tell him you talked to me and that I think you may have scabies. If you'd rather use a more scientific name, tell him you have sarcoptic mange. Good luck!

PART VII

STRANGE, FUNNY,
WEIRD

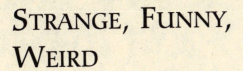

Chapter 28

Full-Moon Saturdays!

It never fails. When Saturday rolls around and it's time to do my talk show, I always check to see if it's anywhere near a full moon. If so, I can be prepared for some very strange calls.

I remember when I was a boy, working with Dr. Baker, the rural veterinarian in Edinburg, Texas. He would be prepared for horses to bleed more profusely during and after surgery near periods of a full moon. Many farmers and ranchers would not let him schedule surgeries two to three days either side of a full moon!

I've spoken with emergency-room physicians and nurses, police officers and others who are in a position to notice human behavior change, and they all agree, weird things happen when the moon is full.

I ran a busy animal emergency hospital in San Antonio, Texas, for two years. The staff and I came on duty at 6 PM and were through at 8 AM. It was a grueling schedule but the work was very rewarding. During a full moon, both human and animal behavior was definitely different.

So it comes as no surprise to me that people who call my show when the moon is full come up with some of the most interesting, entertaining and just plain weird calls I've ever received. I've told many of them they would end up in this book, so they have been forewarned. The names have been changed to protect the innocent. I hope you'll enjoy reading some of the more unusual calls I get on national talk radio on full-moon Saturdays.

RABBITS GO CATATONIC WHEN THEY SEE THE CEILING FANS

"Dr. Jim, we have house rabbits and they are deathly afraid of the ceiling fans. When the fans are off, they're OK. They hop past the fans carefully and just look up in mild fear. But when the fans are turned on, and the rabbits are anywhere in the room, they become so afraid they shake as if having an epileptic fit. Then they just go straight or rigid—like they are dead, but they're still breathing."

What happens then?

"We put them in a quiet room and in about five to ten minutes they slowly come out of it."

MOTHER-IN-LAW CAUSES MAN'S DACHSHUND TO BREAK OUT IN HIVES

George called one afternoon and wanted to know if it were possible for a dog to be allergic to a person. I said I had never heard of that but I've learned almost anything is possible. I prompted George for more information.

"Our Dachshund, Sugar, is really a joy and seems to be quite normal in every way except when my wife's mother comes over. Then she begins to sneeze, run in circles and before long she is breaking out in whelps up and down her back. They are easy to see because of her shiny short hair coat. Do you think the dog is allergic to my mother-in-law?"

A DOG WHO SEES GHOSTS

Dave asked right up front . . . *"Can dogs see ghosts?"*

I don't know, what's going on?

"My three-year-old Poodle, Josh, will, once in a while, suddenly look up at the corner of the room and act very startled. He will give out a low-level growl and keep his eyes

trained on that spot. It's really quite amazing. We just know he sees something."

Do you ever see anything?

"No, we think the dog is just more sensitive to the ghost than we are. Could there be ghosts that only dogs can see?"

I suppose so, although I believe I missed that day in neurophysiology.

Dog Goes Nuts when Star Trek Emergency Warning Comes On

"Dr. Jim, I've got a good one for you. Our dog goes absolutely 'cuckoo' when Star Trek comes on TV and they have an alert on the ship. He goes frantic. He'll jump at the TV set, bark, snap and growl. Why does he do that?"

How does he know there is an emergency on Star Trek?

"It's the siren. You know, the woooop, woooop, woooop. It just drives him nuts!"

A Trekkie dog, I thought I'd heard it all. My dog always runs to the door and barks viciously when the elevator bell dings as it arrives at FYI's floor on Murphy Brown. He hates that. I guess we live with very sensitive dogs. I wonder if Neilson would count that in their ratings' formula?

Gassy Dog Keeps Guests Moving On

One day on my radio show, I was interviewing the representative for AkPharma Inc., the company that makes CurTail, a food enzyme that prevents gas in dogs. After our initial discussion of the gas problem and their unique product, I took this call:

Let's go to Tina in Wanatchie, Washington. Hi there. . . .

"Doctor Jim, I have a very gassy dog, but I don't need your guest's product!" she said confidently.

Maybe she has come up with a good home cure, I thought. . . . Oh, why is that?

"Well, my husband has a lot of old college buddies that like to come and stay with us. This happens more often than I like, and some of them have worn out their welcome. So, I just put the dog in the guest room at night. So far no one has lasted more than two nights!"

DOG IS AGGRESSIVE, SO VET SAID TO CUT THE DOG'S TEETH OFF!

"Dr. Jim, we've got a real problem and we want your opinion. Our dog, Bugsey, has been mean ever since we got him at the Trade Days Fair. He's bit a couple of our friends and also our vet. We asked our vet what we could do, and he told us to cut his teeth off."

WHAT?

"Yeah. He said he'd just take out all of Bugsey's teeth and that would make it so he wouldn't hurt anybody else."

If I were you, I would run, not walk, away from this so-called veterinarian. As soon as you finish talking to me, I would pick up the phone and report this to the Veterinary Medical Association. That is one of the most outrageous things I've ever heard!

"Well, we thought it sounded kind of severe."

Kind of severe! It's cruel, inhumane, unprofessional and stupid. It would do absolutely nothing to correct the problem and would put the dog through a needless anesthetic and risk of severe postop infection. It would change the dog's ability to eat, changing his diet and nutritional health for life. He may even become more aggressive with no teeth to protect himself with.

I suggest you get with a good trainer who knows how to handle aggressive cases and invest the time and effort necessary to train the dog. Take precautions in the meantime so that your dog is supervised and doesn't have the opportunity to bite. Use a muzzle, a leash and a fence to accomplish this.

Dog Has Hiccups—and More!

"Is there any way we can cure hiccups in our eight-year-old Rottweiler? We feel sorry for her, and our vet doesn't seem to know what can be done."

Well, you can try. . . .

"Oh, there is one more thing."

What's that?

"She has, well . . . gas. Every time she hiccups, she passes gas too! That's really why we want to get the hiccups cured."

Grandpa Spread Laundry Detergent All Through House for Fleas

"Doc, my father was visiting with us last week and said he had a surefire cure for our flea problem. While my wife and I were at work, he went out and bought a couple of boxes of Borax and sprinkled it all over our house. It has really made a mess. What was he thinking?"

Your father was using an old farm cure for fleas that has some basis in science. Boron will kill the flea larvae that develop in your carpet. Borax has boron in it, and there must be some effect to using it in the house because I have heard of this before. However, Borax also has detergent in it and anywhere your carpet gets wet, it will make a mess. Plus, it is coarse and granular and will not work down into the carpet fibers where the flea larva are. It may help a little, but there is a better way to use boron.

"DOING IT"

I receive many calls from people who have a question they are too embarrassed to ask a veterinarian in person. Most of these questions are of a sexual nature. When it comes right down to it, most people seem too embarrassed to use the proper terminology. Consequently, I get a lot of calls in which people ask me about their dogs "doing it."

> *"Doctor, help! My dog is in the back yard right now and they are ... well, my neighbor's dog is over here and she is ... well, they were going to get her spayed but they didn't and she's ... well, my dog is on top of her and he's ... well, this has been happening for about ten minutes and they're ... well, DOING IT! What do I do?"*

LICKS AIR

> *"Our dog has licked the air ever since she was a little puppy. Mostly she did it when we would scratch her back, but now, as an adult, she just licks the air like there is something good to eat out there. Why does she do that?"*

I've seen dogs do this and have had this question several times, and I still don't know the answer. My best guess is that they have learned to use their tongue as a means of gathering sensory information. In fact, dogs have glands on the inside of their mouths that allow them to "smell." That's part of the reason dogs don't stop to enjoy the aroma of dog food before wolfing it down. They get to smell it as it is being swallowed! I know that snakes smell important things in the air with their tongues, and I'll guess that your dog has learned to do this as well.

Dog with Back Trouble Learned to Walk on Front Legs

"Our dog can do handstands and walk on his front legs!" the caller said proudly.

Oh really, care to tell me more?

"When he was three years old he was run over by a child on a bicycle and injured his lower back severely. His back legs have some feeling in them but he can't seem to use them at all. Consequently, he has learned to get around by balancing his body weight just right and tipping over onto his front legs. Then he gets some momentum going and walks along on his front legs. It's really something to see."

Another candidate for America's Funniest Home Videos.

Electronic Flea Collars Are Not Recommended for Hiking!

"Dr. Jim, have you ever heard of ultrasonic flea collars?"

Yes I have.

"Well I don't know how well they work on fleas, but they sure do attract other bugs!"

Attract them? How do you mean?

"Well, we do a lot of camping and hiking and I've heard you say how we should protect our dog and ourselves from getting ticks on us because of Lyme disease. I know people who spray their legs down with flea spray and even put a flea collar on each ankle to repel ticks as they hike through the woods. So, being a gadget hound, I decided that ultrasonic electronic flea collars would be even better. I bought two of them and strapped one to each ankle and headed off. When I got back, I had every kind of tick and chigger and bug on my leg you can imagine. All I can figure is that the sound these things make is the universal mating call for the insect world and they came from far and wide to cling to my leg. Can't say that my idea was any good, but I must have made a bunch of bugs happy."

Cat Watches A&E, Dog Watches Golf— They Fight Over the Remote!

"Dr. Jim, we have one for you. Our pets watch TV and they love it!"

Yes I've heard of many pets watching TV, in fact, there is even a home video called Video Catnip that is supposed to attract and mesmerize cats for hours by watching birds in trees and so forth.

"Well our pets are more than just mesmerized, they're obsessed!"

What do you mean?

"The cat will watch A&E for hours and we really believe she has learned to flip the channel over to that station so she can watch it!"

Oh come on!

"No really, but that's not the half of it. Our dog, Arnie, loves to watch golf! Dr. Jim, I swear. On Saturdays, they actually fight over the remote to see who gets to watch what! We've had to buy a new remote cause the first one had so many tooth marks!"

Can You Declaw a Dog?

"Can you declaw a dog?"

Why on Earth would you want to do that?

"We cannot stop our dog from jumping up on us and our friends. I figure if we declaw her, she'll at least do less damage when she jumps up!"

I'm sorry, you cannot declaw a dog! Even if you found a veterinarian that would do such a barbaric surgery, it would not solve your problem. You have a behavior problem, not an anatomical one. Dogs are not cats, and if that is where you got this idea, forget it here and now.

This is one of the easiest unruly dog problems to correct.

SNAKEBITES AND DEWCLAWS

"Doc, I've always heard that the little claw on the side of a dog's leg is there in case he gets snakebit. Is that true?"

I have never heard that one. What's it supposed to do?

"It's supposed to swell up and take up all the venom to keep it from killing the dog."

Well, it makes a good story, but I don't think so. I've treated many dogs with dewclaws that have died because of snakebite. It is just a vestigial finger and is often removed in puppies. Hunting dogs often get them torn when pouncing through the woods. The only time I've ever seen one swell up is when it is infected or injured.

DOG ONLY EATS FOOD WRAPPED IN CELLOPHANE

"Dr. Jim, I know you will think I'm weird, but my dog is very picky. She will only eat very specific types of food and I have to prepare it for her. She likes hot dogs when I fry them in a little oil. She loves any kind of cheese and she'll flip for turkey burgers."

Does she ever get dog food?

"Not anymore. She used to like those cellophane wrapped burgers but since I started cooking for her she likes my cooking best."

Well, I would highly recommend you get this dog back on a professionally formulated, complete and balanced dog food. I recommend you . . . (interrupts).

"No doctor, that's not why I'm calling! I like cooking for her. My problem is that whenever I make goodies for her, she won't eat them unless I wrap them in cellophane!"

You mean that every time you feed your dog one of these homemade meals you have to wrap it in cellophane before she will eat it?

"Yes! What do I do?"

Boy has this dog got you wrapped around its little dewclaw!

Dog Ate Panty Hose

"Doctor, what do we do? Our dog has eaten my panty hose!"

What?

"I was in the bathroom changing clothes to go work in the yard. Our dog was in there with me, watching me change as she always does. She will many times sniff my shoes and my clothes, but I always thought that was normal. Today, before I had a chance to put my dirty clothes in the hamper, the phone rang and I left the room for about fifteen minutes. When I can back, Charlene was kind of gagging and the last little bit of one foot of my panty hose was hanging out of her mouth. Will that hurt her?"

How Do I Get My Dog Up on His Pastures?

"Doctor Jim, how do I get my dog up on his pastures?"

I beg your pardon?

"I went to a dog-showing seminar and the instructor said we should feed our dogs up high so they have to stretch and strengthen their legs to get them up on their pastures!"

Oh, you probably heard the word pasterns, but dogs don't have pasterns—horses do. Maybe this instructor was a horse person and confused canine anatomy with equine anatomy. Strong dogs will stand up straighter with good tone in their lower legs and feet. That's what she probably meant. I know for sure it didn't have anything to do with green pastures.

"Oh!"

Index